Tip-of-the-Tongue States

Phenomenology, Mechanism, and Lexical Retrieval

Tip-of-the-Tongue States

Phenomenology, Mechanism, and Lexical Retrieval

Bennett L. Schwartz
Florida International University

LAWRENCE ERLBAUM ASSOCIATES, PUBLISHERS

2002   Mahwah, New Jersey   London

Lawrence Erlbaum Associates, Inc., Publishers
10 Industrial Avenue
Mahwah, NJ 07430

Cover design by Kathryn Houghtaling Lacey

Library of Congress Cataloging-in-Publication Data

Schwartz, Bennett L.
Tip-of-the-tongue states : Phenomenology, mechanism, and lexical retrieval / Bennett L. Schwartz.
      p. cm.
      Includes bibliographical references and index.
ISBN 0-8058-3445-1 (cloth : alk. paper)
1. Memory disorders. 2. Memory. 3. Recollection (Psychology).
      I. Title.
BF376 .S39   2001
153.1´2—dc21

                                           2001023110
                                                 CIP

Books published by Lawrence Erlbaum Associates are printed on acid-free paper, and their bindings are chosen for strength and durability.

Printed in the United States of America
10 9 8 7 6 5 4 3 2 1

To Leslie D. Frazier and Sarina D. Schwartz,
my wife and daughter, respectively

Contents

Preface

Tip-of-the-tongue experiences (TOTs) are one of those illusive oddities of human cognition. Like slips of the tongue, deja vu, and visual illusions, TOTs dazzle us with their subjective strength, yet at the same time, puzzle us with our frustrating inability to retrieve the desired word. Psychologists have discussed TOTs ever since William James described them so eloquently in his *Principles of Psychology*. As a researcher, I have found TOTs to be both a gold mine of fascinating discoveries and a can of worms of perplexities and oddities. The more experiments I have designed to understand TOTs, the greater the perplexities I have encountered. This book discusses what little is known about TOTs and speculates about much of the rest of the riddle. Cognitive psychologists know a lot about processes. We can tell you what are the processes behind implicit memory, the mechanisms that may be involved in the representation of concepts, or the ways in which syntax is represented in our lexicon. However, cognitive psychology, like behaviorism before it, generally avoids issue of conscious experience and phenomenology. The larger goal of this volume is to use the TOT to relate to the study of human phenomenology. In its essence, the TOT is an experience that all of us encounter from time to time. This book asks the question, "Why do we experience TOTs at all?" in addition to the conventional cognitive question, "What causes them?"

ACKNOWLEDGMENTS

In the course of compiling this manuscript, I had to acknowledge the fact that no one person can write a book by themselves. Only one name appears on the cover, but that does not mean that many others have not had a hand in its conception and its execution (although all errors are my responsibility). Help is not only desirable but imperative. I thank Leslie Frazier and Richard Berg, in particular, for reading through drafts of the entire manuscript. Their reading and rereading were essential to making this volume a reality. I also thank reviewer Richard Carlson of Penn State University for his commentary and criticisms.

Other people, although they did not read drafts, also deserve my thanks. These people were important influences on the way I think about the issues described in this volume. In particular, I thank Janet Metcalfe for putting me on the right track in examining these issues years ago and for getting me back on that track from time to time during the ensuing years. I thank George Wolford for handing me a copy of Brown and McNeill's paper to read in graduate school and first putting me on this journey. I thank Thomas Nelson and Asher Koriat for their encouragement over the years. I thank my chairperson Marvin Dunn for encouraging me to take on the book even if it meant delaying other writing projects usually thought more suitable for a researcher at the current stage of my career. Finally, I thank Judi Amsel, Bonita D'Amil, and Bill Webber at Lawrence Erlbaum Associates. Without them, I would not have had the confidence to begin the project, and the patience to see it through to the end.

The greatest thanks goes to my family, in particular to my parents Foster and Carol Schwartz and my wife's parents, Jack and Nancy Frazier. I also thank my daughter Sarina for being a full-term baby, which allowed me to complete the first draft of this manuscript before she arrived on the scene. Lastly, I thank my wife, Leslie Frazier, who did it all while pregnant and applying for tenure, to make this book a reality.

—*Bennett L. Schwartz*
December 11, 2000

1

What is a TOT?

Several years ago, I was in a bookstore looking for a birthday present for my aunt, a clinical psychologist in Boston. A few months earlier I had read an interesting novel set in the exotic landscape of New Zealand. As I entered the bookstore, I was thinking of the complex interactions between the two main characters, a young boy and an old woman. I started toward the information booth to ask where I might be able to find the book, but realized that I could recall neither the title of the novel nor the author's name. Moreover, I was stuck in a horrible tip-of-the-tongue state for both names. I stammered to the clerk that I was looking for a book written by a woman from New Zealand; not much for the store clerk to go on. I could remember the plot and the names of some of the characters in the book, but I could not remember the two critical pieces of information that I needed—the title or the author. In vain, I simultaneously searched the bookstore shelves and the recesses of my memory, but to no avail. After a half an hour or so of this pursuit, I gave up and left the bookstore. Approximately 1 hour later, while playing basketball with friends and not thinking about the incident in the bookstore, the title popped into my mind with the overwhelming confidence of complete certainty. It was *The Bone People* by Kerri Hulme (1983).

The tip-of-the-tongue experience itself has not escaped literary reference. The Anton Checkov short story, "A Horsey Name" is about a tip-of-the-tongue experience (Pitcher, 1999). In the story, a servant is trying to recall the name of a particularly painless dentist because his employer is suffering from a monstrous toothache. Try as he might, Ivan Yevseich cannot remember the name of the celebrated dentist. All he can remember is that the name of the dentist in some way sounded like something related to horses. Ivan Yevseich has a strong feeling of knowing combined with partial information, a hallmark of the tip-of-the-tongue state. Only after a more painful dentist has pulled the tooth does Ivan spontaneously retrieve the dentist's name, a certain Dr. Oates.

At one time or another, everyone has probably experienced a tip-of-the-tongue state. These stories often cause us a great deal of frustration as we cannot remember something, which we are sure that we know. On other occasions, they may fill us with excitement that we will remember something important soon. Older adults often complain that they experience more tip-of-the-tongue states now than they did when they were younger. Regardless of our age, we all experience tip-of-the-tongue states, and many of us may wonder how and why we cannot remember something we know so well.

This volume concerns what contemporary cognitive psychology knows about the tip-of-the-tongue phenomenon, which its not much, and that is why the book is so slim. However, I think what we do know about the tip-of-the-tongue phenomenon will both surprise and intrigue the readers. Moreover, what we know about the tip-of-the-tongue phenomenon has applications beyond understanding this rather annoying but persistent quirk of the human mind. Investigating the tip-of-the-tongue phenomenon may help us to understand how the human mind works.

The *tip-of-the-tongue phenomenon* (henceforth, *TOT*) straddles the line between what we think of as memory and what we think of as language, two closely related cognitive domains that have been studied somewhat independently of each other. Throughout the volume, a border dispute will become apparent—is the TOT a failure of memory retrieval or is it a failure of language production? Obviously, language production involves a memory retrieval process, and so the processes are intertwined, but scientists who study memory retrieval are not the same scientists who study language production. The implications of whether the TOT is memory-related or language-related has different implications. Consider the following example.

Political pundits used to make fun of former President George H. Bush because of his frequent word-finding failures. Despite his obvious depth of knowledge and expertise, his speech was sometimes characterized by pauses suggesting a failure to recall a known word. His deficit was usually attributed to absent-mindedness, rather than a lack of clear thinking. In other words, it was dismissed as a language-production failure, not a more consequential memory failure. His son, President George W. Bush, suffers from a similar affliction. However, the son's speech errors (e.g., "Kosovarians," "subliminable") are often interpreted as a lack of knowledge, and therefore, a learning deficit; a more consequential one for a president. Speech errors occur for both of the Bushes, but the inference of knowledge by observers is different. A small problem with language (George H.) is considered less detrimental than a small problem with memory (Georg W.). Research into TOTs may tell us much about the nature of speech errors (see Levelt, 1989).

Frequently, people find themselves in a position in which they are sure that they were supposed to remember something, but cannot remember what. We often label this *absent-mindedness*. As a professor, I sometimes get to the end of my lecture and realize I forgot to cover a topic, but I cannot recall what topic I omitted. Most readers will recognize this experience. As you can imagine, this experience would be difficult to study in the lab because it happens so rarely and would be difficult to induce. TOT states may serve as a good model for these situations because the memory and speech error can be easily induced and studied under laboratory conditions.

This book is intended as an exploration of a particular natural phenomenon, the TOT state in human beings. It starts with a natural observation that TOT states occur, and with the question of how and why do they occur. These are the questions that the book will attempt to answer. As we know, in any scientific enterprise, even simple questions can require quite complex and elaborate answers. The human brain is the most complex apparatus that nature has evolved on this earth, and we know that answers to riddles of the human brain are not simple; that most are, in fact, incredibly complex. It is my sincere conviction, however, that simple questions in science help us understand the complex questions. So, this book about TOTs will touch, glance, and hint at bigger questions (although probably not their answers). I also see the TOT phenomenon as sitting at the intersection of memory, language, and the consciousness. Understanding the TOT phenomenon may give us just an inkling of understanding how these parts of the great apparatus of the human mind function and interact.

DESCRIPTIONS AND ANECDOTES

TOTs are ubiquitous. We experience them on a routine basis. Indeed, based on research in which people were asked to record diaries of their TOT experiences, it is apparent that TOTs are likely to occur, on average, once a week for any particular person (Burke, MacKay, Worthley, & Wade, 1991; Schwartz, 1999a). That means the average person experiences approximately 52 TOTs each year, with older adults experiencing as many as 100 per year. Extrapolated across the lifetime, that means several thousand TOTs are experienced in a person's life. Extrapolated to the entire population, human beings experience roughly 300 billion TOTs over the course of a single year. That is a lot of mnemonic frustration.

I suspect that every reader could describe at least several recent or memorable TOTs that they have experienced. However, for completeness and brevity, I will report just a few of the many that have been described to me, just to give the general flavor of TOTs. Here, for example, is a description of a TOT provided to me by one of the participants in my diary study. He reported that "we never watched the old Star Trek—but we watched the Next Generation, you know, Jean-Luc Picard and his crew. We were talking about the old Star Trek, and I couldn't think of the captain's name. I mean, I knew the actor was William Shattner, and I could think of him standing of the bridge on the Enterprise. But, I just can't think of the name." The participant continues by expressing a profound sense of relief when the name "Kirk" was remembered by a friend.

Indeed, over the years, hundreds of people have described their TOTs to me. Sometimes, TOTs drive us crazy. One friend told of getting up in the middle of the night and looking up the name of the first man on the moon, after a particularly frustrating TOT. I have been told about experiencing a TOT for a word in one language, and being able to recall its translation equivalent in another language. Others describe that anticipating a TOT can often prompt them to use an alternate word instead. Some people complain that now that they are older, the number of TOTs they experience has risen dramatically. Their observation is correct; many studies (discussed in chap. 7) suggest that TOTs are more common among older adults than they are among younger adults. Common to all of these descriptions is the frustrating sense of failure combined with the certainty that the elusive word is known. Usually, a sense that eventually the word will be remembered also accompanies a TOT.

The scientific literature on TOTs is replete with colorful descriptions of them. The most famous and oft-quoted passage from William James captures the feeling of the TOT particularly poetically. James (1890/1964) wrote

> The state of our consciousness is peculiar. There is a gap therein; but no mere gap. It is a gap that is intensely active. A sort of wraith of the name is in it, beckoning us in a given direction, making us at moments tingle with the sense of our closeness and then letting us sink back without the longed-for term. If wrong names are proposed to us, this singularly definite gap acts immediately so as to negate them. They do not fit the mould. And the gap of one word does not feel like the gap of another, all empty of content as both might seem necessarily to be when described as gaps. (p. 251)

Brown and McNeill (1966) described TOTs in equally colorful terms: "The signs of it [TOT] were unmistakable; he would appear to be in mild torment, something like the brink of a sneeze, and if he found the word his relief was considerable" (p. 326).

These descriptions of TOTs all appear to share a number of characteristics. each of which will be examined. First, the TOT is a strong subjective experience that is hard to confuse with any other experience. Second, TOTs are generally accompanied by emotional feelings. Emotional frustration may occur when the TOT is first experienced, and relief may be experienced when the TOT is resolved. Third, in general, people have some access to characteristics of the TOT target word. Perhaps they can recall a first letter, what the word sounds like, or how you might say the word in French or Spanish. Fourth, people usually do know the word and eventually retrieve it. Fifth, there is a strong motivation to resolve the TOT, that is, to search and find the elusive target word for yourself.

DEFINITIONS

In all areas of psychology, definitions are important to establish at the outset of any investigation. In TOT research, in some cases, operational definitions of TOTs have varied considerably. Thus, it is important to define what is meant by a TOT in this book. The following is a definition of a TOT that is used throughout this book: A TOT is a strong feeling that a target word, although currently unrecallable, is known and will be recalled.

There are two important aspects of this *definition*. First, the TOT is a wholly subjective feeling, that is, something only "the rememberer" can report as occurring. The person may choose to or choose not to communicate this information to others, but the TOT is only within the subjective domain of the person. Second, it is a feeling about something; in this case, the feeling that a particular unrecalled item is recallable. Thus, it is a subjective experience about retrieval.

Some theorists think that a TOT necessarily involves a feeling of imminence (e.g., Smith, 1994). Imminence is defined as a feeling that this missing word is about to be recalled. Brown and McNeill (1966) instructed study participants that, "If you are unable to think the word but feel sure that you know it and that it is on the verge of coming back to you then you are in a TOT state" (p. 327). This two-part feature of the TOT—inaccessibility and imminence—seems to be the key of some operational definitions of TOTs (A. Brown, 1991). For example, Rastle and Burke (1996) told participants that they were experiencing a TOT "if they were confident that they knew the word and it was on the verge of coming back to them" (p. 591). Schwartz and Smith (1997) defined the TOT as "a feeling that you can recall the answer. It is the feeling of being on the verge of being able to recall the answer that you cannot recall now" (p. 72). These definitions are consistent with the definition given by a dictionary, which defines "on the tip of one's tongue" as "about to be said, because almost but not quite recalled" (Guralnik, 1984). However, Schwartz, Travis, Castro, and Smith (2000) found that many items were rated as TOTs by rememberers, but were not rated as imminent. This suggests that the feeling of imminence may be separable from the TOT experience. Nonetheless, most of the operational definitions given to participants in various studies include instructions about imminence. I, however, do not find it critical—only the feeling that retrieval is possible is critical.

Some researchers define the TOT in relation to any state where the person can demonstrate partial knowledge of the target but cannot recall it, even if the rememberer is not reporting TOT feelings (e.g., Kohn et al., 1987; Vigliocco, Antonini, & Garrett, 1997). I labeled this definition of a TOT a "third-person TOT" (Schwartz, 1999b; see Gardiner & Java, 1993). In studies such as those by Vigliocco and her colleagues (1997), TOTs are said to occur anytime a person reports partial knowledge and later recognizes the target word, irrespective of the feelings associated with that retrieval. In these third-person studies, the emphasis is usually on the word retrieval process (Kohn et al., 1987). Whereas studying impaired retrieval of known words is important to understanding the retrieval process, I argue it is misleading to call this condition a TOT because the TOT should refer to a subjective state of the organism. Another term, like availability without accessibility, would be preferable (e.g., Tulving & Pearlstone, 1966). In this book, I draw on research using this third-person definition and discuss it at length in chapter 4, but at the outset I emphasize that in my view, the TOT should be conceptualized as a subjective phenomena that only the rememberer can decide has occurred.

BROWN AND MCNEILL (1966): SEMINAL RESEARCH ON TOTs

In the 1960s, researchers Roger Brown and David McNeill became interested in the frustrating failure to retrieve known but inaccessible words. For several months, they observed these TOTs in themselves. In their informal observations, they noted some interesting features of TOTs. They observed that when experiencing TOTs, they tended to be able to recall some of the characteristics of the inaccessible target word. For example, one of them experienced a TOT for the name of a street. When he experienced the TOT, he was able to retrieve the words; Congress, Corinth, and Concord, which he was sure sounded like, but were not, the name of the street. Investigation revealed that the actual street name was Cornish Street. Brown and McNeill noted that they could sometimes recall first letters, syllabic stress, and number of syllables when they were experiencing a TOT, although they could not recall the actual target word. They thought both the experience of a TOT and the observation that they usually retrieved related information was important.

When Brown and McNeill began to examine TOTs, there was scant published research on the topic. James (1890/1964) wrote eloquently about

TOTs, he had not carried out any specific research on the topic. Thus, Brown and McNeill's 1966 article achieved many significant landmarks in the study of TOTs. First, Brown and McNeill introduced the first empirical methodology for studying TOTs in the laboratory. Second, the study established the first empirically verifiable observations about TOTs. Third, the article introduced many of the important theoretical issues that have dominated the study of TOTs over the ensuing four decades.

Because it is the seminal article in the area, and because it set the tone of research on TOTs for the next 35 years, I will devote much of the remainder of the first chapter to Brown and McNeill's methodology, findings, and theory. The strong points of their paper have led research in several productive directions, although the weaknesses of their paper have, to some extent, delayed research from expanding in other directions. Therefore, it represents a good place to begin the discussion of research into the TOT phenomenon.

To account for the inability to retrieve, but the strong feeling of knowing, Brown and McNeill conducted their own investigation of TOTs. By doing so, Brown and McNeill (1966) demonstrated that science was capable of studying TOTs. As Jones (1988) reported, "Brown and McNeill showed in their justly famous article that the TOT state, hitherto a feral beast that struck without warning, could be tamed and studied as a creature of conveniently regular habits" (p. 215). In addition, the methodology that Brown and McNeill adopted has become the standard for addressing issues in TOT research (see A. Brown, 1991; Schwartz, 1999b). Finally, Brown and McNeill couched their explanation of their data in a particularly influential theory concerning the origin of TOTs. Although most of the particulars of their theory have been discarded, today many TOT theorists can trace their ideas to those of Brown and McNeill (e.g., Harley & Bown, 1998; Schwartz, 1999b; Vigliocco et al., 1997). Next, we consider the methodology used by Brown and McNeill (see also Freedman & Landauer, 1966; Yarmey, 1973).

Methodology

Brown and McNeill's (1996) "prospected" for TOTs. They did this by reading definitions of words to a class of 56 Harvard and Radcliffe students. The words were difficult and uncommon words, but Brown and McNeill suspected that they might be in the participants' recognition vocabulary, although they might not be able to generate the words on demand. Examples of their stimuli were the definitions for such words as "nepotism," "ambergris," and "cloaca." The definitions were adapted from a dictionary, but Brown and McNeill did not provide any examples of the definitions, just some of the words used. Thus, the definition for "cloaca" might have been something like "the cavity into which both the intestinal and genitourinary tracts empty in reptiles, birds, amphibians, and many fish" (Guralnik, 1984, p. 267). The participants were instructed to raise their hands if they were experiencing a TOT for any particular word and then answer a series of questions pertaining to that word. While the students who were experiencing TOTs were reporting on their experiences, the remaining students waited for the next item. Brown and McNeill defined a TOT as follows: "If you feel you are unable to think of the word but feel sure that you know it and that it is on the verge of coming back to you then you are in a TOT state ... " (p. 327). Today, participants are more likely to report their TOT on a computer keyboard isolated from others, but in Brown and McNeill's case, these instructions were given to a large group. This minimizes any effects of the social milieu. However, Brown and McNeill conducted all of their data gathering in one group setting.

When rememberers identified themselves as experiencing a TOT, they were required to guess the number of syllables and the first letter for the TOT word. They were also invited to write down any words that either sounded like or meant something similar to the TOT target. If they spontaneously retrieved the TOT target word at any time after they had originally experienced it as inaccessible, they were to write the words "Got it" on the response sheet. Before moving on to the next word, Brown and McNeill (1996) read the actual target word and asked those participants in a TOT to indicate whether the target word was indeed the word for which they were experiencing a TOT. If the actual target word was the student's TOT target, they were to indicate that; if not, the student was to indicate that the TOT target was a different, as yet unresolved, word.

Their methodology defined the parameters of TOT research. For example, most TOT studies gather information on partial recall, one of the main concerns of Brown and McNeill (1966). Brown and McNeill were also interested in the type of related words that are recalled, but are incorrect during TOTs. This was followed up by later researchers (e.g., Jones, 1988; Perfect & Hanley, 1992; Reason & Lucus, 1984). On the other hand, Brown and McNeill did not assess the accuracy of TOTs, a topic not addressed until relatively recently (Brown, 1991). Few studies distinguish between varying subjective sub-states of a TOT, a topic Brown and McNeill did not explore (but see Schwartz et al., 2000). Thus, Brown and McNeill's data collection strategies generated a number of important avenues of research, but because of the influence of their article, paradoxically limited other lines of inquiry. However, they speculated on a number of interesting aspects of the TOT that they themselves did not study. For example, in their introduction they described how frustrating the TOT can be (like a "sneeze"), and how much relief retrieving the target word provides although they did not collect ratings on either of these dimensions (presumably because of time limitations in their study and the prevailing lingering behaviorist zeitgeist of the 1960s). In the following 30 years, there was no research on emotionality, frustration, or relief as experienced in TOTs (however, see Schwartz et al., 2000). Similarly, Brown and McNeill distinguished between TOTs that were felt to be "near TOTs," that is, those TOTs whose retrieval is imminent, and "far TOTs," that may not be immediately recalled. They made this distinction on the basis of memory characteristics and not the intensity of the TOT. Nevertheless, Brown and McNeill's seminal article laid the foundation for TOT methodology and their findings made an impact on the future of the field.

Results

Brown and McNeill (1966) showed that it was possible to study TOTs in an experimental setting. Participants readily reported TOTs, and these turned out to mostly correspond to cases in which the person later correctly identified the target word. Moreover, they found that when rememberers are experiencing a TOT, they usually have a wealth of partial information, ranging from the retrieval of similar sounding words to correctly estimating the correct number of syllables of the missing target word. All of their findings turned out to be replicable. In retrospect, it is a shame that Brown and McNeill moved onto other issues after the publication of this article, and they never wrote another article on TOTs. The organization of this section loosely follows the manner in which they reported their data in their article.

Brown and McNeill (1966) collected 360 TOTs from 56 participants. Of these, 233 were considered to be "positive TOTs." Positive TOTs were those in which participants resolved their TOT or recognized the experimenter's word as correct. TOTs were scored as positive even if the participant retrieved a word that was not technically correct but for which the participant was sure that it was the word at which the TOT was directed. Negative TOTs were those in which the participant did not judge the actual word to be the one for which they were experiencing a TOT or that they could not recall the actual word for which they had experienced a TOT. Negative TOTs were far outnumbered by positive TOTs, but it is unclear due to the inclusion of relatively difficult words in the study whether this is a general feature of TOTs.

This distinction between positive and negative TOTs has persisted in more recent investigations (e.g., Perfect & Hanley, 1992; Rastle & Burke, 1996). In their results, Brown and McNeill (1966) specify some analyses in which they only addressed positive TOTs, and therefore, presumably in others, both positive and negative TOTs were included. Some researchers do not think of negative TOTs as TOTs at all, and exclude them from analysis (e.g., Rastle & Burke, 1996). This exclusion is generally motivated by an interest in using positive TOTs to study the retrieval process. Brown and McNeill's reason for distinguishing positive and negative TOTs was probably to address how they differed.

Brown and McNeill (1966) also introduced the distinction between phonological access and semantic access in TOTs (see Burke et al., 1991; Caramazza & Miozzo, 1997). This distinction is that TOTs may elicit two kinds of retrieved information; (a) partial information about the phonology of the word or phonologically related words, and (b) semantic information, such as related information or associatively related words. *Phonological* information includes remembering the first letter, the first syllable, or a word that sounded similar to the target (e.g., "croquet" for "cloaca"). *Semantic* information, such as related information, entails remembering details of the functioning of the digestive system, and associated words might include "intestine" or "crop." Brown and McNeill examined this distinction by asking participants to report words that sounded similar to the target word and words that meant something similar to the target word.

They collected 224 words that were classified by participants as sound matches to an unretrieved TOT target word. They also found 95 words that were similar in meaning to a TOT target. For example, for the word sampan, the participants provided the following phonological matches during TOT states: saipan, sanching, sarong, and sympoon; and the following semantic matches: barge, houseboat, and junk. Brown and McNeill noted that, given the definition of a word, it should not be difficult to produce similar-meaning words because the semantic context is provided. Thus, a high number of semantically-similar words are to be expected. They also suspected that when in a positive TOT, participants are probably more likely to come up with closer matches in meaning, due to the word's higher accessibility, than those not in TOTs, but they did not test this empirically. However, they found that participants were more likely to retrieve phonological matches than semantic matches. This is surprising because no phonological cues are given in the definition. Thus, participants must be retrieving phonological information about the inaccessible TOT word to produce these phonologically similar words. Thus, important questions arise that surface repeatedly in TOT research: (a) why is phonological information retrieved when the entire missing word is unretrieved, and what is the direction of causality? In other words, does the partial retrieval of information create the experience of TOT, or is partial retrieval a symptom of being in a TOT?

Brown and McNeill (1966) found some other interesting correlations between TOTs and what people could retrieve. They found that participants' judgments of the number of syllables in a word was positively correlated with the actual number of syllables (see Table 1.1), but there were some system-

TABLE 1.1

Actual and Guessed Number of Syllables for all TOTs
in the Main Experiment

| | | | Guessed Number of Syllables | | | |
	1	2	3	4	5	Mean
Actual						
1	9	7	1	0	0	1.53
2	2	55	22	2	1	2.33
3	3	19	61	10	1	2.86
4	0	2	12	6	2	3.36
5	0	0	3	0	1	3.50

Note. The data are the number of individual TOTs across participants, not the nmber of prticipants (adapted from Brown and McNeill, 1966, *Journal of Verbal Learning and Verbal Behavior*, p. 329). TOTs = Tip-of-the-tongue phenomena.

atic deviations from perfect accuracy. Participants underestimated the long words and overestimated the short words, although overall they were quite good at getting the correct number of syllables. This finding of Brown and McNeill was replicated a few years later by Koriat (i.e., Koriat & Lieblich, 1974). In addition, Brown and McNeill pointed out that 47% of the similar-sounding words, in contrast to 20% of similar-meaning words, shared the same number of syllables as the target word. They also found that participants' similar-sounding words matched the target words in the pattern of syllabic stress patterns. Thus, participants had knowledge both about the phonology and the prosody of the missing words.

Brown and McNeill's (1966) next analysis concerned whether the participants could correctly guess the first letter of the unrecalled target. For this analysis, they were restricted to examining the positive TOTs, because for the negative TOTs, it is unclear what is the actual TOT target word. This is true because the experimenter-intended word was not the same word as the one for which the participant experienced a TOT. Across all positive TOTs, the first letter was recalled correctly 57% of the time. Although Brown and McNeill did not measure correct performance for items not in TOTs, they suspected that the 57% rate was much higher than baseline. A few years later, Koriat and Lieblich (1974) showed that first-letter recall is indeed higher than the rate expected by chance when they compared correct first-letter recall for TOTs and for unrecalled items that were not judged to be TOTs. Brown and McNeill also found that 49% of similar-sounding words also shared the first letter with the TOT target word, again demonstrating that rememberers have some access to phonology when experiencing a TOT.

Brown and McNeill (1966) also reported a rough correspondence between TOT target words and the first and last letter of the similar-sounding words, with decreased correspondence for letters in the middle of the word. They also looked at differences between guesses of first letters for TOTs in which the target was recognized when the experimenter read it and those that had been recalled earlier by the participant. First-letter recall was improved following a recalled TOT than with a recognized TOT.

In total, Brown and McNeill's (1966) data paint a rather revealing portrait of the TOT. TOT experiences are highly correlated with eventual recognition of the target word. These experiences are often accompanied by the retrieval of words that are either phonologically or semantically related, or both, to the missing target word. Moreover, when a person is in a TOT they can accurately estimate the number of syllables in the word, the stress pattern of those syllables, and the first and last letter of the missing word. Thus, Brown and McNeill demonstrated that the TOT is not an idle subjective experience; rather, it is accompanied by a tremendous amount of objectively verifiable information.

Theory

Brown and McNeill (1966) realized that their study raised more questions than it answered. However, they drew some tentative theoretical conclusions based on the implications of their data. Their theoretical speculation became as influential as their pioneering methodology. Brown and McNeill conducted their study just as information-processing theory was rapidly developing, and therefore, they drew heavily on the information-processing revolution in cognitive science to explain TOTs. In this approach, of course, the emphasis is on hidden cognitive processes, and like much cognitive psychology of the time, does not wish to invoke conscious or phenomenological entities in explanation. Thus, their model is essentially a serial information processing view of the TOTs, in which a system initiates a search that yields only incomplete information.

Brown and McNeill (1966) introduced a concept that they called *generic recall*, that the general sense of the target item is recovered without the specific target word being retrieved. In their view, TOTs occur because the rememberer accesses generic information, but not specific information. In this sense, Brown and McNeill's model is a direct-access model (see chap. 3) because it is the failure of retrieval combined with access to the unretrieved word that elicits the TOT experience. Generic recall drives TOTs, and TOTs are accurate predictors of both recall and recognition performance.

Brown and McNeill (1966) also couched their explanation in terms of extant models of word recognition. Generic recall is generally functional because the letters specifying words in English, as in other languages, usually overspecify the word. By overspecification they mean that, in most cases, the change of a single letter changes a word from a real word to a nonsense word. For example, changing one letter of the word "sextant" yields nonwords such as "textant," "sixtant," and "sektant" (p. 335). Thus, generic recall is beneficial to the rememberer even when specific word knowledge cannot be accessed because often the generic information is all that is required to produce a comprehensible utterance. Thus, if the listeners know I am talking about a nautical navigation tool, saying "sektant" instead of "sextant" probably does not compromise the comprehensibility of the sentence. Theoretically, the influence of this model, which combines information processing theory and a direct access approach to TOTs, persisted until recently. More recent theoretical approaches to TOTs stress their psychological etiology (Harley & Bown, 1998) and their role in metacognition (Schwartz, 1994, 1999b).

Summary of Brown and McNeill's Contribution

Brown and McNeill (1966) made a number of important contributions to the field in their article. First and foremost, they showed that TOTs could be studied in a laboratory context. Indeed, their prospecting methodology has been used many times since by other researchers (see Brown, 1991; Schwartz, 1999b; Smith, 1994; for reviews). Second, their study is the first empirical demonstration that TOTs are accurate at predicting target knowledge. They showed that when people were experiencing TOTs they could remember partial information about the missing word, and were likely to eventually either recall or recognize it. Third, they carefully examined the nature of words that were retrieved when people were in a TOT which, although similar in sound or meaning were not judged to be the TOT target. Brown and McNeill found that these items shared many characteristics with the actual TOT target. However, as with any original approach, some issues that were overlooked by Brown and McNeill. As a consequence, there were two historically unfortunate consequences of their study. The most obvious flaw is that they did not collect generic recall information from those items not in TOTs (often called "n–TOTs"). Thus they did not have control items with which to compare the TOTs. Knowing this information is critical in assessing whether TOTs indeed are correlated with more objective information about the unretrieved target.

This first flaw was corrected a few years later by the work of Koriat and Lieblich (1974). They conducted a study very similar to Brown and McNeill's (1966), but required the reporting of partial information, first letter guesses, and so forth, for unrecalled targets for which participants were experiencing TOTs, and those for which they were not experiencing TOTs. Koriat and Lieblich found that participants were generally above chance at guessing partial information when not in a TOT, but that generic recall was higher during TOTs. Unfortunately, some current researchers use the Brown and McNeill procedure and do not compare TOTs with n–TOTs (or "don't know" states).

A second problem was that Brown and McNeill (1066) failed to reference the nascent literature in feeling-of-knowing judgments. Only a year earlier, J. T. Hart (1965) had published the first article looking at the relation between feeling-of-knowing judgments and memory performance. Hart found that when participants were asked to make judgments concerning future memorability of currently unretrievable items (either answers to general information questions or targets of cue–target word associations), they were able to accurately predict which items would be recognized correctly. The correspondence between TOTs and feeling-of-knowing became judgments is intuitive and natural, but the two literatures have evolved largely independently (Schwartz, 1994, 1999b). Indeed, as the TOT became mainly studied by psycholinguists, and the feeling-of-knowing mainly studied by memory researchers interested in metamemory, the two literatures seldom overlapped (for exceptions, see Gardiner, Craik, & Bleasdale, 1973; Yaniv & Meyer, 1987; for a review, see Schwartz, 1999b). Had Brown and McNeill discussed Hart's work, it is possible that the two literatures would not have become so segregated from each other. Given that Hart published his article just a year earlier in the *Journal of Educational Psychology*, it is likely that Brown and McNeill simply had not seen or read it.

Despite these problems, Brown and McNeill (1966) set the stage for subsequent research in the area, and no paper on TOTs has been more widely referenced or had a greater impact than theirs. I recently surveyed my collection of cognition and memory textbooks and found that roughly 75% discuss the TOT, and most of these pay homage to the seminal work of Brown and McNeill. Alan Brown reported a similar result in a survey he did a few years ago with similar high marks for the Brown and McNeill study (Brown, 1991).

THE DOCTRINE OF CONCORDANCE

Much of the early research on TOTs as exemplified by Brown and McNeill (1966) was concerned with two issues: the cause of TOTs and the nature of word retrieval. In much of the subsequent work using TOTs, the TOT has been considered a method, or "window," for investigating word retrieval processes. Only a minority of the post-Brown and McNeill work considers the etiology or cause of the TOT feeling. I consider this bias in interest to have arisen out of a central problem with theorizing within the field of cognitive psychology, that is, a confusion surrounding cognitive processes and a person's phenomenological experience. Too often the two are considered to be identical or the nature of phenomenological experience is not even considered. With respect to TOTs, this bias is reflected in the central interest in the cognitive process of word retrieval and the lack of interest in the experience of the TOT. The presumed equivalence of cognitive processes and phenomenological experience derives from what Tulving has called the *doctrine of concordance* (Tulving, 1989).

Tulving (1989) expressed dissatisfaction with the doctrine of concordance, an implicit assumption in some contemporary cognitive research, unnamed until Tulving's critique. According to the doctrine, cognitive processes, behavior, and phenomenological experience are highly correlated. Indeed, Tulving argued that research in cognition has assumed that there is a "general, if not perfect, agreement between what people know, how they behave, and what they experience" (p. 8). In this view, cognitive processes are the hidden mental computations that underlie our thought. Behavior is the observable action of a person. Phenomenological experience, or simply *phenomenology*, is the feeling that accompanies the cognitive processes and may motivate behavior. Tulving, however, challenged the doctrine by claiming that, in many cases, there may be dissociations between the underlying cognitive processes and the phenomenological experience that accompanies them.

Figure 1.1 shows two highly simplified models, one consistent with the doctrine of concordance and the other inconsistent with it. In the first model, which is consistent with the doctrine, one underlying process produces both behavior and experience. Given this model, one need only measure behavior because phenomenology only offers redundant information on the underling process. However, the second model is inconsistent with the doctrine. In this model, separate cognitive processes produce behavior and phenomenology. Given this model, it becomes important to investigate both.

In Tulving's (1989) view, cognitive psychology's concern with the mental computation, or cognitive processes, is not to be confused with the study of phenomenological experience. For example, the cognitive process of "retrieval" is not the same as the experience of "recollection." For successful re-

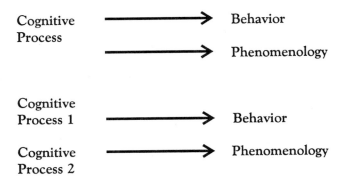

FIG. 1.1.   A simplified model showing the differences between a model consistent with the doctrine of concordance and one, following Tulving (1989), that is inconsistent.

call to occur, the retrieval process combines a cue in the environment with an existing memory trace and elicits a particular response (see Tulving, 1983). The cognitive process of retrieval results in mental activity, which may lead to a behavior such as articulating the target word. However, this retrieval process may not be accompanied by a feeling that recollection from memory has occurred. Words, for example, are retrieved from memory constantly during speech without experiencing recollection. Experienced recollection, or *mental time travel* occurs only in certain retrieval situations involving episodic memory. Mental time travel is the purely subjective experience that accompanies remembering that gives us the feeling of "pastness." Moreover, other nonretrieval factors appear to affect our feelings of pastness (Jacoby, Kelley, & Dywan, 1989). For these reasons, Tulving argued that the doctrine of concordance should no longer be accepted.

Clearly, many of the issues in contemporary cognitive research (i.e., overconfidence, feelings of knowing, implicit memory, and false memory) suggest that many researchers no longer rely on concordance assumptions. As Tulving (1989) pointed out, the assumption of the doctrine of concordance is being put aside in many areas of cognitive psychology, and the study of phenomenology is experiencing a relative renaissance. Within the memory domain, there has been a steady stream of research on flashbulb memories (e.g., Berg, 2000; Conway, 1995) that rely on experiential reports of vivid memories (Larsen, 1998; Rubin, 1998). In eyewitness memory, the apparent lack of a correlation between confidence and accuracy has forced researchers to question concordance (Busey, Tunnicliff, Loftus, & Loftus, 2000; Loftus, Donders, Hoffman, & Schooler, 1989). In decision making, the longstanding debate over overconfidence reflects an acknowledgment concerning the differences between making a decision and having confidence in that decision. Nonetheless, I demonstrate in later chapters of this volume that the assumption is still common in research on TOTs.

In my approach to TOTs, I make a logical extension of Tulving's (1989) critique of the doctrine of concordance. The assumption is that particular cognitive processes (or mental computation) are responsible both for observed behavior and for phenomenology. Under the doctrine of concordance, the likely scenario is that some cognitive processes produce both the observed behavior and the phenomenology. However, following Tulving's challenge, it is reasonable to postulate multiple cognitive processes, some that underlie behavior and others that underlie phenomenological experience. For example, if a particular cognitive process, such as retrieval, is not always accompanied by the same or any kind of phenomenological experience, it is likely that the phenomenological experience has a different underlying mechanism than the cognitive process. In some situations, such as implicit memory tests, retrieval is not accompanied by feelings of pastness. In other situations, of course, such as autobiographical memory tests, retrieval is accompanied by feelings of pastness. Indeed, feelings of pastness are possible without retrieval even taking place (e.g., memory illusions; see Roediger, 1996). Therefore, it is possible that some cognitive processes produce phenomenological experience whereas other cognitive processes effect the actual behavioral response.

Most TOT research implicitly endorses the doctrine. Contemporary research on TOTs has assumed that cognitive processes of retrieval and the phenomenology of TOTs are the same process. When exceptions to the doctrine are acknowledged, they have been considered to be unimportant (e.g., Astell & Harley, 1996; Perfect & Hanley, 1992; Rastle & Burke, 1996). There are two major consequences of this assumption. First, researchers assume variables that affect retrieval also affect TOTs. Therefore, they claim that one can infer the nature of retrieval by studying TOTs. Second, until now, most research studying TOTs has implied that phenomenology is equivalent to retrieval because both tap the same underlying processes. Therefore, little research has been directed toward TOT phenomenology. I claim that new TOT research refutes the doctrine of concordance (thereby supporting Tulving's view) by demonstrating that the processes of retrieval are not always identical to the processes that elicit TOTs. There is growing evidence to suggest that the etiology of TOTs differs from the processes that effect retrieval, leaving open the possibility for a breakdown in concordance. In chapter 3, I present research from my own laboratory and from others suggesting that the TOT phenomenology is dissociable from the processes of word retrieval.

Despite these strong claims, I present the overwhelming evidence that TOTs and retrieval are inextricably linked. Thus, although equivalence between TOTs and retrieval cannot fully explain the phenomenology, there is evidence to suggest that, to a large extent, the process of retrieval does guide TOTs; however, it is not the only causal agent of TOTs. TOT etiology is a complex process, presumably consisting of both retrieval-driven processes and nonretrieval-driven processes. I consider models in which the TOT is based on retrieval processes (chap. 4) and models in which the TOT is largely based on nonconscious inference (chap. 5).

Returning to the classic work of Brown and McNeill (1966), who marveled at the strength of the TOT experience, these researchers commented on the effects of TOT on them and their participants. Brown and McNeill were clearly interested in the phenomenological experience, but their empirical focus was on the types of retrieval processes engaged in during a TOT which has remained the focus of TOT research. This book's goal is to add to that focus and concentrate on why the phenomenological experience is equally important to understand. Nonetheless, to understand the TOT, it is important to relate both its role in language and memory retrieval, in addition to its metacognitive origin.

SUMMARY

TOTs are an interesting phenomena to study. As such, they meet Neisser's (1978) criterion for being an object of experimental inquiry. I think of TOTs as standing at the intersection of theory in memory, language, and metacognition. In this book I intend to demonstrate what we know about TOTs and why they are so important to understand. I also reviewed the seminal research on TOTs. Brown and McNeill (1966) demonstrated that TOTs could be studied in the lab and are usually associated with accurate retrieval of partial information. I also reviewed Tulving's (1989) doctrine of concordance and explained how the doctrine's general failure can be used to understand the complex relation between TOTs and word retrieval.

2

The Properties
of Naturally-Occurring TOTs

Cognitive psychologists are primarily interested in the underlying representations that allow us to think, speak, understand language, remember, and reason. To pursue these interests, cognitive psychologists must carefully design clever experiments that will reveal the workings of hidden representational systems. This ability to design experiments and the interest in the hidden workings of the human mind have made cognitive psychology a vastly successful enterprise. Although scientists are not often (and of course should not be) satisfied with their progress, in just 40 years cognitive psychology has made tremendous contributions to our understanding of the human mind.

The keys to the success of cognitive psychology have been twofold. First, cognitive psychology has addressed countless phenomena that are relevant to everyday life. Even when the paradigms are often quite technical, experimental, and laboratory bound, the clear goal is to understand how the human mind works in everyday situations. For example, within the cognitive psychology framework, Smith, Ward, and Finke (1995) examined the cognitive processes that allow normal people to think creatively and invent novel solutions to problems. Another example is the Loftus misinformation paradigm, in which the goal is to understand how suggestibility affects human memory in eyewitness situations (Loftus, Donders, Hoffman, & Schooler, 1989). Second, cognitive psychology has broken with its behaviorist ancestry by stipulating internal cognitive processes that can be studied scientifically, although they can only be inferred and not observed. This theoretical freedom has allowed cognitive theorists to devise models that are good predictors of human behavior in a variety of situations. It is this attention to the internal processes and representation that has made cognitive psychology what it is today. Most of cognitive psychology has been directed at processes, systems, and representational frameworks. As was discussed in connection with the doctrine of concordance, this research is based on the assumption that science can infer hidden internal processes based on the objective behavior. With this key assumption, behaviorist philosophical dominance gave way to a more powerful cognitive science. However, as Tulving (1989) suggested, the behaviorist jail has not been completely liberated. Most cognitive psychologists consider the issue of phenomenology to be irrelevant. Like the behaviorist, the cognitivist is not interested in either the function or mechanism of phenomenology. Rather, phenomenology at best, is a method for investigating cognitive processes.

To make this point more concrete, consider the recent research on remember and know judgments (see Gardiner & Java, 1993; Rajaram & Roediger, 1997, for a review). Remember and know judgments capitalize on a phenomenological aspect of memory (Gardiner, 1988; Tulving, 1985). Remember judgments are given if a rememberer can access specific and self-referential information pertaining to the recognition target. For example, I "remember" eating a Granny Smith apple this morning. Similarly, an individual may remember seeing a word presented on a list. Know judgments are given if this specific episodic knowledge is absent, but the rememberer "feels" as if the item has been learned. For example, I "know" that Granny Smith apples are green. Similarly, an individual may know that a word is familiar and may have been seen on a list. There has been a debate as to whether differences between "remember" and "know" judgments represent differences between processes of recollection and familiarity (e.g., Jacoby, 1991), implicit and explicit memory (e.g., Gardiner & Java, 1993; Rajaram & Roediger, 1997), or simply represent different criteria along a unidimensional memory scale (Mulligan & Hirshman, 1997). All of these views, however, are not about what causes the different phenomenological states, but rather what these states tell us about the processes of memory retrieval.

This kind of bias, that is, to use phenomenological experience to answer questions about cognitive processes, but not to be interested in the cognitive processes that underlie phenomenological experience, stems from the issues raised by Tulving (1989) concerning the doctrine of concordance. Because the close correlation between phenomenology and cognitive process is assumed, we infer that the phenomenology tells us about the underlying cognitive process.

Thus, one of the themes of this volume is to illustrate through the research on TOTs that the doctrine of concordance is no longer valid (e.g.,

Tulving, 1989). It is imperative that the field of cognitive psychology focus not only on hidden cognitive processes, but also on the complexity of human phenomenology. To be specific, throughout the volume, the point is made that the experience of the TOT and the processes of word retrieval are not identical. Rather, one set of processes drives the retrieval process, and a second set of processes (almost definitely overlapping) drives the phenomenology called the TOT.

I have come to view my own research on TOTs as a case study in issues of human phenomenology. TOTs offer some profound advantages for addressing issues of phenomenology. These advantages include the following. First, they are a naturally occurring experience that occurs quite regularly. Second, they are a universal human experience, across language, culture, and age. Third, they can be studied in both the laboratory and the field. Fourth, because the phenomenology is so salient, it is possible to conduct refined investigations on the rememberer's experience of TOTs. In the remainder of this chapter, I review the reasons for each of the aforementioned four advantages.

TOTs ARE NATURALLY-OCCURRING EXPERIENCES

Recently, while on vacation in the Caribbean, I ordered a glass of soursop juice at a restaurant. Soursop is a sweet and tart tropical fruit that I enjoy. In my home in Miami, the fruit is much more likely to go by the name of the fruit in Spanish. While drinking the juice, I was seized by a TOT for the Spanish word for the fruit. I searched for the word first, then asked my wife, and then the waiter, but neither of them knew the Spanish word. About an hour later, after I had stopped searching for the word, it "hit" me (*guanabana*).

Ask anyone you meet, and chances are that they will be able to instantly describe a recent incident when they were seized by a TOT. What is more, one does not have to explain to them what is meant by "on the tip of the tongue." The expression is learned at quite a young age (Wellman, 1977), and it is a part of everyday speech. Moreover, TOTs are common experiences. They are easy to measure with diary studies and retrospective questionnaires. Much of the data collected in these naturalistic studies correspond to what has been found in laboratory studies.

The claim here is that TOTs are natural and everyday experiences, and therefore, are interesting to cognitive psychology (i.e., Neisser, 1978). Moreover, thanks to the methodology of Brown and McNeill (1966), they can also be brought into the laboratory for more controlled study. Thus, TOTs meet the twin criteria of Banaji and Crowder (1991) for scientific study—they have ecological validity and are subject to experimental control.

THE UNIVERSALITY OF TOTs

Another important reason justifying the study of TOTs is that they appear to be a universal experience across cultures and languages. If TOTs are constant across cultures and languages, then what we find out about English-speaking Americans may indeed generalize to other populations. This is a strong statement to make given that most of the research on TOTs has taken place in Western societies among educated peoples, but I will try to make an argument as to why I think the statement is true. The rationale comes from a handful of studies done on TOTs in different languages, and a recent survey that I conducted (Schwartz, 1999b).

Brown (1991), in his review of TOTs, lamented the paucity of cross-linguistic research on TOTs, and he called for more. At that time, there was one published study with Polish-speaking people (Bak, 1987) and several with Japanese-speaking people (e.g., Murakami, 1980). Since then, TOT research has been conducted in German (Priller & Mittenecker, 1988), Japanese (Iwasaki, Vigliocco, & Garrett, 1998), Italian (Miozzo & Carmazza, 1997; Vigliocco et al., 1997), Spanish (Gonzalez & Miralles, 1997, as cited in Vigliocco et al., 1999), Farsi (Askari, 1999), Hebrew (Faust, Dimitrovsky, & Davidi, 1997; Silverberg, Gollan, & Garrett, 1999), and American Sign Language (Marsh & Emmorey, 2000). Ecke and Garrett (1998) looked at TOTs in translating from one language to another. Taken together, the studies demonstrate striking parallels. In each language, people are able to access semantic, phonological, and, in some cases, syntactical elements of the missing target word.

I choose a different method to address whether the TOT represents a universal experience across language and culture. Rather than run the Brown–McNeill (1966) paradigm in an assortment of languages (which clearly is a desirable strategy), I began by conducting a survey of languages (Schwartz, 1999b). The survey attempted to assay TOT universality by tracing the way that the experience is described in each language. The survey simply asked people to identify the term that they would use to describe a feeling that a word is known, but cannot be recalled at that instant.

At issue here is whether there is a phenomenological basis for referring to an instance of a feeling of temporary inaccessibility by the term "tip of the tongue." Possibly other languages have a literal expression that means "feeling of temporary forgetting" and do not need to employ the metaphor that we use in English. I suspected that it is likely that the term "on the tip of the tongue" is a metaphor that was derived to capture the phenomenological experience. Temporarily forgotten words feel like they are on the tips of our tongues. Metaphors, in memory speech, are actually quite common. For example, you may not be sure of a person's name, but his face may "ring a bell."

If the TOT experience is a universal one, it is likely that the "tongue" metaphor is common to many languages and to examine the existence of the expression "on the tip of the tongue" in different languages may be an effective research tool.

In the survey (Schwartz, 1999b), I contacted as many fluent, preferably native, speakers of as many languages as I could. I tried to contact more than one speaker for each language but for some languages, like the Cheyenne language (a Native American language), that proved impossible. I asked each person if they would provide for me the expression that most closely matched what we (English speakers) mean in the expression "on the tip of the tongue." I made clear that I did not want a literal translation. Rather, I wanted the expression that meant the same thing in that language, that is, how one expresses the feeling of temporary inaccessibility in the non-English language.

There were many obvious flaws in the survey. The sample consisted only of people who were at least partially fluent in English. How knowledge of English influenced their reporting of their other language is anybody's guess. The majority of the informants were professors, students, or otherwise well-educated people, although some languages were provided by a chance encounter, for example, with an Amharic-speaking cab driver or a Hebrew-speaking waiter. Moreover, the sample of languages is not representative. Dozens of Indo–European languages are represented, but only one Native American language, one native Australian language, and one sign language (American Sign Language) are represented. All of the languages are currently living languages. I was unable to find a scholar of ancient Latin, ancient Greek, Aramaic, or Sanskrit who could confidently provide if the term existed in these extinct tongues. Despite all these difficulties, the results of the survey are intriguing.

Across 51 languages known by the informants, 45 languages employed an expression that used the "tongue" metaphor to express the feeling of not being able to retrieve an accessible word (see Table 2.1). Amharic, American Sign Language, Icelandic, two sub-Saharan African languages (Kiswahili, Kalenjin), and Indonesian do not use the metaphor of the tongue to refer to the TOT. The most common term was an equivalent of the English expression, "on the tip of the tongue" (see Table 2.2). For example, the expression in Italian is "sulla punta della lingua," and in Afrikaans, "op die punt van my tong," which both translate to "on the tip or point of the tongue." Other languages use slight variants. For example, Estonian ("keele otsa peal") translates to "at the head of the tongue," whereas Cheyenne ("navonotootse'a") translates as "I have lost it on my tongue." Irish ("ar flaen fy nhafod") refers to the "front of the tongue," whereas Welsh ("ar bharr theanga agam") translates to "on the top of my tongue." Marathi ("jeebhe-war") simply uses

TABLE 2.1

Survey of Spoken Languages

Use of "Tongue Metaphor"	Do Not Use "Tongue" Metaphor
Indo–European Languages	*Indo–European Languages*
Afrikaans	Icelandic
Armenian	
Bulgarian	
Czech	
Danish	
Dutch	
English	
Farsi	
Flemish	
French	
German	
Gujarati	
Haitian Creole	
Hindi	
Irish	
Italian	
Marathi	
Norwegian	
Polish	
Portuguese	
Russian	
Serbo-Croatian	
Slovak	
Spanish	
Swedish	
Urdu	
Welsh	
Yiddish	
Non Indo–European	*Non Indo–European*
Arabic	American Sign Language
Chamarro	Amharic

Cheyanne	Indonesian
Chinese (Cantonese)	Kalenjin
Chinese (Mandarin)	Kiswahili
Estonian	
Finnish	
Hausa	
Hebrew	
Hungarian	
Ibo	
Japanese	
Jaru	
Korean	
Tamil	
Turkish	
Vietnamese	

Note. On the left is a list of languages surveyed that use an expression equivalent to "on the tip of the tongue" to express a state of temporary forgetting. On the right are the languages that do not use the "tongue" metaphor. Adapted from Schwartz, 1999b.

"on the tongue." Perhaps the most poetic is Korean, in which the expression ("Hyeu kkedu-te mam-dol-da") means "sparkling at the end of my tongue." The general similarity of the expressions suggests that the "tongue" metaphor captures a common phenomenology across languages.

Some languages showed a degree of variation, while keeping the general tenor of the metaphor. These languages do not place the missing word on the tongue, but somewhere else in the vocal tract. Five languages (Cantonese Chinese, Mandarin Chinese, Hindi, Hausa, and Ibo) use the expression "in the mouth" to describe the experience. Japanese uses the expression "out of the throat" to describe temporary forgetting. Nonetheless, the overwhelming majority of languages use the "tongue" metaphor just as English does. Some languages use multiple metaphors. For example, Korean uses both the mouth and the tongue metaphor, whereas French speakers use both the tongue metaphor and use the expression "hole in memory" ("trou de memoire") to express temporary forgetting.

Not all languages use the expression "tip of the tongue." Some languages use only the "hole in the head" metaphor (Kiswahili and Kalenjin). According to my Icelandic informant, Icelandic differed from all other Indo–Euro-

TABLE 2.2

Translations of Expressions Using the "Tongue"

"On the Tongue"

Cheyenne

Jaru

Marathi

Norwegian

Slovak

Swedish

"On Tip/Point/Head of the Tongue"

Afrikaans

Arabic

Armenian

Bulgarian

Chamarro

Czech

Danish

Dutch

English

Estonian

Farsi

Finnish

Flemish

French

German

Gujarati

Haitian Creole

Hebrew

Hungarian

Italian

Polish

Portuguese

Russian

Spanish

Tamil

Turkish

Urdu

Vietnamese

Yiddish

"On the Top of the Tongue"

Irish

Serbian

"On the Front of the Tongue"

Welsh

"Sparking at the End of the Tongue"

Korean (1)

"In the Mouth and Throat"

Cantonese Chinese

Mandarin Chinese

Hausa

Hindi

Ibo

Japanese

Korean (2)

Note. Adapted from Schwartz, 1999.

pean languages by its absence of the "tongue" metaphor. Icelandic speakers prefer an optimistic "it's coming, it's coming" when they are experiencing temporary forgetting.

Nonetheless, these data suggest that the term *tip of the tongue* derives from the experience of being unable to remember a known word. In a phenomenological sense, the word genuinely feels as if it is on the tip of one's tongue, regardless of whether one speaks English, Arabic, or Chamarro. Because these languages evolved in different parts of the world at different points in time, and yet each uses the same phrase, it argues for the universality of the experience of the tip of the tongue. Unlike many laboratory phenomena, the TOT exists in most cultures, in most languages, and presumably, in the past languages as well as present ones.

I also wondered what the direction of causality was in the use of this metaphor. Does the feeling precede our choice of words, or does the existing expression "on the tip of the tongue" suggest to us how to describe the experience. In other words, would a person who had never heard another person use the expression "on the tip of the tongue" spontaneously use the expression to describe the frustrating feeling of temporary inaccessibilty? Or, would a person unfamiliar with the expression describe this feeling in a completely different way? It is possible that the existing expressions affect our experience, causing us to attribute the feeling to our tongues. On the other hand, it is possible that the metaphor is driven by a feeling that the word is right there on the tongue. Originally, this question seemed to be quite unanswerable. However, some recent research suggests that the term "tip of the tongue" may reflect actual phenomenology. Marsh and Emmorey (2000) recently looked for "tip-of-the-finger experiences" in deaf users of American Sign Language. Although the term "tip-of-the-finger" does not exist in American Sign Language, the signers indicated that they had often had such experiences, and that the term had some appeal to them. This suggests that the experience of the word being on the tongue ("finger") may exist even in those not familiar with the term TOT.

Based on this survey data and the ready comprehension of the term TOT by the participants, I have become convinced that the TOT represents a universal of human experience, common across languages, cultures, ages, and backgrounds. The expression is much the same from language to language. Thus, it is highly likely that the phenomenological experience of the TOT is similar from person to person and culture to culture. As such, it represents a genuinely unique aspect of cognition that is not specific to literate readers, or rememberers in a particular cultural milieu. It may, therefore, represent a unique lens through which human phenomenology can be studied.

TOTs IN THE FIELD: TOT DIARIES

Whenever I describe my research interests to a new person, the person inevitably describes a recent or particularly memorable TOT experience. I suspect that this is because of the phenomenological salience of TOTs relative to other memory phenomena. Unlike many of the phenomena that we study in our labs, however theoretically important (e.g., suffix effects, phonological priming, ease-of-learning judgments), TOTs are everyday experiences, common across people and across language groups. This allows us to develop research methodologies for TOTs that would be difficult to develop for more laboratory bound phenomena.

Because of this aspect of the TOT, we can use a combination of laboratory and field techniques to study it. I previously outlined the main laboratory technique, the Brown and McNeill (1966) paradigm. In this section I outline a field technique, the diary study, that has been used to study naturally occurring TOTs. In describing the research using diary studies, I provide a portrait of what an ordinary naturally occurring TOT looks like.

In the procedure known as the TOT diary study, rememberers are asked to record natural instances of TOT in their lives over a particular period of time. Participants are asked to write down every TOT experience as they occur normally in conversation and thought. Because TOTs strike without warning, diarists must keep their diaries handy throughout the day to record them as soon as possible after the onset of a TOT. When a TOT does occur, the participant records various features of the TOT on an entry form (e.g., Burke et al., 1991). These features may include partial semantic and phonological information, phenomenological experiences, attempts or successful resolution, and if resolved, what the word is (see Burke et al., 1991; Schwartz, 1999b).

There have been five reported diary studies (Burke et al., 1991; Ecke, 1997; Heine, Ober, & Shenaut, 1999; Reason & Lucas, 1984; Schwartz, 1999a). From these studies, I have extracted a general portrait of the properties of a TOT. To give an initial summary, most TOTs are strong feelings with accompanying emotion. They are typically accompanied by a feeling of imminence, that is, the feeling that the word will be recalled soon. TOTs are generally experienced for proper nouns, although other nouns also make up a sizable portion of the TOTs. Many TOTs are also accompanied by words that seem to block the retrieval of the correct word. Almost all TOTs are resolved, usually within a few minutes of the original experience. TOT resolution is achieved most often by spontaneous retrieval, although active search and consultation with others are often important. Finally, older adults experience more TOTs than younger adults.

This general description should accord with readers' experiences of TOTs because these results are based on ordinary naturally occurring TOTs recorded by diarists. As researchers, of course, we want more than just a description of the experience. We want to know why and how these phenomena occur. Thus we discuss each of these results.

Strength, Emotion, and Imminence

Schwartz (1999a) asked diarists to record whether each TOT experienced was (a) strong or weak, (b) accompanied by a feeling of emotion, or (c) accompanied by a sense of imminence. Strength was defined as the intensity of the TOT feeling; emotionality was defined as a feeling of frustration at being unable to retrieve the target; and imminence was defined as the feeling that retrieval was about to occur. Diarists recorded their answers on an answer sheet when they recorded the TOT.

Schwartz (1999a) found that 66% of TOTs were judged to be strong, 61% were judged to be emotional, and 65% were judged to be imminent. Furthermore strength, emotionality, and imminence were correlated with each other, but not perfectly so. In fact, the correlations were between .20 and .30 for each correlation. Imminence was predictive of successful recognition, but oddly, emotionality was predictive of an inability to resolve the TOT. I speculated that emotionality in TOTs might be indicative of the presence of a retrieved word that blocks or interferes with the retrieval of the correct target.

TOT Words

Diary studies show that TOTs are usually experienced in everyday life for proper nouns. Burke et al. (1991) found that across age groups, 65% of TOTs occurred for proper nouns (e.g., "Chuck Berry"). Abstract words (e.g., "idiomatic") followed, with the fewest TOTs occurring for object names. These findings have also been replicated by Schwartz (1999a), who found a 68% rate for proper names (see Table 2.3). However, Ecke (1997) found only a 33% rate for proper names, but found that another 45% were for nouns. None of the researchers speculated as to why proper nouns are so common TOT in-

TABLE 2.3

Summary of Findings From Diary Studies

	Burke et al. (1991)	Schwartz (1999a)	Heine et al. (1999)	Ecke (1997)
TOTs Per Week (Table 2.3A)				
Young	3.9	4.7	5.2	4.8
Middle-age	5.4			
Older	6.6		6.6	
Oldest			9.3	
TOT Resolution (Table 2.3B)				
Young	92%	89%	91%	90%
Middle-age	95%			
Older	97%		95%	
Oldest			98%	

Note. Data taken from Burke et al., 1991; Ecke, 1997; Heine et al., 1999; and Schwartz, 1999a.

ducers. However, it is likely that proper nouns are often important to remember and are frequently discussed. However, a name is often an arbitrary associate to the item it names. For example, names of people in American culture are somewhat arbitrary designations, such as "Richard Berg." That name tells us almost nothing about the person, except perhaps some of his ancestors may have spoken German. But even people's names are not as seemingly arbitrary as the names of American pop music groups, which were a particularly common TOT target in the Schwartz (1999a) study. The relation of "Afgan Wings," "Counting Crows," "10,000 Maniacs," and "Limp Biskit" to groups of musicians is very arbitrary. I wonder if those societies that name people by salient characteristics of the person (e.g., "Scarface," "Dances with Wolves") show lower rates of proper noun TOTs. This issue could be studied in a laboratory study, in which nicknames are assigned to faces. Those that are based on salient characteristics should be less likely to generate TOTs than those nicknames that are purely arbitrary.

Blocking

One diary study (Reason & Lucas, 1984) explored an issue called *blocking*, which means the retrieval of words known to be incorrect that then interfere with the retrieval of the correct word. For example, somebody might be trying to think of the word "rhinoceros," but failing to retrieve that word might keep retrieving "hippopotamus" (a semantic blocker) or "rhinovirus" (a phonological blocker), which are known to be incorrect (see Table 2.4 for more examples). Some theories of TOT etiology argue that TOTs arise when an incorrect word is retrieved and temporarily blocks retrieval of the correct target. Reason and Lucas (1984) were interested in what percentage of resolved TOTs would be reported as resulting from blocking. They found that over a 4-week period, participants averaged 2.5 resolved TOTs. More specific to their interests, Reason and Lucas found that over 50% of resolved TOTs were preceded by intrusive blocking words; words that kept resurfacing, but were recognized as incorrect. In a second study, with fewer participants and fewer TOTs, they found that 70% of resolved TOTs were preceded by intrusive blockers. However, their sample size was low (only 115 TOTs between two studies), and thus, may be less than representative.

Burke et al. (1991) also looked at blockers, although they called the blockers by a different name (persistent alternates). For the young participants, 67% of TOTs were accompanied by alternates. However, as people got older, the number of alternates decreased. In the older group, only 48% of TOTs were accompanied by alternates. Burke et al. found that nearly 90% of the alternates were from the same syntactic category as the missing word, that over one third shared the initial phoneme, and almost half shared the same number of syllables (see Table 2.4). Burke et. al. suggested that the decreased number of persistent alternates may be due to decreased phonological access in older adults (I explain this view later). This would account for the decrease in alternates when many theories of cognitive aging suggest that older adults become less efficient at screening out alternative retrieved responses (e.g., Salthouse, 1991).

The interpretation of blockers is problematic, however. Both Reason and Lucas (1984) and Burke et al. (1991) demonstrated a correlation between TOTs and blockers, but it is unclear whether the presence of blockers drives the TOT, whether the TOT creates the search for alternates, or whether each is a product of a slowed retrieval process. Nonetheless, the perseverance of these blockers is interesting. Rememberers know that they are not the right word, yet they have difficulties preventing their repeated retrieval when trying to get the target word. The topic of blocking will be revisited in chapter 3.

TABLE 2.4
Percentage of Alternates With Characteristics Identical to TOT Words

Group	Syntactic Category	Initial Phoneme	Number of Syllables
Young	85.2	36.2	50.9
Middle-age	84.1	38.9	37.8
Older	93.0	32.5	40.1
		Example	
Category		alternate	TOT Word
Same Syntactic		lobotomy	dichotomy
		vibrator	blender
		charity	chastity
		Montecito	Mendocino
		Betty Craighead	Besty Crighton
Different Syntactic		despair	discouraged
		Alistair Cooke	Masterpiece Theater
		flame	flamboyant
		rising	sizing
		manganese	magenta

Note. TOT = Tip-of-the-tongue phenomenon. Adapted from FIG. 9 in Burke et al. (1991), p. 558.

Resolution

Burke et al. (1991) found high rates of resolution for TOTs; roughly 95% across the three age groups. They also found a trend toward higher accuracy with age (see Table 2.3). The young adults resolved 92% of TOTs, whereas the middle-aged adults resolved 95%, and the older adults resolved 97% of TOTs. This trend was also replicated by Heine et al. (1999) who found 91% resolution in the younger adults, 95% in the older adults, and 97% resolution in the oldest. Ecke (1997) found 89% of TOTs were resolved in one's native language, but interestingly, 96% of TOTs in a foreign language were resolved. Schwartz (1999a) found an 89% resolution rate when sampling with a young-adult population. Although ceiling effects prevent the definitive conclusion that older adults are more likely to resolve their TOTs than younger adults, the data certainly point in that direction. I delay discussion of why this interesting age difference might occur until chapter 7.

Resolution Time

Diary studies also allow for an analysis of how long it takes people to remember the target word of naturally occurring TOTs. In the laboratory, participants are constrained by the nature of the experiment as to how long they can spend attempting retrieval, but in the natural world, the person may return to the search at any time. Unfortunately, unlike the other measures, retrieval times have differed substantially among the existing diary studies. For example, Schwartz (1999a) found that when deliberate search was the method of resolution, it took participants 14.8 min to resolve the TOT. However, Burke et al. (1991) found that it took participants only 4.3 min. It is unclear why these differences are so large. Alternately, Burke et al. found that spontaneous retrieval took 22.9 min, whereas Schwartz found that it took only 15.3 min. Hopefully, future diary studies will address this issue and find more reliable methods of measuring resolution time.

Resolution Method

Another important issue that can be addressed in diary studies is how people naturally resolve their TOTs. In the laboratory, participants are tested under relatively tight time constraints. Participants know that they have to go through a large number of items, and that they should not delay too much on any particular item. They also do not have access to outside sources. Thus, their ability to resolve TOTs is limited. In diary studies, people can resolve TOTs in a variety of ways over a variety of time frames. The diary studies identify three main methods of TOT resolution. First, participants can engage in active and deliberate search. Second, they can consult with other people or look up the answer in books, on Web sites, or through other outside means. Third, they can wait until spontaneous retrieval or "pop-up" occurs. The data from the three diary studies is presented in Table 2.3. The two main findings are that spontaneous retrieval is the method most often resulting in TOT resolution, and that the reliance on spontaneous retrieval increases with age.

Age

Age differences are perhaps the most studied issue in TOT research. The general finding is that older people experience more TOTs than younger people. This basic finding has been shown in the diary study by Burke et al. (1991) and in the diary study by Heine et al. (1999). In the study by Burke and colleagues, 130 participants were each asked to carry a TOT diary for 4 weeks. The participants were divided into three age groups: college-age adults, middle-aged adults, and older adults. The older (mean age = 71.0) and middle-aged (mean age = 38.7) participants scored higher on the WAIS (Wechsler Adult Intelligence Scale) vocabulary than did the younger adults (mean age = 19.4), but the younger adults had higher digit spans. Education levels were roughly equivalent.

TOTs varied significantly with age. The younger participants experienced only 3.92 TOTs over the 4-week period, for an average of slightly less than 1 per week. Middle-aged participants experienced 5.4 TOTs over the 4-week period, and older adults averaged 6.56 TOTs. Thus, their notion that naturally occurring TOTs would increase with age was confirmed. Heine et al. (1999) found an even higher TOT rate (9.33) for the oldest adults (participants over 80).

Thus, these findings confirm an a priori idea about TOTs. First, older adults do experience more TOTs than younger adults. However, because a longitudinal study has not yet been conducted, it is not quite definitive that this is really a function of age or other factors that might be correlated with age. Because many older people complain they experience more TOTs now than they did when they were younger, such a longitudinal study would be interesting. Alternately, contrary to expectations, it is the older adults who are actually better at resolving their TOTs. There are a number of reasons why this may be so. I return to this issue in chapter 7.

Strengths and Weaknesses of Diary Studies

Diary studies, although few in number, have already generated some interesting and replicable findings. First of all, the diary studies show that proper names are the kind of word retrieval most likely to induce a TOT. Second, most TOTs are eventually resolved (roughly 90%). Third, resolution of TOTs derives from a combination of methods such as deliberate search, spontaneous retrieval, and consulting outside sources. These conclusions were originally shown by Burke et al. (1991) and then replicated more recently by Heine et al. (1999) and Schwartz (1999a). Finally, the various studies converge on the broad generalization that the typical person, on average, experiences a TOT on an almost weekly basis. This rate increases for older individuals.

The diary methodology offers several advantages and disadvantages over laboratory tests of TOTs. I will outline the advantages first. In a diary study, the TOTs originate from everyday life. Therefore, they directly reflect the researcher's interest in the natural phenomena. Analysis, therefore, of the kinds of words for which people experience TOTs is illuminating. Thus, for example, it gives us an accurate reflection of how often TOTs occur for proper and common nouns. In contrast, laboratory studies rely on lists of general-information questions or word definitions. Thus, the ratio of proper nouns to common nouns to other kinds of words may be distorted because the experimenter provides the stimuli, and they are not the kinds of information that people are likely to discuss normally. Thus, the diary methodology gives a more ecologically valid picture of the kinds of materials for which TOTs occur.

Second, diary studies also allow researchers to better address issues of resolution. Because laboratory studies are usually conducted on relatively tight time frames, most researchers are only able to look at immediate resolution, that is, if the TOT is resolved within a few minutes of the onset of the TOT. However, diary studies show that many TOTs are resolved hours, if not days, after the original experience. Diary studies allow for that extended window on resolution. Related to the time course of resolution is the manner in which a TOT is resolved. TOTs may be resolved by an active memory search, spontaneous retrieval, consulting with other people, and by consulting other sources. Some TOTs, of course, may never be resolved.

One of the main drawbacks to the diary study is that it does not allow comparisons between TOTs and n–TOT s (unrecalled words not in TOT states). N–TOTs, or "don't know" states, in which people cannot recall the target but are not experiencing a TOT, provide a crucial comparison to

TOTs. If we wish to know what is unique about a TOT, we must compare it to n–TOTs, regardless of whether we are looking at resolution rates, partial information retrieval, or recognition. For example, we should expect more target knowledge during TOTs than during n–TOTs. However, because the diarist can only record experienced TOTs and not equivalent control items, the diary studies are lacking in the kind of controls that laboratory studies can utilize to clarify results. For example, in a laboratory, one can examine differences in resolution rates for unrecalled targets for both TOTs and n–TOTs. However, in the diary study, it is impossible to get people to record items that they do not know and did not try to recall. Thus, the diary study methodology is most successful when used in combination with laboratory studies (e.g., Burke et al., 1991; Heine et al., 1999).

Another drawback of diary studies is, of course, that by gaining ecological validity, one loses experimental control. The researcher no longer has control over input parameters, the situations in which the diarists find themselves, or the kinds of words that they need to retrieve in ordinary life. Nor is there a sufficient database on TOTs for the researchers to covary any of these variables in a meaningful way. With the exception of age, it is unclear whether any kind of individual difference (e.g., IQ, spatial ability, verbal ability, etc.) is correlated with TOT rate (but see Dahlgren, 1998; Frick-Horbury & Guttentag, 1998). Thus, diary studies do not necessarily give us a complete picture of what a TOT is, but they do provide us with some interesting ideas for laboratory testing and allow us to validate lab findings in the real world.

TOT PHENOMENOLOGY

The final issue to be addressed in this chapter is the clear and strong feeling that defines the TOT. Phenomenological salience can be thought of as being the key element of TOTs. When people enter a TOT, they experience a feeling that they will be able to remember a missing target. Informally, the feeling has been described by numerous researchers; the most well-known being James, quoted in chapter 1. Brown and McNeill (1966) described TOTs in the following way: "The signs of it [TOT] were unmistakable; he would appear to be in mild torment, something like the brink of a sneeze, and if he found the word his relief was considerable" (p. 326). A. S. Brown wrote, in reference to James and to Brown and McNeill that, "Such descriptions are congruent with one's personal introspections of inner turmoil when grappling for an elusive word" (p. 205). However, no empirical research has been directed at whether torment, turmoil, or relief is involved in the experiencing of TOTs. Most research has been content to note the phenomenology but not explore it in any systematic way.

Because the phenomenology of TOTs has been largely ignored, there is little existing research examining the experiential components of TOTs, or how such components might relate to objective retrieval behavior. Therefore, the following section represents a preliminary sketch as to what the important issues in TOT phenomenology may be, based primarily on some of my recent research (Schwartz et al., 2000; see also Burke et al., 1991, p. 560). The focus of my studies over the past few years has been the experience of strength, imminence, and emotionality that appear critical to TOTs. I have also addressed, albeit only descriptively, feelings of relief that may follow TOT resolution and also stability and fluctuation in TOTs over time. Feelings of relief refer to the emotion that occurs once a TOT has been resolved. Stability and fluctuation refer to how long a person actually experiences a TOT once it has been induced.

Research has used the retrieval of target information to divide TOTs into substates. For example, Koriat and Lieblich (1974) divided TOTs into nine different substates depending on whether the target was recognized or not recognized, recalled or not recalled, and whether partial information was recalled or not recalled (see their article for the specifics of the classification scheme). Jones and Langford (1987) divided TOTs into objective TOTs, those for which target information was retrieved, or subjective TOTs, those for which no target information was retrieved (also see Perfect and Hanley, 1992). Burke et al. (1991) defined "proper" TOTs as those followed by successful recognition. Vigliocco et al. (1997) divided TOTs into positive or negative TOTs, depending on whether the participant could correctly verify the TOT target. To the rememberer, however, it is the intense feeling that marks the TOT. Because the TOT is a subjective state and not simply a marker of partial accessibility, the phenomenology of TOTs, separate from the phenomenology of retrieval, is important. Indeed, the TOT feeling is not uniform across all instances and occasions. I suspect that TOTs vary with respect to intensity, emotional content, and feeling of imminence. These three dimensions come from my own experience and empirical studies. It is likely that they do not capture all of the differences in TOT phenomenology, but do provide us with a place to start. The current section addresses whether people can distinguish among phenomenological substates of the TOT, and whether these substates are predictive of memory performance.

One of the most critical aspects of TOT phenomenology is exactly what the role of emotion is in the formation and experience of TOTs. Most descriptions of the TOT include its frustration, or the "turmoil" it generates. Indeed, when we experience TOTs, it is the frustration of not being able to remember that may be most salient. In contrast, at other times, TOTs may be accompanied by a feeling of excitement that the answer will be eventually retrieved.

Emotionality

Many researchers report that rememberers often feel a surge of emotion when they experience a TOT. They report that TOTs do not simply elicit a feeling that a word can be recalled, but that the feeling is tinged with emotionality. Sometimes, this emotionality may be experienced as frustration with not being able to retrieve a word that is so obviously in memory. Alternately, the emotionality may take the form of excitement because of the feeling of imminent retrieval.

In turn, the experience of emotion may influence whether one experiences a TOT or may affect the rate at which people experience TOTs. When people are experiencing emotional stress, they may be more likely to experience TOTs. Anecdotal reports often describe a stressful situation that precedes a TOT. Indeed, in my own case, I often experience TOTs when a student from a previous semester approaches me while walking on campus. When I see the student, and the pressure to retrieve his or her name is there, I cannot do so. Usually a minute or so after the student has walked past, my retrieval system supplies the name. Oddly, research on emotionality and TOTs, or stressful conditions and TOTs, is rare. In this section, I describe research that has been done and its implications.

Emotional Feelings Accompanying TOTs

The first issue to address is whether anecdotal reports and researchers' intuitions have any basis in reality. With this in mind, research in my lab addressed how often participants ascribe an emotional state to TOTs, and whether that emotionality judgment correlates with objective measures of performance (Schwartz et al., 2000). College students answered a series of general information questions such as, "Who was the first person to walk on the moon?" If participants knew the answer (Armstrong), they typed it in and were presented with the next question. If participants could not recall the target word, they indicated whether they were experiencing a TOT. Furthermore, if they did indicate that they were experiencing a TOT, they made a decision as to whether the TOT was emotional or not. Emotionality in TOTs was described by Schwartz et al. (2000) as the following: "Sometimes, you may feel frustrated or emotional that you cannot recall a word that you are sure you know. If you are in a TOT state that is accompanied by this emotional content, indicate a TOT with emotion by pressing the E key" (p. 22). After completing of the questions, they were shown the set of unrecalled questions again. They were given a chance to produce the answers a second time. If resolution was unsuccessful, they then attempted recognition. Rememberers quite readily made the distinction between emotional and nonemotional TOTs, and the judgments were predictive of performance. Roughly half (55%) of TOTs were judged by participants to involve an emotional component. TOTs judged to be emotional were more likely to be resolved and to be recognized than TOTs not judged to be emotional. Nonemotional TOTs were more likely to be resolved and recognized than n–TOTs. Thus, the study suggested that TOTs can be divided into emotional and nonemotional substates, and that these substates are predictive of performance.

In the diary study described earlier (Schwartz, 1999a), participants also decided whether their TOTs were emotional. With the naturally-occurring TOTs, 61% were judged to be emotional, slightly higher than in the laboratory study. Interestingly however, emotionality was counter-predictive of whether the TOT would be resolved. In fact, 89% of unresolved TOTs were judged to be emotional, whereas only 58% of eventually resolved TOTs were judged to be emotional.

In the laboratory study (Schwartz et al., 2000), however, emotionality of TOTs was positively correlated with resolution and recognition. Emotionality was less predictive of resolution than were other phenomenological variables (e.g., imminence, strength). Thus, it is not contradictory with the diary study. One possible explanation, as yet unexplored, is that emotionality in TOTs is associated with blocking, that is, that the retrieval of related but incorrect items interferes with the resolution of the TOT. This interference creates both difficulties in retrieving and induces the emotional state characteristic of TOTs.

In another laboratory study (Schwartz, 2001), I asked participants to make a three-way distinction when they were in a TOT. The participants were asked to distinguish between emotionally frustrating TOTs, emotionally exciting TOTs, and nonemotional TOTs. The definitions provided for the participants were as follows:

> Some TOTs may be accompanied by emotional frustration, because you know the answer, but the failure to retrieve it causes you to be frustrated. Some TOTs may be accompanied by emotional excitement because you sense that you are about to retrieve the answer at any second. Some TOTs may not be accompanied by any experience of emotion at all. Please indicate your emotional state following a TOT.

In analyzing the results, I distinguished between two kinds of memory errors (Krinsky & Nelson, 1985; Riefer, Kevari, & Kramer, 1995). Commission errors are those errors in which the participant provides an answer, but the answer is incorrect. Omission errors are those errors in which the participant does not produce any answer, correct or incorrect. We asked for TOTs after both commission and omission errors. TOTs that followed commission and omission errors differed with respect to their judged emotionailty. Following commission errors, 34% of TOTs were judged to be frustrating and 21% of TOTs were judged to exciting. However, following omission errors, 59% of TOTs were judged to be frustrating, but only 7% of TOTs were judged to be exciting. These differences between TOTs following commission and omission errors were statistically significant. Thus, TOTs following unsuccessful recall are still marked by a sense of excitement or nearness to the target, whereas TOTs for the omission items are those that are simply frustrating, perhaps because the answer is not imminently recallable.

In the case of commission errors, the rememberer has recalled an incorrect answer, and the fluency produced by that response may insure that the rememberer will feel like he or she can retrieve another answer, now the correct one. In this way, ironically, the wrong answer generates the excitement because of the perceived closeness to the answer. In contrast, omission errors are not accompanied by the retrieval of any answers. Therefore, the lack of retrieval combined with the sense of knowing the answer (that is, the TOT) may drive the sense of frustration.

I find these data to be suggestive, although far from conclusive. Something is going on with TOTs and emotionality, but what that is is not yet obvious. Here is what I think is clear from the aforementioned studies (Schwartz, 2001; Schwartz et al., 2000): TOTs can be accompanied by emotional states, some of which are positive and some of which are negative. Emotionality, particularly frustration, appears to be associated with a failure to retrieve or with a block that is precluding retrieval of the target word. Thus, when we are forced to say that we do not know the target, our TOT is frustrating. However, when we are retrieving the blocker or other words that we suspect are close, but not quite there, then the TOT may be experienced as exciting because we feel the correct target is on its way.

However, the direction of causality is unknown from these studies. It is possible that the emotionality is a product of the processes that drive the TOT. On the other hand, it is also possible that processes that produce emotional responses may, to some extent, be also responsible for eliciting the TOT in the first place. Moreover, the relation of emotional excitement to the feeling of imminence of retrieval is only a hypothesis. It is possible that the feeling of imminence drives the emotional excitement or vice versa. These topics are areas for future study.

Stress and TOTs

An unexplored issue is whether the experience of stress or feelings of emotional upheaval influence TOT experiences. Frequently, people report that a TOT occurs for a name that they need immediately under conditions of stress. Once the stress passes, the TOT is resolved. For example, it is a common experience among students that they cannot retrieve answers on tests during the test time, but the answers occur to them after they have left the testing room. Although their professors may be skeptical, those professors may have similar experiences when trying to retrieve student names. It may also be the case that TOTs are more common in stressful environments such as the workplace, whereas relatively fewer TOTs are experienced at home when relaxed. However, there has been no direct research on the relation between stress and TOTs.

Indirectly however, the work of Widner, Smith, and Graziano (1996) is relevant. Widner et al. were concerned that demand characteristics of the experimental context may influence participants' decisions about when to report a TOT. Widner et al. observed that in many TOT paradigms, the items for recall are difficult ones because the experimenter wants a large potential set of unrecalled items. Their point is well taken. For example, in my experiments, I select general-information questions in which students obtain the correct answer around 40% of the time (Schwartz, 1998; 2001; Schwartz et al., 2000). The difficult items allow one to collect more TOTs, but under these circumstances, Widner et al. argued that participants may feel pressured to feel like they know more than they do because of the low levels of recall that they are showing. Thus, to avoid seeming uneducated, there may be some subtle bias to overreport TOTs. Widner et al. reasoned that rememberers should experience more TOTs when the pressures to perform well are perceived as high. Widner et al. claimed that if TOTs are caused by demand characteristics, then at least to some extent, TOTs may be induced by processes other than target retrieval.

Widner et al. (1996) manipulated the participant's expectations of difficulty. In one condition, participants were led to believe that a set of general-information questions were normatively easy. In a second condition, a different group of participants were led to believe that the questions were normatively difficult. The questions were, in fact, identical.

The results were quite revealing. Widner et al. (1996) found that when participants believed that the questions were normatively easy, they were more likely to report TOTs than when they believed that the questions were normatively difficult. There are two interpretations of this result. First, participants may have been reporting TOTs even when they were not really experiencing them just to appear better educated. Second, the greater stress associated with the expectation of easy questions may have indeed induced more TOT experiences.

I suspect that the better explanation of Widner et al.'s (1996) data is the latter interpretation. In addition to collecting TOTs, they also asked participants to report feeling-of-knowing judgments (predictions of subsequent recognition). The feeling-of-knowing judgments were unaffected by the manipulation of expectation. This suggests that the effect on TOTs was not simply be due to wanting to appear more knowledgeable and reporting more TOTs, as this desire should also cause an increase in feeling-of-knowing judgments as well. Rather, I suspect that a potential explanation is the expectations that the questions would be easy created stress when the participants themselves found them to be more difficult than they thought they should be. The stress then increased the rate of TOT experiences. Thus, the participants really did experience more TOTs when they thought the questions were easy, but they were having difficulties retrieving them nonetheless.

I have discussed my interpretation of Widner et al.'s (1996) data with a number of researchers in the field, and I have also made this argument in articles submitted to journals. Most reviewers find fault with my interpretation. I claim that the stress of not being able to retrieve easy items creates an illusion of knowing, subjectively felt as a TOT. Criticisms of my interpretation of the Widner et al. (1996) data have centered around whether the TOTs were really TOTs at all or were simply reported TOTs. This criticism is based on the view that all TOTs must be linked to a particular target in memory for which retrieval has broken down. Under this view, it is unlikely that TOTs could be induced by demand characteristics. Therefore, the TOTs are dismissed as "TOT reports." However, I assert that because TOTs are subjectively defined by the rememberer, if a person reports a TOT, this report must be taken seriously. The TOT may not correspond to knowledge or awareness of the unrecalled target, but it is still an experienced TOT. The difference between the feeling-of-knowing judgments and the TOTs supports this conjecture. Therefore, I have argued that the Widner et al. data support the notion that processes other than retrieval can affect TOTs.

I prefer an interpretation of Widner et al.'s (1996) data in which the change in TOT rates is mediated by the stress experienced by the participant. The "normatively-easy" condition induces a sense of stress in the participants because they think they are doing worse than average. This stress mimics the emotion one feels when a familiar person is approaching, but we cannot retrieve his or her name. This experience of familiarity combined with the failure to retrieve and the subsequent onset of emotion causes the experience of a TOT. In Widner et al's experiment, the increased pressure to perform stimulates the emotional response that helps trigger a TOT. This explanation is highly speculative now, but I have become convinced of the role of affect in TOTs.

If this interpretation is correct, the relation between stress and TOTs may have wide-reaching implications. For example, a wide range of psychosocial variables can increase stress, such as sleep deprivation, poor health, competing life demands, bereavement, and so forth. If stress increases the rate of

TOTs experienced, one might predict that relative to control conditions, people under a variety of stressful conditions may experience more TOTs. Some stressful conditions (e.g., depression) have also been shown to impair retrieval. Indeed, age-related increases in TOTs may be due to the increased stress that older adults experience when their retrieval system does not appear to be functioning as efficiently as when they were younger. The relation of stress, its effect on retrieval, and its effect on TOTs may interact in interesting ways. Might some forms of stress interfere with retrieval without increasing TOT rates, or might some forms of stress increase TOTs without affecting the recall rate? Is some stress necessary for TOTs to be resolved or does too much stress render resolution difficult? Unfortunately, at the time of the writing of this book, the research on TOTs and stress is in its infancy. Hopefully, researchers will begin to address these important and interesting questions.

Gradations of TOTs

Some TOTs are particularly strong overriding feelings whereas other TOTs may be fleeting sensations. Intuitively then, some TOTs are stronger than others. Typically however, following Brown and McNeill (1966), most researchers ask participants to make dichotomous judgments, such as "yes, I'm in a TOT," or "no, I'm not in a TOT." For data analysis purposes, one can look at resolution, recognition, or reported partial information as a function of whether a TOT was reported. Dichotomizing the judgments, however, may cause people to neglect some important features of TOTs. There is no a priori reason to believe that the TOT is an all-or-none state.

An exception to the tradition of dichotomizing comes from a study by Kozlowski (1977), who used a 5-point Likert-type scale to measure TOTs for general-information questions (see also Gardiner et al., 1973). Kozlowski asked participants to answer the following question: "Would you say that the correct answer is on the tip of your tongue (*not at all* = 0 to *completely confident* = 4)?" (p. 478). Participants successfully used this scale, and it predicted recognition performance. When participants gave a 0 (i.e., not at all in a TOT), they recognized only 46% of the correct targets in recognition. When they experienced a "moderate" TOT (1 or 2), they recognized 61% of the correct targets, and when they experienced an "extreme" TOT (3 or 4), they recognized 84% of the correct targets. This finding suggests that TOTs may exist at different levels of strength, and that these levels may correspond to the likelihood of having objective knowledge.

Recent research from my laboratory has begun to use graded scales for TOTs (Schwartz et al., 2000). In a study with general information stimuli, participants who could not recall the target word were asked if they were experiencing a TOT. They marked one of three responses to indicate the strength of their TOT: "strong" to indicate an intense TOT, "weak" to signify a TOT that was less intense, and "no" to indicate that they did not feel that they could recall the target name. Essentially, this boils down to a 3-point scale, only couched in nominal terms instead of a Likert rating system. In the study, rememberers reliably distinguished between strong and weak TOTs. Strong TOTs represented over 60% of all TOTs. Strong TOTs were better resolved than weak TOTs, but interestingly only after errors of commission (23% and 8%, respectively). However, recognition was better for all strong TOTs (35%) than for all weak TOTs (30%), regardless of the status of the error.

The data from Schwartz et al. (2000) and from Kozlowski (1977) suggest that gradations do exist among TOTs, and that stronger TOTs are more likely to be associated with actual target knowledge than the weaker ones. Thus, prior research may have been missing variance in the data by simply dichotomizing TOT states. In addition, that gradations in TOTs track objective knowledge may support a direct-access model of the etiology of TOTs, namely that the retrieval process produces the TOT.

Imminence

A frequent experience during a TOT is the feeling that the word is about to be retrieved. This sense of the closeness of the retrieval has been labeled imminence (Smith, 1994). James (1890), for example, wrote that TOTs are characterized by "making us at moments tingle with the sense of our closeness and then letting us sink back without the longed-for term" (p. 251). Smith (1994) argued imminence may be the key to understanding TOTs, and that some TOTs are accompanied by imminence and others are not. Potentially, rememberers might be able to distinguish between "close" TOTs, those TOTs that are subjectively likely to be resolved soon, and "far" TOTs, those TOTs that are subjectively not likely to be resolved.

The study on imminence followed the same paradigm as the studies on emotionality and strength (Schwartz et al., 2000). Rememberers made TOT judgments after failing to recall general information questions. They were asked to distinguish between imminent TOTs (those immediately resolvable) and nonimminent TOTs (a feeling that the answer is known but that it is not forthcoming immediately). Again, about half of all TOTs were judged imminent (51%). Imminent TOTs (14%) were much more likely to be resolved than nonimminent TOTs (3%) and more likely to be recognized (50% vs. 33%).

This study suggests that the imminence distinction may have phenomenological reality, and that imminence judgments are predictive of objective performance, both of which are quite important. First, the TOT and the feeling of imminence are not identical as roughly half of the TOTs were judged not to be imminent. It is possible that different mechanisms drive TOTs that are imminent and those that are not. For example, imminent TOTs may be driven by direct access to the unretrieved target whereas nonimminent TOTs may be driven by an inference that the target is or should be known. Second, imminence judgments are predictive of performance. People do indeed resolve imminent TOTs more often than the nonimminent TOTs, suggesting that whatever imminence taps into, it is predictive of performance above and beyond the accuracy of TOTs.

Other Phenomenological Aspects, as Yet Unstudied

Two important but neglected aspects of the TOT experience are the "aha" experience that accompanies a spontaneous pop-up and feelings of relief that the TOT has been resolved. Neither of these phenomena has received but the scantiest attention in the scientific literature. Therefore, what follows is almost exclusively conjecture, backed up by only a sliver of data (Schwartz, 1999a).

The "aha" experience occurs when the TOT target is retrieved, and the person feels a strong emotional surge in conjunction with strong confidence in the correctness of the retrieval. The "aha" experience therefore, may be analogous to the "insight" phenomena observed in the problem-solving literature (Metcalfe & Wiebe, 1987; Smith, 1994). According to Metcalfe and Wiebe (1987), certain problems are solved all at once, and only after they are solved does the person's metacognitive system become aware of the solution. Therefore, confidence comes all at once in a sudden "aha." Indeed, Metcalfe and Wiebe (1987) found that when confidence slowly increased for insight-type problems, confidence mispredicted a correct solution to the problems. However, despite speculation concerning the relation of TOTs to insight problem solving (e.g., Smith, 1994), there has been no empirical data collected to date on the "aha" experience with TOTs.

In a diary study (Schwartz, 1999a), rememberers were to indicate whether, on the resolution of a TOT, they felt a feeling of relief. Unfortunately, the diary instructions were somewhat unclear as to what was meant by the term *relief*, but most rememberers interpreted it to mean a sense of emotional relief had been brought about by remembering the forgotten word. In fact, 79% of resolved TOTs were accompanied by feelings of relief. Although it is highly possible that feelings of relief did not mean the same thing to all participants, the high rate coincides with the findings that many TOTs are emotionally frustrating experiences. Therefore, it should not be surprising that the resolution of the frustration is accompanied by relief.

Stability and Fluctuation of TOTs

We now turn from the investigation of TOT substates and specific phenomenological aspects of the TOT to whether the TOT persists over time or whether it changes with time. The question here is, how long does a TOT last, and if the item is not retrieved, will the same TOT reoccur later?

Imagine meeting an old acquaintance on a street corner. You are overcome by a TOT for the person's name, but cannot retrieve it. You handle the situation by mentioning the last time you met, how much fun that was, but carefully avoid addressing the person by name. You part ways still without retrieving the person's name. Has the TOT lasted throughout the entire conversation? Or, once the conversation began, was the TOT for the person's name no longer present, despite the continued inability to retrieve the name? Later, your spouse asks you about your day. You begin to describe the meeting with the old acquaintance. Do you reexperience the TOT for the person's name? Assuming you had not succeeded in resolution, how long does the TOT persist before it wanes. Or does it get stronger and more frustrating with the passage of time?

I have labeled this phenomena fluctuation and stability in TOTs (Schwartz, 1998). Stability means that the same stimulus elicits TOTs over repeated presentations, assuming that the target word has not been resolved. Fluctuation means that the TOT experience appears, dissapears, and then may appear again. There are two separable issues in TOT stability and fluctuation. First, when a person experiences a TOT, does the feeling last throughout the retrieval effort? It is possible that as time progresses and no retrieval is forthcoming, the TOT may wane. Alternately, the emotional feelings of frustration of not being able to retrieve the name may actually cause the TOT to wax. This issue has not been experimentally investigated. Second, are TOTs stable across repeated questioning? That is, if you return to the question later, will you again experience a TOT? One set of experiments conducted by my collaborators and I addressed this question.

We investigated the issue of whether unresolved TOTs repeat themselves on a second presentation of the retrieval cue (Schwartz & Smith, 1998). If a participant could not recall the target word in a general information paradigm, they indicated whether they were experiencing a TOT. After completing the 100 questions, the participants were again shown the set of unrecalled questions. They were given a second chance to produce the answers, and if they could not, they were asked again whether they were in a TOT for that question. Each participant made an initial TOT judgment after the initial questioning and a subsequent TOT judgment after the second round of testing.

The results demonstrated two phenomena. TOTs tended to be stable across time, but there was some fluctuation. Of the targets that were not resolved on the second recall attempt, 60% remained TOTs during the second round. This means that 40% fluctuated from TOTs to n–TOTs. This 40% change represents waning, that is, items that no longer induced a TOT. Interestingly, waxing from a n–TOT to a TOT was less common but did occur. After successful resolutions were accounted for, 8% of the questions that originally did not induce a TOT succeeded in inducing a TOT during the second round of questioning. Therefore, TOTs can both wax (here defined as a transition from n–TOT to TOT) and wane, at least during repeated questioning.

This study is merely preliminary because it has yet to be replicated with other stimuli. However, it documented both waning from a TOT to a n–TOT and waxing from a n–TOT to a TOT. However, it does not indicate any mechanism for why some TOTs would remain stable whereas others changed. What could be going on? The following is a speculative account of these data. It is possible that TOTs are based on the amount and rate of information that the rememberer can retrieve (e.g., Koriat, 1993). If so, as long as information is being retrieved, even if it is repetitive, the TOT may persist. Thus, TOTs will remain stable across repeated questioning if the rememberer again retrieves related information (even if it is the same partial information as in the earlier attempt). However, if the rememberer no longer retrieves any information, the TOT may not reoccur. In contrast, a n–TOT that transforms into a TOT may result because partial information is retrieved now that was not retrieved before. This speculative account is consistent with some mechanistic accounts of TOT formation (Schwartz & Smith, 1997).

This study did not address whether TOTs remain stable across a concerted retrieval effort. It only shows whether a TOT will reoccur when the person is reminded of an otherwise forgotten retrieval attempt. The methodology of an experiment that addressed stability and fluctuation across a single TOT experience would be relatively straightforward. One would "prospect" for TOTs using the Brown–McNeill procedure (Brown & McNeill, 1966). On finding a TOT, the rememberer would be asked to make a concerted effort to retrieve the target word. During this retrieval effort, the rememberer would be asked to make a TOT judgment every 15 sec or so. Metcalfe and Wiebe (1987) used a similar strategy to track "warmth" judgments in problem solving. Using this basic methodology, one could track whether TOTs persisted over the retrieval interval, or whether they faded if the person was unable to recover the target. If the basic methodology worked, the researchers could also track the amount of retrieved information, when that information was retrieved, and how it correlated with TOT stability or fluctuation. Finally, the researchers could call for the rememberers to assess TOT substates, and address how they change over time. Despite the promise and intrigue of this methodology, we have not yet addressed it in my lab, and there has not been any published work on it elsewhere.

The bottom line is that we know little about the nature of TOT phenomenology. We also know little about the causes of TOT phenomenology. What the previous section emphasizes is first to provide a descriptive account of how TOTs are experienced by people, and also to move toward an understanding of the nature and causes of TOT phenomenology. I strongly suspect that the TOT is not a unitary experience, but a combination of various subcomponents, relating to positive or negative emotion, and feelings of imminence, relief, or strength. In some cases, these experiences may grow, whereas in others, they may diminish. How these subcomponents are formed and how they interact to create human experience and to predict cognitive processes is a riddle, the answer to which is just beginning to be unfolded.

I hope that the research reviewed in this section will inspire other researchers to begin exploring TOT phenomenology, as it my belief that such research will provide us with tremendous insight into subjective experience, retrieval, and the nature of conscious experience.

SUMMARY

In this chapter, a case was made for the universality of TOTs. A survey was discussed in which I found a literal translation of the metaphor "on the tip of the tongue" in 90% of living languages. Several diary studies presented a portrait of what a TOT looks like in naturally occurring instances. The nascent literature on TOT phenomenology was reviewed to begin to explore the important aspects of the TOT experience. The chapter ended with some experimental findings describing the paradox of illusory TOTs. This will set the stage for the discussion of issues of TOT etiology in chapter 3.

3

Theories of TOT Etiology

The research discussed in the first two chapters was mainly descriptive. Descriptive research is of crucial importance because it defines the phenomena under investigation and suggests avenues of understanding. Description should always accompany explanation. However, as scientists, our chief interest lies in what is the cause of the phenomena we study. Thus, good science must always move back and forth between description of the phenomena and experimentation on the phenomena's causation. In this chapter, we begin to discuss the theories that have been advanced and tested to understand why TOTs occur.

Following Brown (1991), I use the term *etiology* to refer to the causes of TOTs. Not normally used in cognitive research, the word etiology captures what is meant by the causes that underlie the TOT. Etiology is the set of psychological circumstances that cause a person to experience a TOT for a known (or unknown) target word. Understanding the etiology of TOTs will inform research in lexical retrieval, interference in memory, and the nature of metacognition.

The question as to the mechanisms that drive the TOT may be the most interesting. Answering this question may resolve many of the other debates concerning TOTs. What might such a psychological mechanism entail? The mechanism must be able to monitor word retrieval because the TOT experience is essentially a retrieval experience. Moreover, the mechanism ought to be accurate, that is, when a TOT occurs, it should correlate with the likelihood of subsequent retrieval. Finally, there may be some reason for the conscious experience known as the TOT. In essence, what function does the TOT experience serve the organism? It has been hypothesized that the func-

tion of TOTs is to guide retrieval, to influence the choice of retrieval strategies, or to "buy time" in front of others when knowledge is not forthcoming.

The explanations advanced in this chapter are psychological in nature.
In chapter 7, I discuss the limited neurological evidence on TOTs and prof-
fer some conjectures about the biological causes of TOTs. Chapter 6 discusses control functions of TOTs. In this chapter, however, I focus
exclusively on explanations of TOT etiology at the psychological level. Indeed, there are several compelling psychological theories for which substan-
tial evidence has been gathered. Unlike many sections in this volume, in
which I lament the lack of research, TOT etiology has been well studied.

Nelson, Gerler, and Narens (1984) categorized theories concerning the
bases of metamemory into two main classes. Recently, these classes have been
applied to TOTs (Askari, 1999; Metcalfe, Schwartz, & Joaquin, 1993; Miozzo
& Caramazza, 1997; Schwartz, 1994; Schwartz & Smith, 1997; Smith, 1994).
The two classes of theories are labeled *direct-access* views and *inferential* views.
Direct-access views argue that TOTs arise from sensitivity to the unretrieved
target. Although items have insufficient memory "strength" to be recalled,
they are strong enough to signal their presence as TOTs. Inferential views
claim that TOTs are not based directly on an inaccessible but activated target.
Rather, TOTs arise from clues that the rememberer can piece together. These
clues are information that is accessible to the rememberer, such as information from the retrieval cue or information related to the target that is retrieved. Although direct access and inferential views are not mutually
exclusive, they represent different approaches to the etiology of TOTs, and
have led to different research emphases. The two classes of theories differ with
respect to their position on the doctrine of concordance. Direct-access views
typically, but not always, implicitly endorse concordance, whereas inferential
views usually challenge the doctrine (see Table 3.1).

Direct access views, in effect, do not really postulate any mechanism at all
for TOT formation. They simply posit that the retrieval mechanism simultaneously works to retrieve target words from memory and produces a TOT in

TABLE 3.1

Differences Between Direct Access and Inferential Models of TOTs

Theory	Mode of Action	Implication for Accuracy	Doctrine
Direct-Access	Retrieval causes TOT	Direct link between retrieval and judgment	Endorses
Inferential	Heuristic processes cause TOT	Retrieval and heuristic are correlated	Rejects

Note. TOTs = Tip-of-the-tongue phenomena.

the word's absence. Thus, TOTs are simply a by-product of a faulty retrieval mechanism. In contrast, the inferential view suggests that there are separate processes involved in retrieval and in the formation of a TOT experience. Thus, although the views are not mutually exclusive, and both types of mechanisms may be partially responsible for some TOTs, the hypothesized mechanisms in each view have radically different implications for what a TOT is and how it functions in the organism. For example, if a TOT is simply a point on a continuum from a weak representation to a strong representation, it may not necessarily serve any useful function in cognition, and may only be a simple failure in the retrieval process. On the other hand, if a complex inferential system has evolved to allow us to experience TOTs, it may serve important functions in the regulation of cognitive and linguistic processes.

When I explain the TOT to people, psychologists and laypeople alike, they prefer direct-access explanations. When I started doing research on TOTs in the early 90s, my goal was to find experimental evidence to support direct-access views of TOTs. If a word is on the tip of the tongue, it feels like we can taste the word, sense it with our tongues, but just cannot get our tongue completely around it. It feels to us as if the presence of the word is driving the phenomenological state. I have explained the difference between direct and inferential views to many people. All intuitively feel that the direct access view more accords with their experience. Indeed, they are often incredulous when I explain that based on my research, I now prefer the inferential view.

It is important to again distinguish between process and experience. The TOT feels as if it were the product of a direct access to the unretrieved target. However, that does not mean that, in fact, it is caused by a direct access mechanism. Only careful experimentation can distinguish between the two views.

DIRECT-ACCESS THEORIES

Direct-access approaches fall into three basic theories. The first theory, the blocking hypothesis (Jones, 1989), contends that TOTs occur when a retrieval cue prompts retrieval of an incorrect but closely related word. The realization that the retrieved word is incorrect prompts the experience of the TOT, although the blocking word continues to interfere with the retrieval of the correct word. The second theory, the incomplete activation hypothesis, states that the TOT occurs when rememberers cannot recall the target word, but sense its presence nonetheless. The third direct-access theory has been developed by Burke and her colleagues (Burke et al., 1991; James & Burke, 2000; Rastle & Burke, 1996; see also Askari, 1999; Harley & Bown, 1998; Heine et al., 1999). Burke's theory, the transmission deficit model, argued that TOTs arise from a multi component memory representation. TOTs occur when there is activation of the semantic component of the word, but priming does not pass to the phonological level of the word. For example, on hearing the definition, "a device for protection from the rain or sun," a semantic and perhaps a visual representation of the object may be retrieved, but the definition does not activate the phonological representation (e.g., the word umbrella). Related to Burke's model are recent models by Miozzo and Caramazza (Caramazza & Miozzo, 1997; Miozzo & Caramazza, 1997). These models are similar to Burke's in the etiology of TOTs, although they differ in the mechanism of word retrieval. Like Burke, Miozzo and Caramazza argued that TOTs arise when phonological information does not follow the retrieval of semantic information, but they disagree on the number of stages in the process. The difference between Burke's transmission deficit model and the models of Miozzo and Caramazza are more about the nature of lexical retrieval and less about the etiology of TOTs. Thus, I defer these differences until chapter 4.

Support for the Direct-Access View

There is ample evidence for the view that TOTs are a product arising from the same processes that are involved in retrieval. Three basic kinds of evidence have been used to promote direct access theory: resolution or recall of TOT targets, recognition of TOT targets, and retrieval of partial information. Retrieved partial information may be phonologically, semantically, or syntactically related to the target. Each methodology reveals strong associations between TOTs and retrieval. The evidence to be reviewed here first supports each of the three different direct-access models. After discussing the evidence concerning direct access, I will break down the different versions of direct access and discuss evidence that supports or refutes each model.

   Resolution of TOT Targets.   Support for the assumption that TOTs arise from retrieval processes comes from studies that find strong positive correlations between the likelihood of experiencing a TOT and the likelihood of resolving the target. Resolution is the retrieval of a previously unrecalled TOT item. In diary studies, better than 90% of recorded TOTs were reported as eventually resolved (Burke et al., 1991; Heine et al., 1999; Schwartz, 1999a). This remarkably high percentage indicates a strong correspondence between TOT phenomenology and objective performance. Unfortunately, in diary studies, it is impossible to compare TOT resolution with n–TOT resolution.

   In the laboratory, resolution rates with definitions or general-information questions are typically around 40% (Brown, 1991). Resolution is even lower with episodic-memory stimuli (Ryan, Petty, & Wenzlaff, 1982; Schwartz,

1998). Typically, however, laboratory data are based on studies that investigate immediate resolution, whereas diary studies tap both immediate and delayed resolution, so it is unclear whether these studies are comparable in this regard. In fact, Smith (1994) found that immediate resolution of TOTs for fictional animals was only 9%. Resolution rose to 43% after a 6-min delay. Furthermore, Smith found that resolution was much more likely to occur after a TOT than a n–TOT. Resolution rates for n–TOTs were 3% at the immediate test and 19% at the delayed test. Schwartz (1998) also found lower resolution rates for n–TOTs. Gollan and Silverberg (in press) found that resolution of TOT targets was more than double the resolution of n–TOT targets for both Hebrew and English words. These studies demonstrate a strong correspondence between TOTs and the likelihood of successful resolutions, which supports the view that TOTs reflect target retrieval processes.

Recognition of TOT Targets. Although an item may not be strong enough to be recalled, it may exist in memory and may be accurately recognized. For this reason, a recognition test can assess whether the TOT items are actually of greater strength in memory than items not in a TOT. Some TOT studies have looked at recognition of targets after the rememberers experienced TOTs or n–TOTs (e.g., Burke et al., 1991; Kozlowski, 1977; Schwartz, 1998, 2001; Schwartz & Smith, 1997; Schwartz, et al., 2000; Smith, Balfour, & Brown, 1994; Widner et al., 1996). Recognition of the correct target following a TOT is much more likely than recognition of the correct target when rememberers are not experiencing a TOT (see Table 3.2). Schwartz (1998) measured the gamma correlation between TOTs and recognition, finding a correlation of .66 between TOTs and correct recognition (see Nelson, 1984 for discussion of the gamma correlation). Thus, like resolution, studies that examine recognition also find strong correlations between the presence of TOTs and the likelihood of correct target retrieval.

Partial Information of TOT Targets. In partial information reports, the rememberer is asked to recall specific aspects of the target word. Usually, this involves phonological information, such as the first letter, the number of syllables, and the syllabic stress (Brown & McNeill, 1966). It may also involve semantic information. Participants are asked whether they can retrieve words that sound similar to or that mean something similar to the TOT target. The rationale for this kind of report is the assumption that the TOT reflects activation of a target word, but insufficient activation to achieve full recall. Indeed, almost all studies that elicit partial information find that participants can accurately retrieve some. TOTs have been shown to be correlated with knowledge of first letters, last letters, number of syllables, knowl-

TABLE 3.2

Recognition Rates for TOTs and n–TOTs

		TOTs	n–TOTs
Burke et al. (1991)		81%	Not Reported
Kozlowski (1977)		73%	46
Schwartz (1998)	Exp. 1	81%	63
	Exp. 2	40%	11
Schwartz (2001)	Exp. 1	46%	14
	Exp. 2	55%	31
	Exp. 3	65%	30
	Exp. 4	49%	16
Schwartz & Smith (1997)	Exp 1	81%	70
	Exp. 2	83%	74
	Exp. 3	84%	64
Schwartz et al. (2000)	Exp. 1	33%	10
	Exp. 2	35%	10
	Exp. 3	32%	10
Smith et al. (1994)		78%	57

Note. Percent correct on recognition tests as a function of phenomenological state, TOT Versus n–TOT (items not recalled and not in TOT). Higher recognition performance for TOTs than n–TOTs indicate accurate performance. TOT = Tip-of-the-tongue phenomenon.

edge of similar words, and syllabic stress (see Brown, 1991, for a review). Koriat and Lieblich (1974) showed that more partial information was retrieved when rememberers were in TOTs than could be explained by a guessing strategy based on the frequency of those letters as initial-position letters in the English language. Murakami (1980) found partial recall of letters in Japanese, and Bak (1987) found partial recall of first letters in Polish. Bak (1987) also documented that Polish rememberers were able to retrieve words that sounded similar to or meant something similar to the TOT word. Askari (1999) showed the same type of partial retrieval of information in Farsi.

Other studies examined the relation between TOTs and syntactical features of language. Italian- and Spanish-speaking rememberers have access to the gender of words when in a TOT (Miozzo & Caramazza, 1997; Vigliocco et al., 1997), although Hebrew speakers do not access gender during TOTs (Silverberg et al., 1999). Iwasaki, Vigliocco, and Garrett (1998) found that Japanese rememberers have access to parts of speech, such as whether a word was an adjective or an adjectival noun (a feature in Japanese that indicates that an adjective derives from a noun, as in "rocky"), when in a TOT. Furthermore, Vigliocco et al. (1999) found that English-speaking participants have access to the type of article used for mass (i.e., "some") or "count" (i.e., "the") nouns when in a TOT. For example, the words *peppermint* or *asparagus* are never pluralized; we indicate quantity by terms such as *more*, *some*, and *less*. These are considered mass nouns. Count nouns, such as *cucumber* or *photograph* are pluralized by adding an *s*. In the absence of being able to recall the target word, rememberers are nonetheless able to categorize them as mass or count nouns at a better-than-chance rate when experiencing a TOT.

TOTs have been shown to be accurate predictors of objective memory performance. Moreover, when rememberers are experiencing TOTs, they often successfully recall partial information about the target. This suggests that people experiencing TOTs are retrieving target information. These phenomena are consistent with the position that the retrieval process is causing the TOT for the unrecalled word. Thus, these findings support the view that TOTs reflect target word activation.

To summarize, a large database exists demonstrating strong correlations between TOTs and the likelihood of resolution, recognition, and retrieval of partial information, whether that information is phonological, semantic, or syntactic. This strong correlation is suggestive, but not conclusive, of direct access mechanisms. Because the data only show correlations between retrieval and TOT experience, causal mechanisms cannot be definitively determined. Indeed, inferential mechanisms can also account for these correlations (i.e., Koriat, 1993). Nonetheless, I have included them in this section because of general acceptance that the accessibility of partial information and the eventual retrieval of TOTs support direct-access mechanism (i.e., Brown, 1991; Vigliocco et al., 1997).

Direct-access approaches divide into three separate theories: the blocking hypothesis, the incomplete activation hypothesis, and the two-stage transmission deficit model (Burke et al., 1991). Although all three hypotheses agree that TOTs arise from access to an unretrieved target, each postulates a different mechanism. I now examine each of these three specific theories in greater detail.

Blocking Hypothesis

The blocking hypothesis is based on the common experience of retrieving a persistent, similar, but incorrect word while in a TOT. For example, assume that an individual is experiencing a TOT for a particular breed of cat, such as the Siamese cat. Although the person may be unable to remember the word *Siamese*, the word *Burmese* may be retrieved repeatedly. The rememberer knows that Burmese is incorrect, but that it is quite similar to the actual target. The rememberer also feels as if the repeated retrieval of the incorrect word is actually inhibiting the retrieval of the correct word.

Formally, the blocking hypothesis states that TOTs occur because rememberers retrieve words related to the correct target that are recognized by the rememberer as being incorrect (Jones, 1989). According to the blocking hypothesis, TOTs occur because the rememberer recognizes these blockers as incorrect, but cannot retrieve the correct, but inhibited target. Brown (1991) wrote: "the blocking perspective suggests that the TOT represents a memory search that has become sidetracked" (p. 215). Incorrect intruders have been labeled *blockers* (Reason & Lucas, 1984), *interlopers* (Jones, 1989; Jones & Langford, 1987), *persistent alternatives* (Burke et al., 1991), and *related words* (Brown, 1991). The hypothesis suggests that variables that increase the retrieval of these blockers will both inhibit correct recall and promote TOTs.

Like other direct-access models, the blocking hypothesis easily accounts for why TOTs accurately predict memory performance. Accuracy is promoted because TOTs are caused by activation of target memories. Because TOTs are caused by activation of the sought-after word, a change in retrieval conditions may remove the processes that are inhibiting retrieval. For example, a change in location may remove the cue-dependent inhibition and allow retrieval to occur. In general, retrieval may be inhibited by blockers, but the blockers are recognized as incorrect. Once the inhibition is removed by a change in retrieval cues or by the forgetting of the blocker, TOTs may be resolved.

Evidence Concerning Blocking.   The blocking hypothesis suggests that the rememberer retrieves blockers that are recognized as incorrect but which interfere with correct retrieval. Empirically, however, this is difficult to measure because it is difficult to introduce an experimental manipulation that will increase the number of blockers retrieved while holding correct recall constant. Therefore, most of the research directed at blocking that has provided blockers are thought to be capable of providing interference, and examined whether these words induce TOTs. The assumption in this research is that some of the words presented by the researchers will become blockers for the rememberers, or at least mimic the blocking process. This assumption must be kept in mind when evaluating the research on blocking.

Jones and his colleagues (Jones, 1989, Jones & Langford, 1987) engaged in a series of studies designed to test the blocking hypothesis. They used experimenter-provided blockers. Participants were presented with the definitions of difficult words, and were asked to retrieve a target word. For some of the items ("banal"), Jones presented a word that was semantically related to the target word ("uninspired"), along with the definition. For other items ("bibliophile"), Jones presented a word that was phonologically related ("buffoonery"). If blocking is crucial to TOTs, then presenting a potential blocker should increase the likelihood that the participant reports a TOT. In fact, semantic blockers did not increase the likelihood of a TOT, but phonological blockers did. Therefore, at a first glance, the data supported a partial view of blocking, one in which phonologically-related items blocked retrieval and created TOTs, although semantic blockers had no such effect.

Subsequent research, however, identified a methodological flaw in Jones's work. Jones did not counterbalance the target words from the semantic, phonological, and control conditions, and the results were actually a function of the particular words that were in each condition (see Meyer & Bock, 1992; Perfect & Hanley, 1992). When materials were counterbalanced, Meyer and Bock (1992) found that the condition that led to the highest reported TOT levels, the phonological cueing condition, actually led to the highest number of correct responses, but there were no differences in number of reported TOTs. Moreover, Perfect and Hanley (1992) included a control condition in which the same stimuli that Jones used were shown without the presence of the blocking words. Perfect and Hanley found that the words that Jones had used in the phonological blocking condition resulted in more TOTs even when no blocking words were included. Perfect and Hanley, like Meyer and Bock, argued against any role for blocking in the etiology of TOTs.

Although these studies cast doubt on whether Jones's data supported blocking, they really do not refute it. That Perfect and Hanley (1992) showed that the materials themselves played a role in the number of TOTs is neutral with respect to the blocking hypothesis. Meyer and Bock (1992) showed that phonological priming influences correct recall, but left TOTs unchanged. If one assumes that a TOT represents a criterion along a continuum of target knowledge, and that primes can boost the strength of that target knowledge, then Meyer and Bock's data are ambiguous. Items just below threshold may be boosted from a TOT state into a recalled state, but items further below threshold may be moved from a n–TOT state into a TOT state. Thus, it is possible that more difficult words or less obvious primes might leave recall unaffected but increase TOTs. Indeed, Askari (1999) found exactly that pattern. Phonological priming increased correct recall, but nonsignificantly so. Phonological priming did significantly boost the number of TOTs reported. Because both increased, it is likely that some blockers cued recall, but others induced TOTs via blocking the correct target. Thus, inhibitory or blocking mechanisms may still represent viable explanations.

Smith (1994), moreover, found evidence that supports the blocking hypothesis, using episodic-memory stimuli. Rememberers learned the names of fictional animals (known as *TOTimals*, see Fig. 3.1). Drawings of the fictional animals were combined with a brief description and the name of the kind of animal. Later, at test, participants were presented with the picture of the animal, along with a word that was phonologically similar to the name, the name of another animal, or a word that was unrelated to the target name. Smith (1994) found that the phonologically similar items increased recall, relative to the control, without increasing the reported number of TOTs. The semantically similar cues increased both recall and TOTs. This pattern of results is consistent with the blocking hypothesis. Semantically similar items caused participants to think that the items were recallable. It is not clear, however, that the TOTs resulted from blocking of target retrieval with misleading information, or that the TOTs were induced because semantically similar items serve as subjectively better cues (see section on cue familiarity).

The contradiction between Smith (1994) and Askari (1999) is that Smith found that including semantic blockers increased TOTs, but phonological blockers did not, whereas Askari (1999) found that including phono-

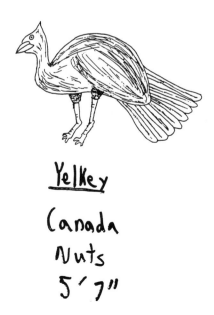

Yelkey

Canada

Nuts

5' 7"

FIG. 3.1 "Yelkey."

logical blockers increased TOTs, but semantic blockers did not. It is not necessarily clear why these data are incompatible with each other, other than the simple difference in stimuli. I offer a clearly ad hoc explanation here, which is left to the reader to evaluate. It is possible that the newly learned material in Smith's experiments did not have sufficient phonological strength to allow for phonological priming to be helpful. The semantic blockers, however, provide clues from which the rememberer might inferentially determine that they are in a TOT. In Askari's experiments, the target words and definitions are much more familiar to the participants. As a consequence, the semantic blockers are recognized as incorrect. Therefore, they are dismissed and do not enter into the TOT equation. However, the phonological primes increase the strength of the target, and through direct-access, increase TOT rates. This explanation is post hoc, but does resolve the apparent contradiction between the two sets of data.

This interpretation, however, cannot account for recent data from Smith's lab. Smith (2000) provided word definitions to participants and asked them to retrieve the target word. For half of the items, he provided them with unrelated words and for the others he provided related words. All of the participants were required to provide definitions of the accompanying words. Smith reasoned that the focusing on the meaning of the words would increase the likelihood that they would block recall. Relative to the targets accompanied by unrelated words, recall decreased and TOTs increased for the targets accompanied by semantic associates. Thus, it may be more likely that participants must focus on semantic aspects of accessible words for them to block retrieval and create TOTs.

Blocking theory states that the rememberer retrieves blockers, and these interfere with retrieval of the correct target. The blocking hypothesis is difficult to evaluate experimentally because it is not clear whether the experimenter-provided blockers serve as blockers or retrieval cues. Furthermore, it is also unclear whether the experimenter-provided blockers actually mimic the role of natural blocking in retrieval and TOT etiology. Therefore, despite the mixed evidence on blocking, it should remain a viable hypothesis. Indeed, it is a hypothesis waiting for a better, as yet undiscovered, methodology.

Incomplete Activation

Incomplete activation is the most simple variant of direct-access theory. The incomplete activation theory states that TOTs are caused by sensitivity to the existence of an unrecalled target in memory, accompanied by the failure to retrieve the target into consciousness. In an incomplete activation model (Brown & McNeill, 1966), TOTs occur because a target word is strong enough to induce a TOT but not strong enough to elicit recall. In-complete activation invokes a direct-access mechanism to account for TOTs, which are simply intermediate states of knowledge.

In incomplete activation, the accuracy with which TOTs predict memory performance is straightforward. TOTs should occur only for target words that are present in memory because TOTs represent intermediate memory strengths. Because target accessibility may fluctuate due to transitory fac-tors, an item that is currently inaccessible, but in a TOT, may increase to greater accessibility or strength and then be resolved. Because TOTs repre-sent higher activation than unrecalled items not in a TOT, TOT targets are more likely to be recognized. Incomplete activation theory is also consistent with the doctrine of concordance, as the phenomenology of TOTs arises from the strength of a memory trace.

Transmission Deficit Model

The transmission deficit model is the most well-articulated and studied ver-sion of direct-access theory. It has also motivated a great deal of recent re-search on the TOT from a number of different labs (e.g., Askari, 1999; Heine et al., 1999; James & Burke, 2000; Rastle & Burke, 1996; White and Abrams, 1999). I consider it here in detail.

In the transmission deficit model (Burke et al., 1991; James & Burke, 2000; Rastle & Burke, 1996), TOTs are induced whenever the semantic representa-tion of a word is activated, but the activation fails to prime the complete pho-nological representation of the target word (see Fig. 3.2). The transmission deficit model differs from the incomplete-activation model because it as-sumes two separate target representations: semantic and phonological. For this reason, Harley and Bown (1998) label the transmission deficit model a two-stage model of TOTs and the incomplete activation a one-stage model. For now, we focus on how the model accounts for TOT production. In chap-ter 4, we discuss its predictions concerning lexical retrieval.

Burke et al. (1991) wrote that the "basic cause of TOTs … is a deficit in the transmission of priming across critical connections required for produc-ing the target word" (p. 545). Therefore, although the model requires a dual representation of the target, TOTs arise from direct access to these particu-lar representations via the same process that is used in retrieval. Because a single process elicits both retrieval and the TOT phenomenology, the trans-mission deficit model is a direct-access model.

The explanation for the accuracy with which TOTs predict later memory performance is similar to the account of accuracy discussed in the section on incomplete activation. When a word definition is given, the semantic repre-sentation of the target word is activated. Priming spreads to an existing pho-

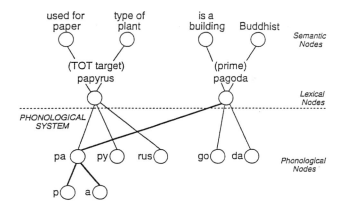

FIG. 3.2.

nological representation. Changes in retrieval conditions will lead to changes in activation and priming, which may result in resolution of TOTs. In other words, accuracy of the TOT is assured because the same processes that elicit retrieval (semantic plus phonological activation) elicit the TOT (which occur when less phonological activation is present).

The model makes some specific predictions concerning the likelihood of TOTs. First, connections between the semantic and phonological representations become stronger with greater use. Therefore, less frequently-used words (e.g., kiosk, sump) should give rise to more TOTs than common words (e.g., house, girl), a finding well-supported in the literature (e.g., Gollan & Silverberg, in press). Second, recency of use strengthens connections. Words that have not been encountered recently should be more likely to induce TOTs than less recently encountered words. Third, aging also weakens connections between the semantic and phonological representations. Therefore, older people should experience more TOTs than younger people. In a series of studies, including both diary methods and experimental techniques, Burke et al. (1991) found support for all three of these hypotheses (reviewed in chap. 2).

Phonological priming data has also been used to support the transmission deficit model. Rastle and Burke (1996) examined the effect of semantic and phonological priming of the target on the likelihood of TOTs in a general-information paradigm. They found that phonological priming increased the number of correct responses and decreased the number of TOTs. Semantic priming had no effects. Rastle and Burke argued that the lowering of TOT rates via phonological priming supports the transmission deficit model because the priming increases the level of phonological activation, which then makes the target word more accessible. James and Burke (2000) replicated this finding with a repetition priming paradigm. Askari (1999) found that phonological priming increased TOT rates without significantly affecting correct recall. The transmission deficit explanation of this discrepancy is that Askari's words were of lower average phonological strength. Thus priming caused them to switch from n–TOTs to TOTs, whereas Rastle and Burke's easier stimuli were boosted from TOTs to correct recalls. To support this view, it is worth noting that Rastle and Burke's participants were fluent native English speakers, whereas Askari's were fluent but nonnative English speakers. The participants in Askari's study probably had weaker connections initially between phonology and semantics for English words.

Harley and Bown (1998) also found results that are consistent with a two-stage model of TOTs, similar to Burke et al.'s (1991) transmission deficit model. Harley and Bown varied the frequency of words and the number of lexical neighbors (i.e., closely related phonological words). They found that TOTs were more likely for low frequency than for high frequency words, and that TOTs were more likely for those items with fewer close phonological neighbors. Both effects are consistent with a view that TOTs are the result of a breakdown between phonological and semantic representations.

One methodological problem clouds the interpretation of data from Rastle and Burke (1996) and Harley and Bown (1998). In both studies, the interest was in the effect of manipulated experimental variables on both recall and the number of TOTs. Because TOTs can only be involved in those items not originally recalled, measured recall and TOTs are not independent of each other. If there are differences in recall, the subset of items for which TOTs can occur may be different. If an experimental variable such as the phonological priming variable in the Rastle and Burke experiments increases recall, then it decreases the set of items on which TOT judgments can be made. In the Rastle and Burke study, it is possible that the unrecalled words in the phonological prime condition represented a harder set of items than the unrecalled unprimed words. Thus, the lower rate of TOTs may be a function of the more difficult items and not the manipulated variable (see Schwartz and Metcalfe, 1994). When evaluating etiologic issues in TOTs, it important to equate recall or recognition across experimental conditions.

These problems were corrected in a recent study by White and Abrams (1999; see also James & Burke, Exp. 2, for a similar paradigm). They compared three age groups: young adults (ages 18–25), older adults (ages 60–72), and oldest adults (age 73–83). In their study, participants were given definitions of words and asked to retrieve the word (e.g., "What word means to formally renounce a throne?"—Abdicate). If they could not re-trieve the word, they were asked whether they were experiencing a TOT. After that, they were given a phonological prime, and then an opportunity to resolve the TOT. In this study, TOTs were collected in advance of the priming, so the priming could not directly affect the TOT judgments. The results were quite clear: Phonological priming increased resolution of TOTs relative to n–TOTs for the younger participants, and to some extent for the older participants. The oldest participants could not resolve more TOTs af-ter phonological priming. The study represents a better test of transmission deficit theory because, unlike Rastle and Burke (1996), who confounded TOT rates with TOT resolution, White and Abrams kept TOT rates con-stant across the primed and unprimed conditions. Moreover, White and Abrams looked at resolution of n–TOTs as well as TOTs.

White and Abrams' (1991) data support the transmission deficit model for several reasons. In younger adults, TOT resolution was increased by phonological priming. If TOTs are caused by activation of a semantic node, but with insufficient activation of the phonological node, then priming the phonology should increase access to the word. Additionally, Burke et al. hy-pothesized that the connections between semantics and phonology weaken with age. In this study, phonological priming benefitted the older adults, but only when it was the first syllable that was primed. Finally, priming did not benefit the oldest adults at all, presumably because their baseline phonologi-cal activation was lowest of all. For the oldest adults, resolution rates were no higher after priming than no priming. White and Abrams found that phonological priming improved TOT resolution relative to n–TOT resolu-tion and did so more in the younger than the older adults. This pattern is logically predicted by the transmission deficit model.

Like White and Abrams (1999), James and Burke (2000) also introduced phonological priming after an initial retrieval failure. Consistent with the transmission deficit theory, more TOTs were resolved following phonologi-cal priming than when the primes were phonologically unrelated. Moreover, for n–TOTs (or "don't know" items), phonological priming did not influ-ence resolution. This suggests that it may unactivated phonological infor-mation that induces TOTs.

Smith et al. (1994), using their TOTimal paradigm, also found evidence that supports the transmission deficit model. Participants were presented with TOTimal pictures and the names of animals (e.g., see Fig. 3.1). In one experiment, participants were asked to rehearse the stimuli by writing the names of the fictional animals. In this experiment, writing practice in-creased the rate of correct recall and reduced the number of TOTs, without affecting the number of n–TOTs ("don't know") responses. Thus, the writ-ing practice shifted TOTs to correct recall, but did not shift the n–TOTs to

TOTs. Smith et al. (1994) reasoned that if the picture produces a semantic representation, a TOT or a correct recall can occur. The writing practice only influences phonological activation, thus it only shifts TOTs to correct recall, without affecting the n–TOTs. Smith et al.'s findings support a view in which semantic and phonological representations are separate, as suggested by Burke et al. (1991).

Brennan, Baguley, Bright, and Bruce (1990) conducted a study on TOTs, paying particular attention to the roles of face cues in TOT resolution. They presented participants with general-information questions such as, "Who is the actor who played 'The Bionic Man?'" (Lee Majors). Participants who were unable to retrieve the target answer were given one of two kinds of cues. Either the participant was shown a photograph depicting the question, such as a photograph of the actor, Lee Majors, or the participant was given the initials of the person (L. M.). Brennan et al. then compared the rate of TOT resolution. They found that TOT resolution was higher when the initials (phonological cues; 46.6%) were given than when the faces (14.5%) were given as cues. Brennan et al. were most interested in models of face recognition, but their data strongly support the importance of phonology in TOTs, as subsequently emphasized by Burke et al. (1991). The face cues might be considered visual, or perhaps even semantic. It is possible that the participants experiencing TOTs were visualizing the bionic man, running in slow motion, presumably at high speeds. However, the TOT was for the name, a phonological entry. Thus, access to the photo did not help in the resolution of TOTs. However, the first initials provided the cues to overcome the retrieval problem and resolve the TOT. Burke et al. argued that it is a lack of phonological activation that induces TOTs. Here, phonological priming resolves TOTs, but face priming does not.

The transmission deficit model can account for much of the data on TOTs. It succinctly accounts for frequency effects, neighborhood effects, phonological priming on TOT rates and resolution, the accessibility of partial information, and differences in TOTs between younger and older rememberers. However, it cannot explain some of the data, such as cue priming, which provide support for inferential theories and challenge the doctrine of concordance. Therefore, it is likely that any adequate explanation of TOTs will need to include both a mechanism similar to the transmission deficit model and a mechanism that produces TOTs inferentially.

Direct-access models postulate that the TOT is caused by the same processes that cause word retrieval. By assuming that identical processes are involved in each, some direct-access models implicitly endorse the doctrine of concordance. Nonetheless, direct-access models can account for a large amount of the TOT database, although much of the data really concerns retrieval processes and not the processes that affect TOT phenomenology. For example, the White and Abrams (1999) and the Brennan et al. (1990) data show that the transmission deficit model can account for TOT resolution, but it does not really speak to TOT etiology. In the following section, I discuss inferential models, a class of models directly theorized to explain phenomenology within a framework that does not assume concordance.

INFERENTIAL VIEWS

In the inferential approach, the TOTs are not based on sensitivity to inaccessible but activated targets. Instead, rememberers infer the target's existence from a host of clues that inform them that it is likely to be in memory. The clues that are used to make the inference may include the cue, which may include the question itself and information implicit in the question (e.g., Metcalfe et al., 1993), retrieved partial information about the target (Koriat, 1993), or any generated information related to the target name (Schwartz & Smith, 1997). Cues can be considered anything in the environment that may help the rememberer retrieve the sought-after target. Generated information may consist of bits and fragments of the sought-after target or may consist of words, pictures, and other kinds of information that are related to the target.

The inferential approach does not mean that the process producing a TOT is a conscious one. Instead, the inferential process is assumed to be largely nonconscious. The cues and clues are processed by a nonconscious mechanism evolved to assess the likelihood of recall. If the nonconscious process yields a "positive," the result is the feeling of the TOT, which signals to the rememberer that the target is in the memory store. I argue that the processes are hidden or nonconscious although the product (the TOT) is by definition, conscious.

We may use a similar process consciously to make feeling-of-knowing judgments. For example, if the question is "What is the planet closest to the sun? (Mercury)," I may employ a host of conscious inferential strategies. First, how much I know about astronomy may influence my judgment. Second, because I know that most of the planets are named after Roman gods and goddesses, I may try to retrieve a few of these names and try to match them up with the right planets. Third, if I have some phonological information, such as the first letter, I may consider my feeling of knowing to be quite strong. The inferential view stipulates that we unconsciously use a similar process to determine whether we are experiencing a TOT. This unconscious inference makes us feel as if the target word is actually right there—on the tip of the tongue—giving rise to the phenomenology that feels like direct-access.

Inferential approaches to metacognition have been shown to be useful in explaining the bases of several different metacognitive judgments, including speeded feelings of knowing (Reder, 1987; Reder & Ritter, 1992), slower feeling-of-knowing judgments for unrecalled targets (Koriat, 1993; Metcalfe, 1993; Metcalfe et al., 1993; Schwartz, 1994; Schwartz & Metcalfe, 1992), and judgments of learning (Benjamin, Bjork, & Schwartz, 1998; Koriat, 1997). Inferential explanations, developed within a metacognitive perspective, are inconsistent with the doctrine of concordance. The inferential approach assumes that TOTs are caused by a process in addition to the retrieval process. Therefore, consistent with Tulving (1989), the phenomenology of TOTs is elicited by one process, and target retrieval occurs due to another.

Unlike the straightforward manner in which direct-access views account for the accuracy with which TOTs predict recognition, the inferential account of accuracy requires an additional step. The inferential view claims that the processes that produce TOTs and the processes that effect target retrieval are generally correlated. Thus, when cues are familiar and considerable related information is retrieved, the rememberer will usually have a representation of the target word in memory. Unfamiliar cues that do not elicit related information are, correspondingly, less likely to induce TOTs, but it is also likely that the rememberer will not have the target representation. In this way, TOTs are thought to be the product of a heuristic. The experience of a TOT generally means that target retrieval is likely; however, because the TOT is not based on target retrieval, occasions will arise when a TOT is elicited by certain factors when no representation of the target is present. Thus, inferential mechanisms can also account for the high correlation between resolution, recognition, and access to partial information, if we assume that the processes that cause TOTs are correlated with the processes that evoke retrieval. In addition, TOTs can account for instances in which the correct target is not known, but the person experiences a TOT anyway (Perfect & Hanley, 1992; Schwartz, 1998).

There are two main hypotheses within the inferential framework. These two hypotheses are not mutually exclusive, but involve different cognitive mechanisms. Cue familiarity theory suggests that some TOTs arise because of a strong feeling elicited by recognizing a familiar cue (Metcalfe et al., 1993). Koriat (1993) argued for an accessibility heuristic, which states that TOTs arise from inferences made based on the amount and kind of information retrieved from memory when the target is not recalled. In the next two sections, I consider the evidence for each of these views.

Cue Familiarity

The cue familiarity hypothesis states that TOTs are based on an assessment of the level of recognition of a particular cue or question (Metcalfe et al.,

1993). This approach dismisses the relevance of the unretrieved target altogether and instead emphasizes the role of the cue. In its purest form, the cue familiarity hypothesis suggests that a familiar cue should induce a TOT regardless of whether the target is known. There is much data describing the importance of cue familiarity in feeling-of-knowing judgments (Connor, Balota, & Neely, 1992; Metcalfe, 1993; Metcalfe et al., 1993; Reder, 1987; Reder & Ritter, 1992; Schwartz & Metcalfe, 1992). However, less data exist linking cue familiarity with TOTs.

Koriat and Lieblich (1977) examined the relation between TOTs and the cues or questions that elicited the TOTs. They labeled the questions as *pointers* because they point or cue the relevant target answer. Koriat and Lieblich analyzed the pointers along several dimensions, but the most relevant finding is that redundancy within the question led to more TOTs for unrecalled items than did more succinct definitions. For example, definitions with repetitive elements, such as "a circle, or any indication of radiant light, around the heads of divinities, saints, sovereigns in pictures, medal, etc." (nimbus) tended to produce more TOTs than did more concise definitions such as, "the science of coins" (numismatics). This trend toward more TOTs in questions with repetitive elements in the cue was the same across TOTs that were resolved (i.e., eventually recalled or recognized) and those that were not. Thus, Koriat and Lieblich's results suggest that cue factors play a role in causing TOTs.

Metcalfe et al. (1993) directly tested the roles of cue-based sources in TOTs in an episodic memory paradigm. Participants studied cue-target word pairs. In one condition, both the cue and the target were repeated ("captain–carbon," "captain–carbon;" A–B, A–B). In a second condition, the cue was repeated, but with a new unrelated target ("pasture–dragon," "pasture–movie;" A–B, A–D). In a third condition, neither the cue nor the target was repeated ("trouble–camel," "garden–miser;" A–B, C–D). In accordance with results from interference paradigms, Metcalfe et al. found that the A–B, A–D condition showed the lowest recall. Recall was highest in the A–B, A–B condition, presumably because both cue and target are repeated. If TOTs are based on the strength of the representation, as predicted by incomplete activation, the A–B, A–B condition should show the highest number of TOTs. Cue familiarity, however, predicts that because the cue is repeated in both conditions (A–B, A–B and A–B, A–D), TOTs will be high for each when compared to the condition in which the cue is presented only once (A–B, C–D). Indeed, Metcalfe et al. found that both the repetition condition (A–B, A–B) and the interference condition (A–B, A–D) each showed a high percentage of TOTs relative to the once-presented condition (A–B, C–D). Further supporting the cue-familiarity explanation, Metcalfe et al. also found that recognition of the unrecalled targets mirrored the pattern observed in recall and not the pattern observed in the TOT judgments. Thus, they found that cue repetition led to more TOTs, regardless of the level of memorability.

Schwartz and Smith (1997) also found evidence that supports cue familiarity. In this study, country names were used as cues to retrieve the names of TOTimals that supposedly came from those countries. Prior to the test, participants were asked to judge a list of country names for pleasantness. The participants were asked if the countries would be good places to go for vacation (Italy, by the way, was judged the most desirable vacation country). Some of the counties were habitats (cues) for TOTimals, whereas others were controls. Following the pleasantness rating task, participants attempted to retrieve the names of TOTimals that came from the primed countries and to retrieve the names of unprimed TOTimals. Relative to the unprimed countries, there were more TOTs experienced for TOTimals cued by those countries that had been primed in the unrelated task. Given that memorability of the TOTimal names was equivalent between the primed and unprimed cues, this data also supports a cue familiarity component to TOT etiology (cf. Harley & Bown, 1998; Rastle & Burke, 1996). This means that there were no differences in memorability across the conditions, and therefore any differences in TOT rates must be caused by nonmnemonic factors. Furthermore, because the phonological representations of the target names were studied the same number of times, theories such as transmission deficit theory would not have predicted differences simply on the basis of the familiarity of the cue. Thus, a separate inferential mechanism must be invoked to explain these data.

Accessibility Heuristic

Koriat (1993, 1995) argued that feeling-of-knowing judgments are based on the amount and intensity of partial information that rememberers retrieve when they cannot recall a target answer. Koriat's view is inferential because the judgment is only made based on accessible information, and it is not based on inaccessible but available targets. This is an important distinction. In direct-access models, a present lexical representation in memory is sufficient to cause a TOT. In Koriat's model, an inference is made based on accessible information (i.e., that which can be retrieved). Thus, this view falls in the inferential camp rather than the direct-access camp. Schwartz and Smith (1997) also hypothesized a similar basis for TOTs, arguing that the amount and intensity of retrieved information may play a role in the etiology of TOTs. In our view, TOTs are caused by any information that is retrieved, including information that may actually be tangential to the sought-after target.

To test this hypothesis, Schwartz and Smith (1997) used the TOTimal methodology. They presented participants with lists of fictional animal names. Each name was paired with the name of a country, and some of the names were also accompanied by line drawings of fictional animals. For example, participants might have seen "Yelkey–Panama," which indicated that the "yelkey" is an animal that lives in Panama. Of the animals for which line drawings were provided, half were also accompanied by information pertaining to the size and diet of the animal. The three encoding conditions were minimum information (just the name–country pair), medium information (the name–country pair and line drawing), and maximum information (the name–country pair, line drawing, and diet and size information). The conditions were designed to allow different amounts of information to be retrieved when the participants were given the country name as a cue for the retrieval of the animal name. If the participants could not retrieve the name of the animal associated to a given country cue, they were then asked for a TOT judgment and asked to guess the first letter of the animal's name. The participants were also asked to retrieve as much related information as they could. Related information included both biographical information and descriptions of the appearance of the animal.

The encoding manipulation (amount of related information) did not affect recall of animal names and it did not affect the recognition of unrecalled names. This suggests that three conditions were composed of roughly equivalent items for which possible TOTs could exist. However, the rates of TOTs differed among the conditions. Consistent with Koriat's (1993) accessibility theory, there were more TOTs reported in both the medium and maximum information conditions than in the minimum information condition. In addition, the number of reported TOTs was correlated with the amount of related information retrieved. Thus, when more information was accessible to participants, they were more likely to experience TOTs. This basic finding was found in three separate experiments. Again, direct access theory, based on the strength of the representation, would not have predicted differences in conditions that were equated for correct recall and recognition. However, the conditions differed in the amount of related information that was recalled. Therefore, it is not the strength of the phonological representation that is driving the differences in TOTs; it is more likely that it is the accessibility of the related information.

In a recent study, MacLin (2000) also tested Koriat's (1993) accessibility theory as it applied to TOTs. MacLin presented famous faces as cues for the retrieval of the names of these people. For faces for which the name was not recalled, MacLin asked for TOT judgments, and he asked the participants to report any related information that they might recall about the person. MacLin found that, like Schwartz and Smith (1997), the retrieval of related information was positively correlated with the experience of a TOT, thus supporting Koriat's accessibility view.

The accessibility framework, developed by Koriat (1993), offers an alternative explanation for the findings linking the retrieval of partial information with the likelihood of a TOT (i.e., Brown & McNeill, 1966; Koriat & Lieblich, 1974; Rubin, 1975; Vigliocco et. al., 1997; Vigliocco et al., 1999). If partial related information is retrieved, it may be the presence of that information itself, regardless of whether the representation is activated, that induces the TOT. Therefore, much of the data that supports the direct-access view can also support the accessibility view. Indeed, blocking effects on TOTs are also amenable to the accessibility view. However, only one published study (Schwartz & Smith, 1997) and one as yet unpublished study (MacLin, 2000) directly supports the role of the retrieval of related information in the formation of TOTs. Therefore, the hypothesis should be considered tentative at best. Nonetheless, the research accumulating on inferential views of TOTs suggests that, in some circumstances, TOTs are based on clues of memorability rather than memorability.

The Heuristic Account of Accuracy

Inferential views, compared to direct-access theories, require a more complicated explanation as to why TOTs are relatively accurate predictors of performance. For inferential views, the actual presence of the target is not a given, and therefore, predictive accuracy must rely on the natural correlation among the factors that cause rememberers to have TOTs and the factors that actually influence temporary forgetting and subsequent retrieval. Accessibility theory, which centers on the evaluation of partial information, accounts for this accuracy by suggesting that people tend to retrieve more correct than incorrect information (Koriat, 1993). If more correct than incorrect information is retrieved, TOTs will tend to be accurate in predicting eventual resolution or recall. The TOT experience may indicate—correctly most of the time—that retrieval is indeed imminent.

Consider an example: Imagine experiencing a TOT for the name of the first person on the moon. You may remember being spellbound watching him walking on the moon many years ago. You may remember his famous quote, you may remember the names of his fellow astronauts, and you may remember that the mission was named "Apollo." However, you still cannot remember the name of the first man on the moon. However, it is likely that you do know the name given that you remember all of the other details. Inferential theory stipulates that there is a strong correlation between the accumulation of all that information in memory and the likelihood that the target name will also be in memory. Sooner or later, one of the various pieces of retrieved information will serve as the cue that triggers the retrieval of the name Armstrong. Thus, the reliance on retrieved information is adaptive because partial and related information correlate with knowledge of the TOT target word, and the retrieved information may cue the TOT word.

The TOT has been referred to as a cognitive heuristic (e.g., Schwartz, 1999b; Smith, 1994). The heuristic account cogently explains why some TOTs are not resolved or recognized. These TOTs may be spurious experiences caused by familiar cues or the retrieval of related information. Indeed, in the case of illusory TOTs, the person cannot know the target answer (Schwartz, 1998). Thus, cases of "negative" TOTs (Vigliocco et al., 1997), TOTs for incorrect items (Rastle & Burke, 1996), and illusory TOTs (Schwartz, 1998) may be best thought of as an error produced by inferential heuristics. Heuristics can, therefore, account for both the general accuracy of TOTs and the existence of unresolved, unrecognized, or illusory TOTs.

Illusory TOTs in particular provide some empirical support to the heuristic concept. Schwartz (1998) included questions for which there was no correct answer among normal general-information questions. For example, one of the questions was, "What is the only living reptile that flies?" The correct answer is that there is no such animal. However, frequently participants reported TOTs for these questions. Regardless of whether they were experiencing TOTs via direct access for an incorrect target (e.g., sugar glider) or were basing their TOTs on inferential means (lots of related information, e.g., that the Komodo dragon is the world's largest lizard), the TOT is an error because the target does not exist. Thus, metacognitively speaking, some TOTs are errors. Errors in cognition suggest a mechanism that typically works well, but can be "thrown a curve." Indeed, that is the case for TOTs. Most studies show high accuracy, but Schwartz' study showed that errors can occur as well.

The heuristic approach to TOTs is also consistent with Tulving's (1989) view on the doctrine of concordance. TOTs are accurate at predicting memory performance because they arise from processes correlated with retrieval, but not directly from retrieval itself. This correlation does not imply that the cognitive processes are identical, but only that they are linked. In fact, the linkage may occur only because of features of the external environment. Concordance does not preclude significant correlations between cognitive processes and phenomenology. Rather, it suggests that the processes may be separable, as indeed they appear to be with some TOTs.

Finally, the heuristic approach converges with the importance of heuristic processing in a number of other cognitive domains, from decision making to cognitive mapping. In cognitive mapping, for example, people appear to rely on heuristics to determine compass directions (Tversky, 1981, 1991). Thus, people will judge that Miami, FL is east of Pittsburgh, PA, based on the heuristic that east coast cities are further east than inland cities. In fact, Miami is further west than Pittsburgh. In the decision-making literature, people's reliance on cognitive heuristics has been the focus of intense research for many years (e.g., Kahneman & Tversky, 1973; 1984; Piattelli-Palmarini, 1994). In the face of uncertainty, research has demonstrated reliance on heuristics such as availability, representativeness, and anchoring and adjustment, instead of the laws of probability theory. For example, based on its availability, people will judge airplane travel to be more dangerous right after a plane crash covered extensively by the media.

The general principle in all of these heuristic processes is that people do not have direct access to the information being judged. Most people do not have degrees of longitude and latitude memorized for every American city. Most people do not intuitively know the laws of probability (however, see Pinker, 1997). Thus, heuristics play an important role in making decisions. Most coastal cities will be further east than inland cities among Atlantic states. And, experiencing a TOT is predictive of later remembering the word.

SUMMARY

The focus of this chapter was theoretical accounts of TOT etiology. TOT etiology refers to the processes that cause the phenomenology of the TOT. Two basic classes of theories were evaluated: direct-access theory and inferential theory. Direct-access theory states that TOTs occur when a target's strength is above some hypothetical knowledge threshold but below a retrieval threshold. The theory has been instantiated in a number of specific models, most notably Burke et al.'s (1991) transmission deficit theory, which postulates that TOTs are caused by access to a semantic representation but a failure to retrieve the phonological representation. I reviewed the rather extensive evidence that supported this model. Inferential theory hypothesizes that TOTs are caused by the accumulation of indirect clues that the rememberer uses to reconstruct the likelihood of recalling the target. Evidence, which supports inferential theory, exists in both cue familiarity studies and from studies which manipulate the retrieval of related information. Inferential theory accounts for accuracy by suggesting that the TOT serves a heuristic function, usually correctly informing us which unrecalled targets we can eventually recall. Direct-access and inferential views are not mutually exclusive, and any complete explanation of the TOT is likely to require both.

4

TOTs as a Window
on Retrieval

In most arenas of our life, it is not our confidence or our potential that matters. Indeed, it has become almost a truism of modern society that it is results that count. For a professional athlete, it does not matter how well he or she performs in practice. It is performance in the big game that counts. Similarly, for a researcher, it is not the creativity of his or her ideas, but whether these ideas can be translated into published articles and funded grants. No less for our cognitive systems. Our TOTs are meaningless unless they really do tell us something about the retrieval process. In chapter 3, TOTs were discussed as heuristics; heuristics are only good when they are accurate predictors of the future. Therefore, in this chapter, I detour from my primary concern with the etiology, phenomenology, and function of TOTs. Here, I focus on the lexical retrieval process. In particular, I discuss how TOT research informs theories of lexical retrieval. Therefore, to paraphrase a famous president, let us ask not what TOTs are, but what they tell us about the cognitive processes that allows us to speak.

Before we return to the gritty details of theory, recall that precarious pedestal on which I have placed TOTs. They sit atop a carefully constructed tripod of research in memory, language, and metacognition. Brown and McNeill (1966) realized that the TOT was a crucial phenomenon in both memory and language research. The TOT can be thought of as a memory lapse, but it is a memory lapse for a linguistic entity. TOTs can also be thought of as speech production error, one in which the speaker fails to retrieve a particular word. Obviously, this issue is two sides of the same coin. Elsewhere in this volume I make the case that metacognition represents a different coin altogether; however in this chapter I focus what most of the research on TOTs has been directed, namely, theories of lexical retrieval. Thus in this section, the concern is on the nature of the memory lapse or speech production error, and less on whether that condition also includes a TOT experience.

MODELS OF LEXICAL RETRIEVAL

Think about retrieving a word from memory, perhaps the name of someone with whom you work or the name of one of your first cousins. Introspectively, the retrieval process is a black box. When you are asked, "What is the name of your first cousin?" the phonology of the names simply appears, or pops up at the conscious level. Most of the cognition involved in word retrieval occurs at a level below the threshold of consciousness. In some cases, you may not be able to retrieve a name at first, in which case, you may try cueing yourself through a variety of conscious strategies, such as going through the alphabet. But this case is the exception. Usually, word retrieval is a well-oiled machine. It is the failure of this efficient machine that may contribute to the frustration experienced during a TOT. Nonetheless, theories of word retrieval are not constrained by phenomenology because of the lack of conscious introspection into the normal functioning of lexical processes.

Models of lexical retrieval face a daunting task. They must account for several features of ordinary speech. First, consider the rapid speed of ordinary speech. During such speech, adults produce 15 sounds per sec (Matlin, 1998), or potentially several words per sec. Any model of lexical retrieval must account for the rapid and continuous retrieval of words. Second, consider the size of the retrieval set. The average adult may know more than 75,000 words in his or her native language (Matlin, 1998) . How does the lexical retrieval system hone in on just the right word among the thousands of wrong words? Third, natural language is not simply a string of words. It is a complex pattern of words and phrases, woven together by verbs, joined by conjunctions, and within a system of syntax. Lexical retrieval processes must be able to select correct transformations of words on the fly, as in "there are media present at the conference" or "there is a medium to express those ideas." Thus, a model of word retrieval must take into account how syntax constrains and changes the particular word to be retrieved (e.g., Pinker, 1999). It is likely that we will need complex models to account for such an incredibly complex phenomenon.

Most current theories of language production stipulate two distinct processes that occur during lexical retrieval (e.g., Garrett, 1992; Levelt, 1989; MacKay & Burke, 1990). The first process is a semantic retrieval process, whereby the speaker activates the appropriate semantic information relevant to the intended speech act. The second process is a phonological re-trieval process in which the particular phonological form of the spoken word is specifically accessed. Successful phonological access allows the word to be actually spoken. Although the particulars of the models vary, the basic model of semantic retrieval first, followed by phonological retrieval is gener-ally agreed upon (see Caramazza & Miozzo, 1997).

Much recent research has been directed at supporting the notion that the retrieval of words occurs in this two-stage process (Garrett, 1992; Harley & Bown, 1998; Levelt, 1989; Martin, Dell, Saffran, & Schwartz, 1994; Schachter, 1990). In these models, the first retrieval produces a representa-tion known as a *lemma*. A lemma is a hypothetical entity containing only se-mantic and syntactical information without any information concerning the particular phonology of the to-be-retrieved word. In a second stage of retrieval, the product is called a *lexeme*. The lexeme is a representation that includes the phonological form of the word, which can then be outputted by the speech production system (see Fig. 4.1).

Consider a person asked the question, "What animal is the closest living relative to humans?" The question initiates a lexical retrieval process. Ac-cording to the general model, the first stage involves the retrieval of particu-lar semantic information. The speaker accesses various semantic attributes of the concept to be articulated. In the example given, semantic concepts may be accessed such as animal, primate, smart, uses tools, wild, cute, and so forth. This initial process of retrieval results in the lemma (Caramazza & Miozzo, 1997; Levelt, 1989). The lemma maintains an abstract representa-tion of the to-be-spoken word that combines both the semantic information and various syntactic components (e.g., pluralization, grammatical gender, part of speech, etc.). In this case, that would include information such as noun, regular pluralization, and animate). According to theory, however, the lemma does not contain any phonological information.

Once the lemma representation has been formed, the second stage of lex-ical retrieval is initiated. In this second stage, the rememberer compiles an abstract description of how the target word chimpanzee is constructed pho-nologically. This lexeme is then processed by a motor production unit that actually articulates the word (see Fig. 4.1).

Normal lexical retrieval is an extremely rapid process, and therefore it is difficult to break down the lexical retrieval process experimentally into its component parts, although this is a major thrust of modern psycholinguistic research (Martin et al. 1994). It is precisely because normal lexical retrieval is so rapid that the TOT plays such an important role in delineating theories of lexical retrieval. During TOTs, the retrieval process is slowed. This slow-ing of an otherwise rapid retrieval process may allow researchers to examine the lemma-level retrieval and the lexeme-level retrieval independent of

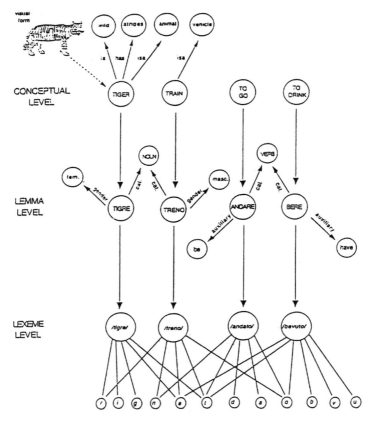

FIG. 4.1   Part of the lexical system showing the relation between the lemma and other levels
of lexical representation. The lemma and lexeme levels show the Italian words for the lexical
concepts tiger, train, to go, and to drink. Adapted from Bock and Levelt (1994), Jescheniak
and Leveit (1994), and Roelofs (1992).

each other. Thus, for scholars interested in lexical retrieval, the TOT holds
the promise of allowing researchers to examine what the lexical retrieval
process looks like in slow motion. Indeed, Brown (1991) wrote that "examining it [word retrieval] in a temporary 'holding pattern' imposed by the
TOT has the potential to reveal subtleties of normal retrieval functions,
similar to how slow-motion photography clarifies the dimensions of a hum-
mingbird's flight" (p. 204). During retrieval of a TOT word, the lexical retrieval process has been slowed significantly.

Despite the agreement on this basic hierarchy of lemmas and lexemes,
there are a great many variants of lexical retrieval models. In some versions

of the models, the two stages are serial, that is, the lemma must be retrieved in advance of the initiation of the phonological retrieval (see Butterworth, 1989, 1992; Miozzo & Caramazza, 1997). In interactive models, activation flows back and forth between different levels (e.g., Burke et al., 1991). In interactive models, the search for the lexeme is partially dependent on the success of the first stage. Thus, in both serial and interactive models, the lemma represents an important preliminary step in accessing word forms (see Harley & Bown, 1998; Miozzo & Caramazza, 1997).

Recently, Caramazza and Miozzo (1997) challenged the general view that lexical retrieval involves two distinct stages. They claim that the two-stage view has too often been assumed and then imposed on existing data. They find no compelling reason in the literature to support a two-stage view. Instead, they think of lexical retrieval as not requiring a lemma or lexeme distinction. They base this challenge to the existing theory on TOT data. Their study and rationale will be reviewed later in this chapter in a more thorough manner.

Most researchers agree that much of the evidence used to support two-stage models comes from errors in ordinary speech (see Caramazza & Miozzo, 1997). Garrett (1975) argued that two kinds of errors are observable. The first are called word-exchange errors, which involve substituting a word of the same grammatical class but of a different phonology, thus corresponding to lemmas. For example, one might substitute blanket for pillow (Tweney, Tkacz, & Zaruba, 1975). The second are exchange errors which involve substitutions of similar but incorrect phonological structures, with no relation to meaning, thus corresponding to lexemes (see Caramazza & Miozzo, 1997). For example, one might substitute mittens for muffins (Tweney et al., 1975). In this research tradition, TOTs are also seen as speech errors, in which the lemma has been retrieved, but the complete lexeme has not. Studying what is accessible during TOTs tells us what kinds of information (other than phonological) are represented at the level of the lemma. Indeed, James (1890) wrote that "the rhythm of the lost word may be there without the sound to clothe it; or the evanescent sense of something which is the initial vowel or consonant may mock us fitfully, without growing more distinct" (p. 251). James's quote is consistent with the view that TOTs are seen as instances in which we can analyze the lemma, largely uninterrupted by the processes that generate the lexeme. Thus, according to this view, lemmas are activated and lexemes are only partially activated in TOTs.

In chapter 3, I presented Burke et al.'s (1991) transmission deficit model in discussing the etiology of TOTs. In this context, the transmission deficit model is an example of a two-stage interactive model of word retrieval. In the model, priming spreads from an initial semantic representation (lemma) to a second phonological level (lexeme). If sufficient priming spreads from the semantic level to the phonological level, activation of a word form oc-curs, and the rememberer can say the word. In the model, priming is a graded phenomenon, but activation is all or none; that is, a particular word may be highly primed, but below the activation threshold and therefore not recalled. It is this state of high priming, which is still below activation thresh-old, that triggers a TOT in the model (refer to Fig. 3.2, this volume). In sum-mary, TOTs occur when lemmas are retrieved, but there is insufficient retrieval of the lexeme.

According to most theorists, syntactical and semantic information is repre-sented at the level of the lemma. When a rememberer experiences a TOT, se-mantic and syntactical information should be relatively easy to report, despite the inability to report the whole word, or even any of its phonological features. The models predict that semantic information will always be accessible in TOTs, that syntactical information also should be readily accessible during TOTs, but complete phonological information may not be accessible. On the other hand, aspects of the phonological lexeme may be accessed, albeit not completely during a TOT. Therefore, the models also predict that partial pho-nological information will be accessible during some TOTs. This chapter first considers phonological access in TOTs and then syntactic access.

Phonological Access in TOTs

The purpose of TOT research within the context of lexical retrieval models is that TOTs represent instances in which the normal lexical retrieval pro-cess has slowed down or is experiencing a selective failure (Burke et al., 1991). In this framework, analysis of the kinds of information accessible during a TOT may shed light on the process whereby words are retrieved. In particular, because the assumption is that during a TOT the lemma has been fully retrieved, it is possible to focus on the nature of the phonological retrieval process when a rememberer is experiencing a TOT. Indeed, Rastle and Burke (1996) wrote that "TOTs provide a means of isolating phonolog-ical processes within a conceptually-driven task" (p. 594).

Both one-stage (Caramazza & Miozzo, 1997) and two-stage (Burke et al., 1991) theories predict that during a TOT, participants should be able to re-trieve phonological information about the unrecalled target. In the two-stage views, a lemma is retrieved, but the lexeme is not completely re-trieved. However, the rememberer may be able to activate some aspects of the lexeme, such as the first letter or first syllable. Similarly, a related phono-logical word may be activated. The one-stage view is also compatible with the retrieval of phonological information. That is, the retrieval process si-multaneously pulls out both semantic and phonological information, each of which may be complete or incomplete.

The data support the hypothesis that rememberers access aspects of the phonology during a TOT (see Brown, 1991; Schachter, 1990). Although much of this data has already been discussed, it is important to review it again in this context. In chapter 2, the concern was whether the retrieval of any partial information was more supportive of direct access or inferential theories. In the current context, it is important to distinguish between different kinds of linguistic information such as phonological, orthographic, semantic, or syntactic information. Phonological information includes similar-sounding words, initial phonemes of the word, the final phoneme of the word, as well as syllabic information, all of which have been demonstrated in the lab. Note, of course, that the phonology itself does not distinguish between one- and two-stage views, a point to which I shall return.

Retrieval of Phonologically-Related Words.   In chapter 3, the blocking hypothesis was introduced. The blocking hypothesis contends that TOTs are caused by the retrieval of items known to be incorrect. Although the evidence that blocking causes TOTs or lexical retrieval failures is lacking, there is considerable data that suggest that TOTs are often accompanied by persistent alternates (blockers), most often related to the target phonologically. Schachter (1990) presented a series of examples: In one case, a TOT was for the target name "Rex Harrison." The persistent alternate was "Rock Hudson" (in this case, there is both a phonological and semantic relation). Another TOT target was the name "Deese," and the persistent alternate was "Reese."

In laboratory studies, blockers or persistent alternates often occur for more than half of the TOT targets. Brown and McNeill (1966) found that 70% of retrieved related words were phonologically-related to the missing target . In contrast, Harley and Bown (1998) found a much lower rate of phonological alternates. Indeed, of 325 interlopers observed by Harley and Bown, only 43 were phonologically related to the target. Why there would be such a difference between the two studies is unclear. Nonetheless, diary investigations show that half of all TOTs are accompanied by known incorrect words (e.g., Burke et al., 1991; Reason & Lucas, 1984, see Brown, 1991).

Retrieval of First Letters.   Rememberers are often able to retrieve the first letter or the first phoneme in the absence of being able to retrieve the complete word when they are experiencing a TOT. In Brown's review (1991), he found that, across a series of studies on the TOT, rememberers could correctly identify the first letter between 50% and 71% of the time during a TOT. In a recent study with Italian speakers, Miozzo and Caramazza (1997) found a 76% rate of correct first phoneme identifications, although Caramazza and Miozzo (1997) found a much lower rate (28%) in one experiment and a slightly lower rate (57.5%) in another, also with Italian-speaking participants. Given the base rate of guessing the correct target, first letter retrieval is accurate. Indeed, Koriat and Lieblich (1974) found that for n–TOTs, the first letter was guessed correctly only 10% of the time. Similarly, Burke et al.(1991) found that the initial phoneme of the related word retrieved matched the TOT target 36% of the time, whereas chance was only 6%. Caramazza and Miozzo (1997) also found a 10% rate for n–TOTs in Italian. Thus, there is strong evidence to suggest that TOTs are often accompanied by the retrieval of phonological information. Interestingly, in a different domain, Marsh and Emmorey (2000) found that American Sign Language signers retrieve partial information about hand position when experiencing a TOT.

Retrieval of Last Letters. Caramazza and Miozzo (1997) found that the final phoneme for TOTs was retrieved correctly 67% of the time, significantly higher than the rate for n–TOTs (49%). Koriat and Lieblich (1974) found that their participants retrieved the final phoneme on 69% of the TOT targets, significantly higher than the 17% rate for n–TOTs. Finally, Rubin (1975) also found a 31% correct rate for last letters, significantly higher than chance, although lower than the other studies. Again, these data suggest that during TOTs participants do have access to phonological information, however incomplete.

Number of Syllables. There is also evidence suggesting that, during a TOT, rememberers have access to the number of syllables of the missing target. For example, Koriat and Lieblich (1974) found that rememberers were accurate 80% of the time in identifying the correct number of syllables for targets for which they were experiencing TOTs, but only 38% of the time when they were not experiencing TOTs. A similar pattern had been observed by Brown and McNeill (1966), who found a 60% correct rate in syllable estimation. On the other hand, Caramazza and Miozzo (1997), using Italian stimuli, found that the correct syllable was retrieved 37% of the time for a positive TOT and 34% for a n–TOT. English may be relatively rare in its speakers' ability to identify the number of syllables during a TOT. Recently, Gollan and Silverberg (in press) found that for English monolinguals and English–Hebrew bilinguals, the correlation between TOTs and correct identification of the number of syllables was significantly above chance and significantly better than the same correlation for n–TOTs. However, in Hebrew (most participants' native language), there was no difference between the correlation for TOTs and for n–TOTs. Gollan and Silverberg speculated that because Hebrew has more multisyllable words than English, it may be more difficult to distinguish between two and three syllable words in Hebrew.

Orthographic Features.   A frequently neglected aspect of the partial retrieval of information is that orthographic features may also be partially retrieved. Orthography here refers to the physical form of the written words. The relation of TOTs and orthography has not been addressed in any experiments. However, Schachter (1990) did provide several examples of persistent alternates that were based on similarities in orthography rather than phonology. For example, he discussed a TOT target word "Chris" in which the persistent alternate is "Charles." These two names are orthographically similar ("Ch") but the "ch" is pronounced differently in each. In another example, the target was "Phyllis" and the alternate was "Peg."

In summary, there is much data demonstrating that rememberers experiencing a TOT do have partial access to the phonological information that they cannot completely retrieve. This information takes the form of retrieving phonologically-related words as well as the retrieval of parts of the word, such as its first or last letter, or the number of syllables. In word retrieval models, this phonological information comes from partial activation of the lexeme after the lemma (semantics and syntax) has been successfully retrieved. The retrieval of the lemma, however, contains no phonological information, and therefore its retrieval does not guarantee the word will be remembered and spoken.

Syntactical Access in TOTs

The crux of the debate between those who argue for a two-stage model of lexical retrieval and those who argue for a one-stage theory partially hinges on the issue of syntactical access during a TOT (Caramazza & Miozzo, 1997). In the two-stage theory, the lemma represents a prephonological stage in which semantic and syntactical information have been compiled. Syntax here means information pertaining to the part of speech, article required, grammatical gender (e.g., whether nouns are masculine or feminine), and whether the word agrees with the sentence context in tense and number. After this information is assembled in the lemma, the retrieval of the lexeme (or phonology) ensues. In the one-stage view, the syntax is added to the retrieval process in parallel with the retrieval of the phonological information and compiled into the lexeme.

According to the basic two-stage model (Levelt, 1989), syntactical information is represented along with semantic information in the lemma. Therefore, if the lemma is completely activated in a TOT, syntactical information about the word should be accessible even if phonological information is not accessed. Recall that phonological information is not accessed later at the level of the lexeme. In the two-stage model, both semantic and syntactic information are accessible before phonology. Thus, rememberers experiencing a TOT should have access to syntactical information, regardless of whether they have access to phonological information. On the other hand, in a one-stage model syntactical and phonological information are not retrieved sequentially, and therefore may be independent of each other. Thus, the relation between the retrieval of syntactical information and the retrieval of phonological information can inform us about the underlying processes. Caramazza and Miozzo (1997) stressed the importance of looking for correlations between the retrieval of the two kinds of information during TOTs. If there is no correlation between them, then it is likely that they are retrieved independently and in parallel, in keeping with a one-stage model.

Grammatical Gender.   In some languages, a key element of a word is its grammatical gender. In some of these languages, a noun may be male, female, or neuter, whereas in other languages, words are either male or female. For most nouns, there is no relation to biological gender and grammatical gender. Thus, a common word such as table may be masculine in one language (e.g., French) but feminine in another (e.g., Spanish). Because gender is a key aspect of syntax, many theorists postulate that grammatical gender is stored in the lemma for each word (Garrett, 1992; Levelt, 1989). If so, it is possible that people experiencing TOTs in those languages with grammatical gender will often be able to correctly recall the gender of a missing word (Miozzo & Caramazza, 1997; Vigliocco et al., 1997; Vinson & Vigliocco, 1999).

Three initial studies in this area were conducted with Italian speakers (Caramazza and Miozzo, 1997; Miozzo and Caramazza, 1997; Vigliocco et al., 1997). Each study examined grammatical gender and its relation to the TOT. In Italian, all nouns are either masculine or feminine, and as Vigliocco et al. (1997) pointed out, the assignment is seemingly arbitrary and not based on any conceptual distinctions. For example, there is an Italian word *stella*, which is feminine, and a word *astro*, which is masculine. Both translate to the English word *star*. Usually, gender is correlated with noun endings. Masculine words end in "o" and feminine words end in "a," but there are many exceptions (e.g., the word *plasma* is masculine). Grammatical gender has important syntactical consequences in sentence formation, as it determines agreement within the sentence (Vigliocco et al., 1997).

Now consider an Italian speaker in a TOT for a particular word, say, *amniocentesi* (amniocentesis), which is feminine and irregular (Caramazza & Miozzo, 1997). Even if the speaker can retrieve the final phoneme of the target word, it does not provide that speaker with any information concerning grammatical gender. According to two-stage theory, the lemma stage compiles semantic and syntactical information prior to the retrieval of phonological information. Thus, the speaker should be able to retrieve the grammatical gender in the absence of retrieving the specific phonological form of the word. The data from these studies will now be evaluated.

Vigliocco et al. (1997) presented participants with definitions of words and asked them to retrieve the target word. If the participants could successfully retrieve the word, they were then given the next definition. If they could not recall the target for a particular definition, the participants were asked to rate their feeling of knowing on a 1 to 5 scale, with 5 indicating a TOT. Then they guessed the grammatical gender, the number of syllables, as many letters of the word as they could, and any related words that came to mind.

Problematically however, Vigliocco et al. (1997) did not use rememberers' ratings of how well they knew the word to determine whether the rememberers were experiencing a TOT. In their published report, they completely ignore whether the participants felt they were in a TOT. Instead, TOTs were assigned to all unretrieved targets for which the rememberer made partial information guesses. Positive TOTs were defined as those that were later recognized as correct, and negative TOTs were those in which the rememberer did not associate the target word with a hypothetical intended word.

Allow me to add an aside here. Although not really relevant to the interests of Vigliocco, this study tells us nothing about what kinds of information are accessible during a TOT, or what is the etiology of the TOT. It does shed light on the nature of syntactical access in words for which the phonology is lacking, however, and therefore is relevant for debates concerning the nature of word retrieval.

Vigliocco et al. (1997) found that gender was retrieved correctly 84% of the time when rememberers were in (experimenter-defined) positive TOT but only 53% of the time when in a negative TOT. This suggests that rememberers do have access to syntax even when the phonological form is missing. In further support of this claim, Vigliocco et al. reported that rememberers retrieved gender correctly 80% for the positive TOTs, when only those TOTs for which no phonological information was reported, not significantly different from the overall rate. Moreover, when they considered only those irregular words in which grammatical gender could not be determined by retrieving the last letter, the rate was still 80%. Thus, the results support the notion that syntactical and phonological information are represented at different levels of the word-retrieval system, and that it is possible to accurately retrieve syntactical information without retrieving the full phonological form.

Fortunately, the problem of relying on experimenter-defined TOTs in the Vigliocco et al. (1997) article was corrected in a pair of articles on the accessibility of gender in Italian during TOTs (Caramazza & Miozzo, 1997; Miozzo & Caramazza, 1997). I discuss the Miozzo and Caramazza article first, as it mainly dealt with empirical issues, and then turn to the more theoretical article of Caramazza & Miozzo.

Miozzo and Caramazza (1997) used a very similar paradigm, asking Italian-speaking participants to provide the words matching stimulus definitions or pictures. If they did not recall the target word, they indicated whether they were in a TOT, and then were required to guess the gender and the initial phoneme. However, unlike Vigliocco et al. (1997) Miozzo and Caramazza used rememberers' subjective judgments of TOTs to classify the unrecalled items. They compared those items that the participants rated as TOTs with the set of "don't know" responses (n–TOTs), which occurred when the participant indicated that he or she could not retrieve the target and was not in a TOT. Miozzo and Caramazza refer to the n–TOTs as "don't know" or "DK" responses, but I will use n–TOTs to remain consistent with other sections in this book. Miozzo and Caramazza found that grammatical gender was correctly reported in 71% of the TOTs, but only 47% (chance) for the n–TOTs responses. Moreover, rememberers guessed the initial phoneme 72% for TOTs, but only 58% for n–TOTs.

Miozzo and Caramazza's (1997) data are more convincing than Vigliocco et al.'s (1997) work because the comparison is between subjectively-defined TOTs and n–TOTs and not between experimenter-defined TOTs and items for which no partial information was reported. Nonetheless, both studies suggest that syntactical information, in this case grammatical gender, can be correctly reported in the absence of the retrieval of the target word. Thus, at a first glance, the data could be taken to support a two-stage model of lexical access in which phonology is retrieved only after a lemma, complete with syntactical information, is retrieved. However, Miozzo and Caramazza urged caution.

In fact, Miozzo and Caramazza (1997) argued that the data suggest that syntax and phonology may indeed dissociable. This suggestion is based on the observation that, in their Experiment 2, the correct gender was correctly reported 77.8% of the time, and the correct first letter was reported 78.8% of the time. According to the two-stage theory, this could not happen because for phonological information to be retrieved, an intact lemma must first be retrieved, in which the syntax is already known. Therefore, for two-stage models to be correct, the syntactical retrieval must be higher than the phonological retrieval. Moreover, if there is control for guessing, the 1% difference would actually yield a great advantage for the retrieval of phonological information during TOTs. In other words, guessing the gender correctly will occur 50% of the time, but guessing the first letter is much less likely, given there are 26 possible first letters.

Thus, Miozzo and Caramazza (1997) rejected serial models of word retrieval because phonological access during TOTs and n–TOT responses were higher than syntactical access. If the lemma is always retrieved in TOTs, and it is phonological access that is deficient, one would not expect better retrieval of phonology than any aspect of syntax. This led Miozzo and Caramazza to follow with a second study in which they directly tested the relation between retrieved syntax and retrieved phonology (Caramazza & Miozzo, 1997).

Caramazza and Miozzo's (1997) experiments were similar to the earlier study, except that, in the new article, they were able to correlate gender retrieval with initial phoneme retrieval. They considered this a crucial test of the role of syntax in the lemma, and whether it is necessary to consider the lemma stage at all. If the two-stage model is correct, and a lemma contains syntactic information, then there should be a strong positive correlation between the retrieval of gender and the retrieval of phonology during TOTs. That is, if the syntax precedes the phonology, then phonological retrieval should occur only after syntactical retrieval. In a one-stage model, the retrieval of syntax and phonology is potentially independent. Thus, a low or zero correlation would support a one-stage view.

In their first experiment, Caramazza and Miozzo (1997) found that gender was retrieved correctly for positive TOTs nearly 74% of the time, whereas the correct initial letter was retrieved only 28.3% of the time, roughly consistent with a two-stage model. However, when they examined the correlations they found that the correlation between the likelihood of retrieving the correct gender and the likelihood of retrieving the correct phoneme was -.085, not significantly different from zero. This zero correlation supports the one-stage view which suggests that the retrieval of syntax and phonology are independent of each other. In other words, retrieval of phonological information during a TOT does not depend on the prior retrieval of a syntax-driven lemma.

Caramazza and Miozzo (1997), however were concerned about the low rate of retrieval of the initial phoneme. In a second more simple experiment, the rate of initial phoneme retrieval rose to 57.5%, only slightly lower than the 67.8% correct gender retrieval. Nonetheless, the correlation was still not significantly different from zero (.034), again finding no comfort for the two-stage models of lexical retrieval. Therefore, Caramazza and Miozzo concluded that two-stage models are not necessary to account for the retrieval of syntax and phonology during TOTs. The retrieval of each seems to be independent of each other, supporting a one-stage model.

Interestingly, the story is not complete. Recently, Silverberg et al. (1999) attempted to replicate the retrieval of gender during TOTs in another language, Hebrew. Unlike Italian, Hebrew speakers were unable to access gender during TOTs. In fact, in their study, gender access was just slightly above chance for both TOTs and n–TOTs. This suggests that, unlike other aspects of TOTs which may be universal (e.g., phenomenology), access to gender is variable depending on the structure of the language. Silverberg et al.'s data can also be interpreted to support Caramazza and Miozzo's (1997) view that a lemma stage is not necessary to explain lexical access. If it were, then syntax would be assembled there, and Hebrew speakers would have access to gender even when they did not have full phonological access.

The relation between TOTs and grammatical gender is unclear. In Italian, rememberers have access to grammatical gender during TOTs. Recently, this has been replicated in Spanish (Gonzalez & Miralles, as cited in Vigliocco et al., 1999; Schwartz, Castillo-Andrade, & Gonzalez, 1998). However, Hebrew speakers do not access gender while experiencing TOTs. Caramazza and Miozzo (1997) argued that the data on gender suggest that it is not necessary to invoke a lemma stage in retrieval to explain TOT data. Nonetheless, as we see in the following section, there is strong support for the notion that some syntactical information is accessible to rememberers, regardless of language. We turn to other syntactical features now.

Other Aspects of Syntax.   An interesting aspect of language is the way in which we pluralize certain nouns. Linguists distinguish between mass and count nouns (Pinker, 1999; Vigliocco et al., 1999). Count nouns are objects that are countable and are those that get pluralized normally in speech. For example, the plural of the word cucumber is cucumbers and the plural of bird is birds. Mass nouns refer to those objects that are not countable and usually exist in groups; they do not get pluralized. For example, the plural of asparagus is asparagus and the plural of thunder is thunder. As you can see from these examples, there are many instances in which the division of words into mass or count nouns seems arbitrary. Thus, it is likely that this syntactical division must be represented in memory for each word.

Vigliocco et al. (1999) examined whether participants could determine if a noun was a mass or a count noun, in the absence of retrieving the actual word in English. That is, if participants could not retrieve the target word, they were asked to guess whether the word was pluralized in a mass or count fashion. Rather than get a determination of TOTs from participants, Vigliocco et al. (1999) classified all instances in which partial information was retrieved or successful recognition took place as "positive TOTs," and all instances in which no partial information was retrieved and the target was not recognized correctly as "negative TOTs." Not pleased with their definition of TOTs, I recently replicated the study, but used subjective TOTs as the criterion instead of experimenter-determined TOTs (Schwartz & Castillo-Andrade, 1999).

Vigliocco et al. (1999) found that participants were significantly more likely to correctly guess the syntactical state for the positive TOTs (85%) than for the negative TOTs (70%), although both rates were significantly above chance. In my replication, using subjective TOTs the correct syntax was reported for 74% of TOTs and 65% of n–TOTs. Again, both rates were above chance, and the rate for TOTs was significantly above that of the n–TOTs. Thus, during TOTs rememberers do have access to mass and count syntax. In the Vigliocco et al. (1999) study, retrieval of the first phoneme was independent of the retrieval of grammar. Caramazza and Miozzo (1997) argued that if syntax was always retrieved prior to phonological retrieval, then syntactical information should always be accessible when phonological information has been retrieved. In Vigliocco's study, the two forms of retrieval were independent of each other, thus further supporting Caramazza and Miozzo's notion of a single stage in retrieval.

One more study is relevant here. Iwasaki et al. (1998) looked at a grammatical aspect of the Japanese language, which is not present in English. In Japanese, some adjectives are based on nouns (adjectival nouns) and other adjectives are pure adjectives. A rough equivalent of adjectival nouns in English would be words such as bookish, colorful, and fishy, which are adjectives based on a noun. Pure adjectives include such words as good, special, and modern. This is a clearly marked feature of the Japanese language, but the origin of an adjective is independent of its meaning. Like the aforementioned features, Iwasaki et al. asserted that there is no a priori basis for knowing whether an adjective is an adjectival noun or a pure adjective. Therefore, Iwasaki et al. examined access to this syntactical feature when participants where in experimenter defined positive or negative TOTs. As in the earlier studies, positive TOTs were associated with better access to syntactical information than were negative TOTs. However, to the best of my knowledge, this study has not been replicated with subjective TOTs.

In conclusion, there is now evidence to suggest that rememberers have access to syntactical information when they are experiencing a TOT. However, most of the data comes from experimenter-defined TOTs, and the only data on subjective TOTs and grammatical access is the work of Miozzo and Caramazza (Caramazza & Miozzo, 1997; Miozzo & Caramazza, 1997) and my own unpublished work (Schwartz & Castillo-Andrade, 1999; Schwartz et al., 1998).

Much of the research supports the one-stage view of lexical access. I concur with the Caramazza and Miozzo (1997) position: the TOT data support Caramazza and Miozzo's assertion that a one-stage model is more predictive than two-stage models. In their view, a semantic intention (that is, to produce a particular linguistic idea) is followed by two parallel processes, one that invokes the correct syntax, and one that calls the correct phonology. During a TOT, either or both of these processes may be partially or completely disrupted. That there is no correlation between the retrieval of partial syntactic information and the retrieval of partial phonological information suggests that syntax is not compiled at a lemma stage prior to phonological retrieval.

TOTs AND THEORIES OF BILINGUAL SEMANTIC
REPRESENTATION

TOTs have played a role in the development of two other lexical theories. TOTs recently contributed to our understanding of lexical representation in bilinguals (e.g. Askari, 1999; Gollan & Silverberg, in press). TOTs also play a role in the understanding of the relation between hand gestures and spoken language (Beattie & Coughlan, 1999; Frick-Horbury & Guttentag, 1998). I discuss the issues of TOT and bilingual representation first and then address gestures.

One of the cognitive issues being studied about bilinguals is the nature of semantic representation. One the one hand, the single-store view is that bilinguals represent meaning of words in both languages in a common representational system (e.g., Altarriba, 1992, Altarriba & Mathis, 1997; Chen & Ng, 1989). On the other hand, the dual-store view postulates that meaning is represented separately for each language the person knows (Askari, 1999; Tulving & Colotla, 1970). Contemporary views favor the single-store view, at least for speakers who are native or fully fluent in both languages (Altarriba, 1992; Gollan & Silverberg, in press). Whether this is true for those who are less fluent in a second language is beyond the scope of this discussion. I have no intention or expertise in delineating the important experiments and ideas in this area. However, recently two studies have looked at this issue using TOT methodologies, and each study drew opposite conclusions about the nature of bilingual semantic representation (Askari, 1999; Gollan & Silverberg, in press).

Askari (1999) examined semantic and phonological priming in Farsi–English bilinguals. Farsi is an Indo–European language, a descendent of Persian, now spoken in Iran. Askari's bilinguals were mostly Farsi-dominant, but had been speaking English since childhood. Her study had two objectives. First, she wished to test models of bilingual representation. Second, she wished to test whether Burke et al.'s (1991) transmission deficit model best explained the pattern of TOTs.

Askari (1999) compared three priming conditions: a semantic prime, a phonological prime, and a no-prime condition. The primes were words that were presented along with a definition. For example, if the definition was "Shallow body of water, near or connected to a larger body of water" (lagoon), then the phonological prime was "platoon." If the definition was "homesickness, an excessively sentimental condition, yearning for return to or of some past period or irrecoverable condition" (nostalgia), the semantic prime was "memories." The sentences were presented in either English or Farsi, and the primes were presented in either English or Farsi, in a fully crossed (three prime conditions by two prime languages by two definition languages). This yields 12 conditions for which Askari obtained both correct recall and TOT rates (see Table 4.1) The participants were instructed to answer in whatever language in which the definition was provided.

The results were rather complex (see Table 4.1). As far as recall was concerned, the participants recalled far more words in Farsi than they did in English. Priming also increased recall of the target word in English, but did not have any effect in Farsi. The TOT data were intriguing. When English primes were used to prime English definitions, there was a small increase in TOTs when semantic priming occurred, but a large increase in TOTs when phonological priming occurred. Thus, when the definition was of the word "lagoon," presenting the word "platoon" increased TOTs. However, when the definition was for the word "nostalgia," presenting the word "memories" only slightly boosted TOTs. This is consistent with other studies of priming and TOTs (e.g., Rastle & Burke, 1996; White & Abrams, 1999). However, for Farsi, when Farsi primes were used, semantic priming increased the number of TOTs, but phonological priming had no effect at all, in stark contrast to the English-language data.

Askari (1999) interpreted these data as supporting Burke's transmission deficit model (Burke et al., 1991) because the primes did not inhibit word retrieval. However, the result that Farsi semantic priming increased TOTs, but phonological priming did not, contradicts the Burke et al. model, which postulates that phonological deficits, not semantic deficits, cause TOTs. In contrast, an inferential model might better explain these data. Because the participants were stronger in Farsi than in English, they might have sus-

TABLE 4.1

Askari's Results on Bilingual TOTs

	English Prime				Farsi Prime		
	SR	RP	UR		SR	PR	UR
			English definition				
Correct .21	.19	.06	.38		.33	.23	
TOT	.14	.38	.08		.28	.29	.13
			Farsi definition				
Correct .56	.48	.50	.42		.40	.50	
TOT	.27	.20	.27		.29	.18	.15

Note. *Note.* Mean proportion of correct responses and TOTs as a function of definition language (English, Farsi), prime language (English, Farsi), and prime (SR = semantically related, PR = phonologically related, and UR = unrelated). Adapted from Askari (1999), *Journal of Psycholinguistic Research.* TOT = Tip-of-the-tongue phenomena.

pected that what they lacked in their weak language was phonological aspects of the word, especially as they may have retrieved the word already in Farsi. Thus, phonological priming helps in a second language. However, when the participants could not retrieve the Farsi word, it may have had more to do with not being clear on the definition (i.e., see the aforementioned definition of lagoon—it could also cue "inlet"). Thus, more semantic information might facilitate a greater sense of confidence in retrieval. Of course, why the Farsi pattern is different from the English pattern in studies of English monolinguals (Rastle & Burke, 1996; White and Abrams, 1999) is a mystery.

In terms of a single- or dual-storage view of bilingualism, Askari (1999) argued that her data support a single-store view. First, cross-language priming did occur for correct recall. English primes marginally improved retrieval of Farsi definitions, and Farsi primes significantly improved retrieval of English definitions. A dual-storage view would not have predicted any cross-language priming because retrieval occurs wholly within that language's representational system. The TOT data is not directly relevant, although Askari noted that anecdotally, her participants often used translations from one language to cue retrieval of the word in the other target language, which also supports a single-storage view.

The other study, which used TOTs to study bilingual representations, was Gollan and Silverberg's (in press) study of TOTs in Hebrew–English bilinguals. This study also compared bilingual performance to monolingual performance in a TOT task. The methodology was different enough from other TOT studies to warrant mention. The participants were Hebrew–English bilinguals, most of whom rated their proficiency in Hebrew to be stronger than their proficiency in English. They were given definitions in either Hebrew or English, but asked to retrieve the words in both languages. TOTs were subjective decisions that an unretrieved target felt retrievable.

The most interesting feature of their data is that the bilingual participants experienced more TOTs overall than did the monolingual participants, even when the greater number of to-be-retrieved words was taken into account. This was true even for "super-bilinguals," that is, those participants who were highly proficient in both English and Hebrew. Resolution rates, however, were equivalent for the two groups. As in their earlier study (Silverberg et al., 1999), Gollan and Silverberg (in press) also found that Hebrew-speaking participants did not have access to grammatical gender during TOTs.

Gollan and Silverberg (in press) presented a variety of explanations for the higher rate of TOTs in the bilingual participants. These included general fatigue because of the greater number of retrievals and the dual nature of the task that required them to retrieve words in both languages. Gollan and

Silverberg suspected that inhibitory mechanisms may be necessary to account for these data. They wondered if the increased TOT rates in bilinguals is due to inhibitory competition between the words in the two languages. They remain cautious, however, because of the accumulated wisdom that inhibition (or blocking) does not explain TOTs (e.g., Askari, 1999; Brown, 1991; Burke et al., 1991; Heine et al., 1999; Perfect & Hanley, 1992).

Cautiously, Gollan and Silverberg (in press) suggested that, contrary to current orthodoxy, the current data are more in line with a dual-store view of a bilingual's lexicon. They suspected that competition between retrieval of the target word in one language and retrieval in the other should not happen if they share a common semantic representation. If they do not share representations, inhibition is more likely, as in the Hebrew–English bilinguals studied by Gollan and Silverberg. Thus, their interpretation of the TOT rates of monolinguals and bilinguals suggests that the dual-store view of bilingual representation might better account for these data.

Clearly, these two studies alone are insufficient to answer any questions about whether bilinguals' lexicons are unified or separate for each language. They do, however, suggest another promising avenue in which TOTs can be used to study word retrieval phenomena. On the other hand, the differences between TOTs in different languages is an interesting phenomenon unto itself. Earlier, I made the argument that the TOT may represent a universal cognitive experience. Two studies discussed here may suggest otherwise. First, phonological priming increased TOTs only in Farsi for English–Farsi bilinguals (Askari, 1999), similar to the pattern with English monolinguals (Rastle & Burke, 1996). I proffered earlier that this may suggest that bilinguals use different inferential strategies in producing TOTs. Askari (1999) also commented on the better metalinguistic capabilities of bilinguals. Second, Gollan and Silverberg (in press) found that Hebrew speakers, unlike Italian and Spanish speakers, cannot access grammatical gender during TOTs. What linguistic differences among various languages create this difference remains to be understood.

THE RELATION OF GESTURES, TOTs, AND WORD RETRIEVAL

During normal human speech, most people combine their spoken language (articulation) with an array of hand gestures (gesticulations; Frick-Horbury & Guttentag, 1998). Many researchers have wondered about exactly what is the interplay between hand gestures and spoken language (e.g., Krauss, Dushay, Chen, & Rauscher, 1995). Some theorists hypothesize that gestures help us retrieve words by providing the speaker with retrieval cues (Krauss et al., 1995) Two new studies have examined the relation between iconic hand and arm gestures and the likelihood of a TOT (Beattie & Coughlin, 1999; Frick-Horbury & Guttentag, 1998). Gestures include clasping hands, raising hands above the head, scratching eyebrows, and drumming fingers. Iconic gestures include indicating size by gesturing outward with the hands and pantomime gestures to demonstrate the potential use of an object when the name cannot be retrieved.

Frick-Horbury and Guttentag (1998) conducted a standard Brown–McNeill (1966) type study, in which participants were asked to recall low-frequency targets when presented with their definitions. Because Frick-Horbury and Guttentag were primarily interested in the role that gestures play in the retrieval of words, half of the participants were prevented from making gestures while doing the task, and the other group was free to move their hands as they pleased. This experimental manipulation had no effect on overall TOT rates or TOT resolution. However, when Frick-Horbury and Guttentag looked only at those participants who were free to gesture, they found that many more TOTs were accompanied by gestures than were n–TOTs. Thus, a TOT compels us to wave our hands trying to retrieve the target, although the hand gestures apparently do not help us resolve TOTs. Frick-Horbury and Guttentag's (1998) fascinating study is unique in that it examines the hand movements that accompany subjective TOTs and frustrating word retrieval. Beattie and Coughlin (1999) also looked at the relation of hand gestures and lexical retrieval, but they did not ask the participants to make TOT judgments. TOTs were determined by the experimenter when they engaged in some unspecified combination of verbal statements (e.g., "oh God, I know it"), facial expressions (such as winces), body movements, head movements, and foot and leg movements.

Beattie and Coughlan (1999) found that when rememberers were "free to gesture," they recalled no more targets than when they were instructed to "keep their arms folded." However, when they were free to gesture, they experienced substantially more TOTs than when they were to keep their arms folded (112 to 72). Moreover, more TOTs were resolved when they were free to gesture. Thus, TOTs and TOT resolution increases when people are free to gesticulate.

On the surface, there is again a contradiction between Frick-Horbury and Guttentag's (1998) data and that of Beattie and Coughlan (1999). One study found that restricting hand gestures did not affect TOT rates and resolution, but the other did. I suspect the difference lies in the methodology. Because Beattie and Coughlan did not rely on subjective TOTs, it is possible that they classified as TOTs items that Frick-Horbury and Guttentag's participants would have labeled n–TOTs. Although there are only two studies from which to draw inferences, it is the Frick-Horbury and Guttentag study that is more relevant to those interested in the TOT, as they actually measured TOTs. Nonetheless, further study is necessary to resolve this discrepancy.

In terms of the standard two-stage model of retrieval, it is possible to consider that gestures, like semantics and syntax, are represented at an early level of the word retrieval process (i.e., the lemma). Thus, allowing for gestures strengthens the representation of the lemma, allowing for stronger activation of phonological levels, which then increase TOTs and the likelihood of resolution. However, it is also possible to interpret these results in terms of inferential models. Gestures may serve as cues that the target item is known and is in memory, and they increase the probability of resolution of unrecalled items. The gestures may increase TOTs because rememberers correlate their likelihood of retrieval with their state of gesturing. If they find themselves gesturing, it is assumed that they are likely experiencing a TOT. Thus, the very freedom to gesture increases TOT rates.

The common ground in both Frick-Horbury and Guttentag (1998) and Beattie and Coughlan (1999) is that gestures increased when people were experiencing TOTs. It is unclear how to best interpret these data. It is possible that the gestures are used to help infer that a TOT is present, as just discussed. It is also possible that people intuit that gestures help them retrieve words. Given that TOTs are feelings that a word is retrievable, it may be that people choose to gesture more when experiencing a TOT. If, as Beattie and Coughlan suggested, gestures do help recall, then it is good strategy to gesture during TOTs.

THE TIP-OF-THE-PEN PHENOMENON IN CHINESE WRITING

Reading and writing has been extensively studied in Chinese because Chinese, unlike most languages, uses a logographic writing (Xu, Pollatsek, & Potter, 1999; Zhang, Perfetti, & Yang, 1999). Most languages, such as English, use a phonological alphabet, in which each letter represents a particular sound in each word. In Chinese, however, characters refer to concepts, not to sounds. Sun, Vinson, and Vigliocco (1998) examined a fascinating phenomenon in Chinese writing called the tip-of-the-pen phenomenon (TOP). According to Sun et al., there is an idiom in Chinese (Ti-Bi-Wang-Zi) that means literally, "Pick up a pen but forget how to write a character." Thus, the TOP refers to the "condition in which a speaker knows a word but cannot write it." In other words, the Chinese speaker can say the word aloud, but cannot remember the character used to write the word. Sun et al. found that Chinese participants were able to retrieve partial orthographic information when in a TOP, similar to the partial phonological information retrieved during a TOT. Thus, the TOP may mirror the TOT in both phenomenology and its relation to partial retrieval. TOPs have never been reported in alphabetic languages, because knowing the pronunciation always gives you at least a head start on how to write it. However, it would be interesting to see if TOPs could be induced for exception or irregular words in English (e.g., mood, blood, good), perhaps in nonnative writers.

SUMMARY

The main goal of this chapter is to describe the ways in which TOT research has been used to explore issues of word retrieval, in general, and to assess two- versus one-stage theories of word retrieval, in particular. I also touched on how TOTs have been used to address issues in bilingual representation. In these research frameworks, TOTs have been used as a "window" on word retrieval, that is, TOTs allow researchers to address what happens when retrieval is slowed or blocked. As has been shown in this chapter, research has indicated that both phonological and syntactical aspects of the to-be-retrieved word are accessible during TOTs, and that this has been interpreted as supporting both one- and two-stage views.

In this chapter, I discussed theories of lexical retrieval. Two-stage theory stipulates that word retrieval occurs in two stages. In the first stage, a lemma is retrieved. Lemmas contain both semantic and syntactical information specifying a target word. In the second stage, a lexeme is retrieved, which specifies the phonological form of the word. In the one-stage view, the lemma is removed, and syntactical information is not retrieved until the level of the lexeme.

TOTs have been used to address this issue. The studies find that both phonological and syntactical information is accessible during a TOT. Partial gestural information is retrievable for American Sign Language signers in TOTs. Some researchers contend that this pattern of findings supports the two-stage view. Caramazza and Miozzo (1997), alternately, argued that the statistical independence of phonological and syntactic retrieval suggests that the one-stage model might better account for the data. If syntax were retrieved before phonology, then the retrieval of phonology would be partially dependent on the prior access to syntax. Similar logic has been used to compare single-store and dual-store views of bilingual representation. TOTs are more common in bilinguals suggesting greater access to a common semantic access when individual phonological access in each language may be lacking.

5

Theories of Metacognition

An old saying about men is that they never stop to ask for directions, no matter how lost they actually are. The proverbial "lost man" in this joke is so sure that he knows where he is that it does not occur to him to stop somewhere and ask for directions. The man's failure can be considered an instance of poor metacognition. To an outside observer, the man is clearly lost, but that is not subjectively salient to our man. Thus, his metacognitive experience is inaccurate. Moreover, because he does not know that he is lost, he does nothing to ameliorate the situation, such as calling and getting new directions. The man has poor metacognitive monitoring skills, and he cannot adequately control his performance.

Although we each may know people similar to the one in the joke, research has shown that fortunately, our metacognitive systems are actually quite good at informing us about what we know, do not know well, or do not know at all. Moreover, the research also suggests that based on our metacognitive awareness, we often make quite sophisticated decisions about how to go about learning, remembering, or probably finding our way when lost. This chapter provides an overview of recent theory and research in the domain of metacognition.

In chapter 4, the discussion centered on how TOT has been used as a means to study the processes of lexical retrieval. In this chapter, I adopt the metacognitive perspective, which views the TOTs as a metacognitive experience about word retrieval. The metacognitive approach will be introduced in general and not directly applied to TOTs until chapter 6, although the metacognitive perspective has been discussed previously in the context of the importance of phenomenology (chap. 2) and etiology (chap. 3).

I consider the theory of monitoring and control, mostly drawing on the theoretical work of Thomas Nelson and Louis Narens (e.g., Barnes, Nelson, Dunlosky, Mazzoni, & Narens, 1999; Nelson, 1996; Nelson & Narens, 1990; 1994), drawing mostly from the literature on feelings of knowing and judgments of learning. Nelson and Narens stressed the importance of the function of metacognition. In chapter 6, I apply it to the work on TOTs and the focus will be on the possible functions that TOTs may serve to keep the human mind working efficiently and effectively.

MONITORING AND CONTROL

Nelson (1996) stressed the importance of two potential and integrated functions of metacognition, which he referred to as monitoring and control. Monitoring refers to peoples' ability to become aware of how well their cognitive processes are working. To do this, the monitoring process builds a model of how the basic process is working. For monitoring to be accurate, information must flow from the "object" level process to the "meta" level process. Monitoring process, then, can serve the basis for conscious metacognitive judgments, although in some cases, the monitoring may be hidden from conscious access (e.g., Reder & Schunn, 1996). Control refers to the decision that the person makes based on the output of the monitoring system. If the monitor informs the person that learning is going poorly, the control processes can redirect attention to the to-be-learned items. Control is a process whereby the object level process affects changes in the meta level process. Control, then, changes how the system works. For control to be effective, it must be able to change the object level processes and change it in adaptive ways. Control processes may be conscious (e.g., Mazzoni & Cornoldi, 1993) or nonconscious (Reder & Schunn, 1996). In either case, their effectiveness is partially dictated by the monitoring effectiveness and partially by the choice of good strategies.

The key function of metacognition, then, is to monitor what the cognitive processes are doing and then if needed affect change in them. For a system to be able to monitor and control itself, it must construct a model of its own ongoing function (Nelson & Narens, 1994). This monitoring system can represent what the organism is doing in real time. For this model to work, Nelson hypothesized that at least two levels of organization must exist—an "object-level" and a "meta-level." The object-level is ordinary cognition, retrieving information, making decisions, and recognizing objects. The meta-level models the activity of the object-level and therefore can make predictions about its future.

The second feature of Nelson's framework is that the object-level and the meta-level must be connected such that information can continuously flow from the object-level to the meta-level, and that information can flow back from the meta-level to the object-level (see Fig. 5.1). This flow of information from the object to the metalevel is what is called monitoring; that is, the meta-level needs constant input from the object-level system to construct a model of its function. The flow from the meta-level to the object-level is considered the control function; that is, the meta-level can now direct the object-level to change or redirect its processing in line with what the meta-level computes to be a more desirable goal.

Nelson and Narens (1990, 1994) defined monitoring in the following way: "The fundamental notion underlying monitoring ... is that the meta-level is *informed* by the object-level." (Nelson & Narens, 1990, p. 127; emphasis in the original). They defined control in the following manner: "The fundamental notion underlying control ... is that the meta-level *modifies* the object-level, but not vice-versa" (Nelson & Narens, 1994, p. 12, emphasis in the original). Thus, the meta-level represents and changes the object-level.

Nelson and Narens (1994) compared the metacognition model to the workings of an ordinary home thermostat. A thermometer, which serves as the monitoring function, measures the ambient temperature of the room. The thermometer can be thought of as a model of the outside world. Information flows from the world (average motion of molecules) to the thermometer, allowing the thermometer to maintain a model (albeit a simplified one) of one dimension of the outside world. For the thermostat to work, the system must have a control element as well. Indeed, when the temperature rises above or falls below a certain threshold temperature, the thermostat mechanism,

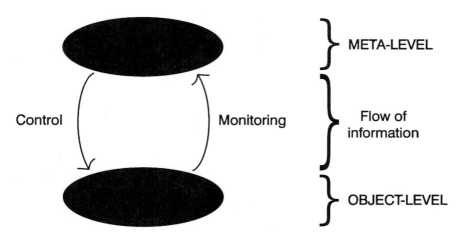

FIG. 5.1.

which serves as the control function, turns on the appropriate heating or cooling unit. When the air conditioner is turned on, the system affects the outside world by lowering the temperature. By analogy, metacognitive judgments such as judgments of learning, feelings of knowing, or tip-of-the-tongue states, can serve the purpose of monitoring object-level cognition.

In this model, the two levels are continuously interacting with each other. Once the air conditioner has been turned on, the thermometer continues to measure the now-falling temperature. When the temperature returns to a predetermined base level, the thermostat shuts off the air conditioner and allows the process to begin anew. Similarly, according to the Nelson–Narens framework, mental monitoring and control are engaged in continuous dance. A control function may alter behaviors by causing the remember to focus on more difficult study items. This may, in turn, affect the memory strength of items being studied, which in turn alters the items selected by the control level as items to be restudied (e.g., Thiede & Dunlosky, 1999).

Nelson and Narens (1990) introduced one more nuance into this theory. They asserted that the concepts of meta-level and object-level are relative, and that a particular level that is meta to one level, may be the object of another level. This hierarchy of levels exists for both monitoring and control. Thus, one level, called Lx, may be superordinate to one level, Ly, but superordinate to another level, Lz. Thus, information continually flows from lower levels to higher levels, in the form of monitoring, and back again, in the form of control. In this way, Nelson and Narens related their conception of monitoring and control to earlier notions of control (e.g., Atkinson & Shiffrin, 1968). In practice however, most research has simply looked at whether metacognitive monitoring is accurate and the extent to which it directs control.

An example of this system in action comes from the quickness with which people can say that they do not know something (e.g., Klin, Guzman, & Levine, 1997; Kolers & Palef, 1976; Glucksberg & McCloskey, 1981). In these studies, participants are asked to decide as quickly as possible whether they know the answer to a question. Monitoring allows people to quickly decide that some answers are simply not known, and there is no need to initiate a memory search. For example, given the question, "What was Benjamin Franklin's horse's name?" most people would quickly respond "don't know."

It is also possible, although Nelson and Narens are not explicit about it, to describe the monitoring/control framework in an evolutionary perspective (e.g., Pinker, 1997; Tooby & Cosmides, 1995). This is one of the inherent advantages of Nelson and Narens' functional approach, despite the difficulty in experimentally testing such evolutionary ideas concerning the human mind. Specifically, the argument is that the ability to monitor and control cognitive processes may have given our human ancestors an evolutionary advantage over those with less well developed monitoring and control abilities. For example, consider two Pleistocene hunter-gatherers heading out from the settlement in search of food. If one expresses more confidence in his knowledge of the likely way home, he will be followed. This is only adaptive if confidence correlates with accuracy. If not, following either member will do. A hunter-gatherer with poorer accuracy risks causing the whole group to go hungry. Of course, many animals find their way to food and back home without the benefit of metacognition. But, the organism with metacognition has far more options and the ability to choose its destiny rather than simply following its strongest instinct.

At this point, any discussion of evolutionary advantages for a monitoring and control system are pure speculation. Nonetheless, the functional approach advocated by Nelson and Narens is interpretable within such evolutionary thinking. Following the lead of Tooby and Cosmides (1995), it may be possible to design metacognition experiments to tap into these primordial metacognitive problems. For example, one might test how well people can monitor their knowledge of spatial locations, or whether they feel they have learned sufficiently how to discriminate between edible and poisonous mushrooms, monitoring and control skills that would have given our ancestors some advantages. However these studies remain to be done.

I do not attempt an exhaustive review of the huge literature on metacognition (see Metcalfe, 1996, 2000; Nelson, 1996; Schwartz, 1994 for such overviews). In the current section, I will outline some of the basic methodologies used to address metacognitive monitoring and metacognitive control as illustrative of the basic Nelson-Narens model. I will draw from experiments concerning judgments of learning and feeling of knowing. These studies will provide the flavor of how monitoring/control theory has been applied to metacognitive judgments.

Monitoring

The study of monitoring in memory dates back to the seminal work of J. T. Hart in the mid- 1960s. Like Brown and McNeill on the east coast of the United States, Hart, on the west coast, set out to examine the accuracy of feeling-of-knowing judgments (FOK). He was interested in whether rememberers could accurately predict whether they would recognize targets that they could not recall. Thus, aside from some definitional differences between what a TOT was and what a FOK was, Hart (1965) and Brown and McNeill (1966) started out with very similar paradigms. Hart (1965) asked participants to retrieve the answers to general-information questions (e.g., What is the capital of Denmark?). If they recalled the answer (Copenhagen), they moved on to the next item. If they could not recall it, they were asked to make a FOK for recognition of the item. Hart simply asked people to indicate "Yes" for a positive FOK or "No" for a negative FOK. He then gave them a recognition test to assess their accuracy. Hart found that people were better at recognizing targets when they had experienced a FOK than when they did not.

Unlike Brown and McNeill, who were primarily interested in the information accessible during a TOT, Hart (1965) was mostly interested in whether the FOK accurately predicted recognition performance, and thus, his interest was in the relation between the judgment and performance. In this way, Hart initiated the study of metacognitive monitoring, that is, how well people know what they know and what they do not know. Hart, indeed, (1967) coined the phrase "the memory monitoring system."

Prospective and Retrospective Monitoring. Nelson and Narens (1990, 1994) divided monitoring into two basic categories, prospective and retrospective monitoring. Prospective monitoring has been the classic domain of metamemory (e.g., Arbuckle & Cuddy, 1969; Hart, 1965, Underwood, 1966). Prospective monitoring concerns judgments about how likely information will be remembered in the future. Retrospective monitoring refers to the subjective accuracy of already-retrieved information. Because most of the research from theorists who adopted a monitoring/control perspective has involved prospective monitoring, I will focus on it here. Nonetheless, ideas concerning monitoring and control equally apply to retrospective judgments.

The main foci of research on prospective monitoring have been two classes of monitoring judgments; feelings of knowing and judgments of learning (see Schwartz, 1994 for a review). Although there are many other kinds of prospective monitoring judgments, such as judgments of interest (Son & Metcalfe, 2000) and judgments of comprehension (Maki, 1998), I will confine the discussion to feelings of knowing and judgments of learning.

Judgments in the Nelson-Narens Model. Nelson and Narens (1990, 1994) neatly divided monitoring judgments in memory according to when they occur in information processing (see Fig. 5.2). Thus some judgments accompany the process of encoding, whereas others accompany the process of retrieval. The middle of Fig. 5.2 shows the object-level processes, such as acquisition (or learning), retention, and retrieval. The top of the figure shows the judgments designed to tap the monitoring process for each phase of learning, and the bottom shows the kinds of control tasks that have been looked at to see the effectiveness of control. Thus, ease-of-learning judgments are made just prior to a study trial, in advance of actual learning. During ease-of-learning judgments, participants are asked to make an im-

Metamemory Framework

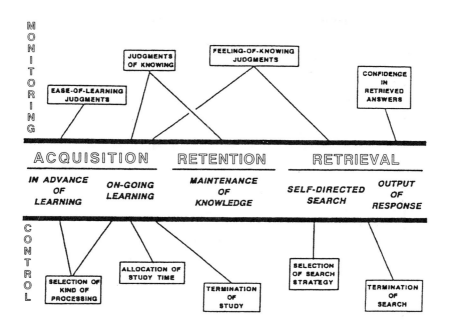

FIG. 5.2.

mediate assessment of how much study will be required to learn presented information, typically cue-target pairs (Leonesio & Nelson, 1990; Underwood, 1966). Judgments of learning occur during the acquisition of knowledge. They are predictions made during learning as to whether an item will be remembered in the future. Feeling-of-knowing judgments are made at the time of retrieval. They are judgments as to whether a currently unrecallable items will be recognized later. These have been the three most common ways of tapping monitoring (see Nelson & Narens, 1994).

Researchers have designed the judgment tasks to tap into metacognitive monitoring. For example, judgments of learning tap into the confidence that rememberers have that an item has been sufficiently studied. Nonetheless, the judgments themselves may not necessarily be pure measures of monitoring. Factors other than monitoring may affect the judgment process. For example, reported judgments may be arbitrarily high in order for the rememberer to appear more knowledgeable. It is also conceivable that stopping the monitoring process in order to make the judgment may interfere with accurate monitoring. Preliminary evidence suggests that this is not the case (Begg, Duft, Lalond, Melnick, & Sanvito, 1989). Indeed, making judgments may enhance the learning and monitoring (Spellman & Bjork, 1992).

The above discussion suggests that one source of inaccuracy of judgments is that the judgments themselves may only partially tap the underlying monitoring function. Of course, before sources of inaccuracy in metacognitive judgments are considered, it is necessary to demonstrate that metacognitive judgments do reflect ongoing cognition, in the first place, that is, whether they are indeed accurate. Some researchers have questioned whether metacognition is accurate. When Nelson and Narens first began investigating metamemory, they were surprised at how poor accuracy appeared to be (see Nelson and Narens, 1990). Indeed, they considered the possibility that monitoring is like looking at oneself in funhouse mirror—the monitoring may be replicable, but a gross distortion of the object-level processes. The practical implications of metacognition-as-funhouse mirror are enormous. If monitoring is inaccurate, we should not teach students to rely on their innate monitoring and control functions. Nelson and Narens (1990), however, did find when they asked the right questions that metacognition was accurate, sometimes highly so. Therefore, they abandoned the funhouse metaphor.

Monitoring Accuracy.   This section involves a whirlwind tour of research done on the accuracy metacognitive judgments in predicting memory performance. I consider feeling-of-knowing judgments and judgments of learning, which have been the mainstay of metacognition research. To summarize, these judgments tend to be accurate most of the time. For example, feelings-of-knowing tend to be correlated with recognition about $+.40$ to $+.50$ (e.g., Nelson, 1984, 1988; Schwartz & Metcalfe, 1994). Judgments of learning also tend to be accurate, with the correlation being often greater than .9 (Nelson & Dunlosky, 1991; Dunlosky & Nelson, 1994). Ease-of-learning judgments have not been as well studied, but the studies that have been published suggest better-than-chance accuracy as well (Leonesio & Nelson, 1990). However, metacognitive judgments are far from perfect, and there are circumstances in which judgments may actually mispredict performance (e.g., Benjamin et al., 1998; Koriat, 1995).

I will interject a brief methodological note. In metacognition research, there has developed a consensus to use gamma correlations to assess the accuracy of judgments (see Nelson, 1984; Schwartz & Metcalfe, 1994). Gamma correlations yield -1 to 0 to 1 values, and are therefore comparable to other correlation statistics. They are nonparametric, allowing researchers to draw inferences from ordinal data, such as metacognitive judgments.

Recently, within the field of metacognition, considerable research has been devoted to the delayed judgment of learning (JOL) effect (e.g., Dunlosky & Nelson, 1994; Nelson & Dunlosky, 1991; Nelson, Dunlosky, Graf, & Narens, 1994; Spellman & Bjork, 1992). This is a monitoring effect, in which the gamma correlations between judgments and performance are extremely high. The contrast between immediate and delayed JOLs is instructive in understanding both monitoring and control. I have chosen to devote space to reviewing the delayed JOL effect for two reasons. First, the effect demonstrates how subtle manipulations can alter the accuracy of metacognitive judgments. Second, explanations of the effect bring into play the role of mechanistic theories in accounting for metacognitive monitoring.

In a typical JOL task, participants are given word pairs to learn, such as "dog-spoon." Later, they are given the cue word "dog" and asked to make a judgment as to the likelihood that they will recall the target word at some point later. In an immediate JOL, the judgment is called for immediately after the participant has studied the pair. In a delayed JOL, the judgments is called for at some point much later after the participant has studied the word pair (5 min, 15 min, 24 hrs). The differences in the accuracy of the judgments is remarkable. Gamma correlations for the immediate JOLs are respectably better than chance, usually around $+.5$. However, the delayed JOLs show an astonishing accuracy, with gamma correlations usually exceeding $+.9$ (e.g., Dunlosky & Nelson, 1994). The only difference is the delay between the time of learning and time of judgment.

Explanations have varied, but they all center on one major component of the difference between the immediate and delayed judgments (e.g., Bjork, 1994; 1999; Dunlosky & Nelson, 1997). In an immediate JOL, the target is still likely to be in short-term memory. Thus, when the participant makes the judgment, it is made with the answer clearly in mind. Bjork (1994) argued that this interferes with the assessment of how difficult the retrieval will be because the participant cannot test its difficulty by practicing the retrieval. However, when a delayed JOL is made, the target answer is no longer in short-term memory, and must be retrieved from long-term memory. Under these circumstances, the judgments can be made on the basis of an actual retrieval attempt. Successful retrieval of the target at the time of judgment then makes a much better predictor of later retrieval than the judgment made without the benefit of the attempt. Given the similarity between what the rememberer does when the JOL is made and the later task of retrieving the target, accuracy is extremely good.

I am simplifying the theories here for the sake of brevity, and there is considerable debate about the specifics of the explanation of the accuracy differences between the two types of JOLs. However, the common ground among the theories is the notion that the delayed JOL situation allows rememberers to make accurate judgments by making the monitoring maximally straightforward. Participants can use the retrieval process itself to serve as the monitoring process in a delayed JOL. However, in an immediate JOL, this option is not open to the rememberer because the target word is easily accessible in short-term memory. In the immediate JOL, the rememberer must use strategies, which are not only less accurate, but more attention demanding of the individual because the situation does not allow for easy monitoring.

Supporting this idea concerning the accuracy of delayed JOLs and the relative difficulty of immediate JOLs, Nelson et al. (1998) found that alcohol intoxication has different effects on immediate and delayed JOLs. In their study, alcohol impairment did not affect the accuracy of delayed JOLs at all. However, for immediate JOL, sober controls showed much better accuracy than did their alcohol-impaired compatriots. This suggests at the reason for the high accuracy of the delayed JOLs. If one can recall the target at the time of judgment, then there is a good chance that it will be recalled at the time of test. However, for immediate JOLs, when one cannot benefit from a dry run at retrieval (no pun intended), more sophisticated monitoring strategies must be employed, which are disrupted by the alcohol.

Incidentally, the above reasoning suggests that TOTs may be relatively difficult judgments to make. In TOTs, the target word is not accessible. Therefore, the strategies used to infer its presence must tap into sophisticated strategies, regardless of whether they are direct access or inferential mechanism. Thus, the delayed JOL findings can be interpreted to predict that TOT accuracy should be above chance, but less than perfect. Indeed, in studies in which gamma correlations have been computed, TOT accuracy usually comes out around +.6 (e.g., Schwartz, 1998; 2001). Thus, when viewed as metacognitive judgments, TOTs are accurate, but not perfectly so.

Under normal circumstances, both feelings of knowing and judgments of learning show high correlations between the judgments made and the later memory performance. Indeed, in the case of delayed JOLs, the accuracy is near perfect. This rosy picture of metacognitive monitoring stands in contrast to earlier views of human introspective ability, which showed some major deficits in insight (e.g., Nisbett & Wilson, 1977). However, most researchers agree that metacognition is an inferential task, and thus is subject to error.

Metacognitive perspectives of monitoring emphasize both the demonstration of accuracy of judgments and an acknowledgment that accuracy may deviate from perfection, or that some judgments may not reflect object-level cognition at all (see Nelson & Narens, 1994; Nisbett & Wilson, 1977). Indeed, this latter contention leaves open the possibility that some monitoring may not only not reflect accurate ongoing cognition, but may actually distort the object-level cognition. Therefore, the monitoring/control perspective fits neatly with Tulving's criticism of the doctrine of concordance (Tulving, 1989). Monitoring research does not assume the judgments made by people will necessarily reflect the object-level cognition.

When will metacognitive monitoring actually mispredict performance? The delayed JOL effect suggests that accuracy will be high in circumstances in which the basis of monitoring is related to the to-be-predicted task in a straightforward manner. Circumstances that call for complex monitoring processes will show lower accuracy. If the experimental situations can be constructed such that rememberers are using the wrong bases for monitoring, judgments that participants make may, in fact, be negatively related to the task that they are predicting.

Several studies have now identified situations in which monitoring not only does not predict performance, but it mispredicts it consistently (Benjamin et al., 1998; Koriat, 1995). Koriat's study found that usually accurate feeling-of-knowing judgments could be mispredict performance if "trick" questions were used. Koriat (1995) presented Israeli participants with deliberately chosen "trick" questions, such as "What is the capital of Australia?" or "In what U.S. state does one find Yale University?" More Israelis incorrectly respond "Sydney" and "Massachusetts" than they do with the correct answers (Canberra and Connecticut, respectively). Moreover, they express high confidence in these incorrect answers or in their ability to recognize correct answers. Other questions, such as "What is the process by which plants produce food?" (photosynthesis) may elicit less confidence in their abilities, but more correct answers. Koriat asked participants to make feeling-of-knowing judgments (predictions of future recognizability) for misleading and non-misleading questions. For the misleading questions, the feeling-of-knowing judgments was negatively correlated with recognition performance, that is, confidence was higher for those questions that were later answered incorrectly than those answered correctly. Thus, at least in this specific situation, metacognitive monitoring was inaccurate.

Benjamin et al. (1998) also uncovered a number of situations in which metacognitive monitoring was inaccurate, but their focus was on JOLs. In one study, Benjamin et al. asked people to retrieve answers to general-information questions. However, the JOLs were directed at whether the participant would be able to free recall the target answer later in the absence of the question. If they did not recall the answer themselves, the answer was provided. The logic of this experiment was as follows. Some questions (e.g., What is the capital of France) will be easy, and others (e.g., What is the capital of Argentina?) may be more difficult. The JOL task, however, is directed at the likelihood of free recalling Paris and Buenos Aires. Some research (Gardiner et al., 1973) suggested that the more difficult items in cued recall become the easier items in free recall. Benjamin et al. suspected that participants would use the ease of retrieving in cued recall to predict the likelihood of free recall. If this is so, then the JOLs should mispredict free recall. To operationalize difficulty in cued recall, Benjamin et al. used the amount of time it took participants to retrieve the answer or decide that they did not know. More difficult items took longer whereas easier items required less time. For example, compare the speed of your response to a question such as "What is the capital of France?" versus a question like "What is the capital of Argentina?" For most Americans, at any rate, Paris will be quickly retrieved, but Buenos Aires may take some time.

Under these circumstances, the participants mispredicted their performance. They gave high probability judgments to the ones that had been easy to retrieve initially, and low judgments to those that had been retrieved with difficulty. In the free recall test, they were more likely to recall the originally-difficult ones, like "Buenos Aires" and less likely to recall the originally-easy ones, like "Paris." Therefore, the data supported the original hypothesis of Benjamin et al. (1998). Under certain misleading circumstances, the processes for monitoring involve errors, and these errors result in inaccurate monitoring.

To summarize, metacognitive monitoring is generally accurate. This is true for both judgments of learning and feeling of knowing. Under some circumstances, it can be highly accurate (e.g., Dunlosky & Nelson, 1994). However, accuracy only occurs when the monitoring process constructs an accurate model of the object-level process. There are circumstances in which this does not occur, and accuracy can be at or below chance (Benjamin et al., 1998; Koriat, 1995).

Control

In the metacognition model, monitoring allows us to build an accurate model of our cognitive processes, but it is the ability to implement control over these processes that allows us to use metacognition to improve our abilities or increase our rate of learning. Monitoring alone is like a thermometer, it can only tell you whether it is cold or warm outside. Control processes allow us to choose whether a sweater or t-shirt is appropriate for the day.

To illustrate the importance of control, imagine a student studying for an exam. It is well past midnight, she has been studying for hours, and is exhausted. The decision that this student must make is whether she has studied the material for the exam sufficiently and should go to sleep, or if she must brew another pot of coffee and keep studying. Metacognitive control is critical. The student must decide if the material is generally well-learned, and if not, which information necessitates further study. These metacognitive decisions influence not only the student's caffeine intake but also her studying behavior and, ultimately, her test performance (see Nelson, 1993).

The research on metacognitive control is not as well developed as the research on metacognitive monitoring. Recently, there has been considerable progress in delineating the kinds of control processes available to the human rememberer and in detailing when and how these processes are used (Barnes et al., 1999; Koriat & Goldsmith, 1996; Mazzoni & Cornoldi, 1993; Nelson, 1993; Nelson et al., 1994; Son & Metcalfe, 2000; Thiede & Dunlosky, 1999). Control processes may be directed at both the process of encoding (Mazzoni & Cornoldi, 1993; Nelson et al., 1994) or at the process of retrieval (Barnes et al., 1999; Koriat & Goldsmith, 1996). In general, the literature on control suggests that rememberers use highly adaptive and sophisticated control strategies to improve learning and retrieval and are often very accurate in directing these processes. However, as with monitoring, there is often room for improvement (e.g., Mazzoni, Cornoldi, & Marchetilli, 1990). In the next chapter, control functions of TOTs will be discussed.

Referring to Figure 5.2, Nelson and Narens (1990) described two kinds of control behaviors at the time of encoding, selective encoding and allocation of study time. Selective encoding refers to the kinds of processing used for incoming information. For example, one may choose to engage in mindless rote repetition if one is just trying to remember the pizza delivery number, or one may choose to engage in elaborative encoding if studying for an exam. Thus, selective encoding refers to the kinds of processes that can be utilized, whereas allocation of study time refers to when those processes are deployed. Rememberers may selectively choose some items to study more than others, based on the input from their monitoring system. If the monitoring is accurate, the differential allocation of study time should improve learning.

Control at Encoding. In an important series of papers, Mazzoni, Nelson and their colleagues investigated the relation between the monitoring processes and control processes in the encoding of new information (Nelson, 1993; Nelson et al., 1994; Nelson & Leonesio, 1988; Mazzoni et al., 1990; Mazzoni & Cornoldi, 1993; Mazzoni & Nelson, 1995). Mazzoni et al. (1990) presented participants with sentences to remember, such as "The policeman stood under the lamp." The participants gave a judgment of learning (prediction of future remembering) for each sentence. In a second phase, they were re-presented with the sentences, and given a choice as to how much time to allocate to studying that item. Although the overall time was limited, the participants could allocate study time differentially among the items, with the overall goal of maximizing memory performance. After the study phase, participants recalled the sentences. This paradigm is typical of the studies that address allocation of study time, although usually cued recall is used instead of free recall (e.g., Mazzoni & Cornoldi, 1993).

Mazzoni et al. found a strong negative correlation between the JOLs and the amount of time that the rememberers studied the items. The rememberers chose to study those sentences given low JOLs (i.e., the difficult items) for longer durations than those sentences given high JOLs (i.e., the easy ones). Presumably, the participants thought that they could recall the easy ones without much study, but that the difficult ones required more study. This negative correlation between JOLs and allocation of study time is the typical finding in these studies and has been replicated many times (see Nelson, 1993; Son & Metcalfe, 2000). Therefore, it appears that rememberers are able and willing to use their metacognitive monitoring, as measured by the JOLs, to their advantage, by using monitoring to influence control decisions that they make.

However, just as monitoring is not completely effective, neither is control. Nelson and Leonesio (1988) identified a phenomenon that they labeled the "labor-in-vain" effect. This refers to the observation that participants may allocate more study time to the difficult to-be-learned items, but that does not ensure that they will, in fact, learn these items. Indeed, in all of the studies correlating JOLs to study time allocation, the participants fail to completely compensate for the original difficulty differences. This means that although they study the more difficult items for longer durations than the easy items, they still recall more of the easy items. Thus, Nelson and Leonesio argued that control, like monitoring, is not perfect.

I have found an everyday analog to this labor-in-vain effect when I learn the names of students in my class. In a typical psychology class at my university, there are usually about five women for every one man. As a function of that disparity, I find that I learn the names of the men more quickly than the names of the women. Knowing this, I emphasize the women's names in my learning attempts because my judgments of learning tells me that they are harder. Nonetheless, I still learn each individual man's name more quickly than each individual woman's name despite my efforts to compensate.

In general, the strategy that learners adopt is to focus on the items that they judge to be more difficult. They assume that the easy items require less time or less effort. This strategy is presumably highly effective when the learner has sufficient time to study and learn the difficult items. However, what happens when the overall amount of time is more limited? One possibility is that learners will continue to focus on the difficult items. Another possibility is that people will realize the hopelessness of learning the difficult ones in the allotted time and will focus their efforts on the easy ones.

Thiede and Dunlosky (1999) tested these two possible scenarios by observing how participants selected items for restudy, that is, which items the participants choose to restudy, not necessarily how long they studied each item. In their experiments, they varied the amount of total time that participants had to master a list of word pairs. In some conditions, the total study time was very limited, whereas in other conditions, participants had almost unlimited time to study the items. When study time was unlimited, Thiede and Dunlosky found the usual negative correlation between JOLs and selection of items for restudy. However, when study time was limited, participants opted for a different strategy and choose the easy items for study, generating a positive correlation between JOLs and study selection.

Son and Metcalfe (2000) conducted a similar study, in which students were asked to allocate study time to a number of different short expository essays. Like Thiede and Dunlosky (1999), Son and Metcalfe found that the allocation of study time was positively correlated to the judgments of learning when overall time was limited. The students spent more time studying those items that they felt would be easier to remember. In simple terms, the participants realized that they would not have sufficient time to master the difficult items, and therefore, chose to concentrate their efforts on those items that they thought they had a better chance of remembering anyway. Interestingly, however, Son and Metcalfe found that judgments of interest were more predictive of study than judgments of learning. Thus, although the participants did use some strategies to enhance learning, they were more likely to follow their interests when expository text was used. In other words, a grade of "B" might be satisfactory for Physics, but students want "A's" in their Psychology classes. These data suggest that rememberers have complex control mechanisms at their disposal (see also Nelson et al., 1994). They will switch control strategies depending on the time constraints and on the intrinsic interest of the materials being studied.

Control at Retrieval.   Recent studies also suggest that control functions influence decisions at the time of retrieval (e.g., Barnes et al., 1999; Reder, 1987, 1988; Reder & Schunn, 1996). Monitoring can help people to determine whether particular information is accessible in memory. If the answer is positive, participants may spend more time attempting retrieval and may try more retrieval strategies to recall the item. Although equally important, control at retrieval has received less attention from researchers than control at encoding, but there have been a few relevant studies. Rememberers must decide at the time of retrieval whether it is worth the effort to attempt retrieval, how to recall items, and whether to admit that one does not know. These decisions may have important cognitive and social implications. I briefly describe some of the research designed to test retrieval control.

Reder and her colleagues (1987, 1988; Reder & Schunn, 1996) were interested in how metacognition affected strategic decisions in the regulation of recall. In particular, they were interested in whether people relied on memory search or opted for other strategies such as calculation (in math problems) or inference (in general-information problems). For example, some questions may be so difficult (How many minutes have passed since the Big Bang?) that most people will quickly respond "I don't know." Other questions ("How many legs do antelopes possess?") may not be stored in memory, but may be easily inferred once the question is posed. Similarly, a question such as, "How many windows does your current home have?" may not be stored in memory and hence not immediately retrievable, but may be easily determined by mental counting. Other questions ("Who was the first president of the United States) draw forth a quick and definitive response from memory. One of the functions of metacognition, according to Reder and Schunn, is that it allows us to make rapid decisions about our state of knowledge. For Reder and Schunn, metacognition directs the strategies that people use to solve problems or answer questions. Interestingly, Reder and Schunn argued that most metacognition is outside of the domain of consciousness. One does not necessarily access one's confidence when answering such questions. Nonetheless, the metacognitive process is directing retrieval strategies.

Barnes et al. (1999) designed an experiment to test the strategic regulation of memory retrieval. They presented participants with general-information questions for retrieval. They provided penalties for lack of speed, and rewards for number of correct answers. Thus, participants were penalized for each second the question was on the screen, but were rewarded whenever they provided a correct answer. They compared conditions in which the penalty for slowness was low vs. high, and when the reward for correctness was low vs. high in two separate experiments. These incentives were predicted affected the metacognitive control processes.

Barnes et al. found that when the incentive for speed was high, the rememberers spent less time at retrieval, and the number of correct answers decreased. However, when the incentive for correct answers was high, the rememberers spent more time attempting retrieval and generated more correct answers as a consequence. In a second experiment, Barnes et al. found that when the incentive was high, participants made fewer commission errors, although they recalled less overall. These findings suggest that rememberers are capable of using sophisticated control processes at retrieval as well.

In the Barnes et al. (1999) study, explicit measures of metacognition were not made. However, other research has demonstrated correlations between the magnitude of feeling of knowing and retrieval latency. Nelson et al. (1984) and Nelson et al. (1998) showed that FOK judgments were positively correlated with retrieval latency for omission errors, that is, the longer the response time to recall, the higher the FOK judgment had been. These results were replicated by Costermans et al. (1992). I will present similar evidence for TOTs in the next chapter.

I discuss one more study concerning control processes and metacognition. The study (Koriat & Goldsmith, 1996) differs from the others reviewed here because it concerns retrospective monitoring and its effect on control rather than prospective monitoring. Retrospective monitoring refers to judgments made about the correctness of an already-retrieved target. These judgments are often called simply confidence judgments and have been studied heavily in the eyewitness memory area (e.g., Loftus et al., 1989). Confidence in a retrieved answer can affect control decisions. Koriat and Goldsmith were interested in whether these confidence judgments would affect decisions to output answers when the situation called for different criteria of correctness.

Consider a question such as "What is the capital of California?" (Sacramento). There are three possible categories of answers, a correct one, an incorrect one (commission error), and a "don't know" response (omission error). A "don't know" response is not incorrect, and therefore does not count as an "inaccurate" memory. On the other hand, if one says "San Francisco," one has committed a commission error, which does count against the accuracy score. Now consider the person who, when asked this question, originally thinks of San Francisco, and then realizes that the capital is a smaller, less well-known city, but is not sure of its name. If forced to guess, the person may say San Francisco, even though the confidence is low for that name. Thus, Koriat and Goldsmith's (1996) interest was in how participants withhold low-confidence answers like San Francisco. The withholding of answers is defined as the control function, whereas the confidence judgment is the monitoring process that informs the control process. This monitoring/control function applies to both incorrect and correct answers.

In their experiment, Koriat and Goldsmith presented participants with general-information questions. They were required to answer all questions and then were asked to make a confidence judgment (on a 0 to 100% scale) for each question. Thus, even if they had no idea what the answer was, they were required to make a guess. Presumably, such guesses elicited answers accompanied by low confidence judgments. After they answered all of the questions, the instructions switched to free-report conditions. The questions were shown again, and now the participants were free to answer only those questions that they were sure were correct. Koriat and Goldsmith could then examine the relation between the original confidence judgments and the subsequent decision to report or withhold. To make matters more interesting, in one condition, the participants were offered a financial incentive to answer correctly, coupled with an equal disincentive for wrong answers (moderate-incentive condition). In a second condition, the disincentive was much larger than the incentive (high-incentive condition).

The results were quite striking. First, the participants were accurate with their confidence judgments. Those answers given high confidence ratings were much more likely to be correct than those given lower confidence ratings. Indeed, the gamma correlation was .87 for recall. There was also a strong positive correlation between confidence and whether the answer would be volunteered in the second phase. Moreover, in the high-incentive condition, the participants screened out more of their incorrect answers, resulting in an increase in overall accuracy. This came at a cost of a decrease in quantity, but it does show that the participants were able to monitor their output (via confidence) and control their accuracy (via volunteering or withholding answers).

Koriat and Goldsmith (1996) argued that these data are consistent with a metacognitive model. Rememberers monitor the accuracy of their answers, reflected in their confidence judgments. Then, depending on the incentives, they can use their confidence judgments to decide which answers they will output and which they will withhold. Control is represented by the volunteering or withholding of answers. Therefore, we see the usefulness of the metacognitive model of monitoring and control in both prospective judgments (feelings of knowing and judgments of learning) and retrospective judgments (post-answer confidence).

To summarize, there has been a recent surge of interest in the processes by which metacognition is used to control the processes of learning and remembering. The studies suggest that people can monitor their mnemonic processes accurately, and that people can use the output of monitoring to effectively control the ongoing learning and remembering. The majority of the work from the metacognition literature is based on studies that assess FOK judgments at the time of retrieval or JOLs at the time of encoding.

The question to be addressed in chapter 6 is whether the metacognitive model of monitoring and control can be successfully applied to TOTs. In my work, I treat TOTs as a metacognitive state, akin to judgments of learning and feelings of knowing (e.g., Schwartz, 1994, 1999; Schwartz & Smith, 1997). However, many researchers prefer to think of TOTs simply as deficits in lexical retrieval (e.g., Vigliocco et al., 1997). Thus, to demonstrate that TOTs do belong under the rubric of metacognitive theory, monitoring and control in particular, it is important to show that TOTs serve both monitoring and control functions for the cognitive processes of a human rememberer.

SUMMARY

In this chapter, I outlined a general theory of metacognition, originally de-vised by Nelson and his colleagues (e.g., Nelson, 1996; Nelson & Narens, 1990). The theory focuses on the functions of metacognition for the remem-berer. The theory postulates two hypothetical functions of metacognition, monitoring and control. Monitoring builds a model of what the cognitive pro-cesses are doing. Judgments are often based on this monitoring process. If the internal model is representative of what the cognitive processes are doing, the judgments will be accurate. Control allows the metacognitive system to redi-rect the cognitive processes, thereby improving them. Accurate monitoring is necessary for effective control. In this chapter, we discussed research that supports Nelson's view of metacognition, and shows that people are good at monitoring their mnemonic processes. I also have shown that people are good at controlling their cognitive processes, based on their metacognition. In the next chapter, I apply this model to TOTs.

6

Functional Aspects
of the TOT

Consider the following familiar scenario. You see an acquaintance approaching. Instantly, you are hit with a TOT. You cannot retrieve the person's name, although you are sure that you know it. What do you do? Chances are you will try to cue yourself in some way. Where do I know this person from? What letter does the name start with? Compare this with your preparation for an acquaintance for whom you are not experiencing a TOT. Here you might be planning on how to be friendly and social, but avoid revealing that you do not know the name.

This example gets at the crux of the possible control function of the TOT. TOTs are not arbitrary side effects of lexical retrieval failure. Rather, they can be thought of as metacognitive experiences that inform the rememberer about the likelihood of eventual recall. In this way, they serve a useful control function for the rememberer. TOTs alert us to which items we may be able to remember, and thus, TOTs may direct our retrieval processes in directions that maximize performance. Indeed, they may direct the selection of retrieval strategies, and possibly to serve certain social functions as well.

For the TOT to usefully serve these functions it must be an accurate reflection of accessibility in memory. This is the issue, discussed in chapter 5, of the close interplay between monitoring and control. For TOTs, the monitoring is the ability to accurately predict the likelihood of recall, whereas the control function is the hypothesized ability to direct search in the appropriate direction. In this chapter, the metacognitive model of monitoring and control will be applied to issues in TOT research. First, I take a new look at the existing data on TOTs from the perspective of monitoring. Much of the research previously used to support lexical access views is also interpretable as supporting accurate monitoring. This research, which demonstrates the accessibility of the TOT target and partial and related aspects of the TOT target, can be reinterpreted as evidence of the good monitoring ability of TOT experiences. Some of this research is better interpreted from a monitoring perspective than from a lexical access perspective. Second, the issue of TOTs and control is discussed. Although this issue has not received much attention as of yet, there are some intriguing findings that suggest that TOTs may indeed direct retrieval, as suggested by a monitoring and control model. Much of this research on TOTs and control comes from recent studies in my lab.

MONITORING AND TOTs

In the Nelson–Narens framework, monitoring processes form a model of the object-level process and thereby predict what may happen next (Nelson & Narens, 1990, 1994; see chap. 5). In the case of the TOT, the monitoring process alerts the rememberer of the possible presence of the target in memory, despite its temporary inaccessibility. Accurate monitoring means that TOTs will occur when the target is in memory and potentially accessible, and that TOTs will not occur when the target is not accessible. Therefore, monitoring is only successful if the monitoring system constructs a good model, which can accurately predict what the object-level process will do. The empirical question to ask is, how well do TOTs predict retrieval, the object-level performance in question?

For the most part, this question has already been answered under a different guise, and the answer is a positive one. In chapter 3, the evidence that supports direct-access was discussed. Much of the evidence comes in the form of correlations between the experience of a TOT and the likelihood of resolution, recognition, or the retrieval of partial or related information. Also discussed in chapter 4 was the accessibility of partial phonological and syntactic information. These correlations also support the idea that TOTs serve a monitoring function. In almost every study that has compared TOTs and n–TOTs, TOTs are associated with greater resolution, recognition, and partial item recovery. This strongly suggests that TOTs inform the rememberer which items are likely to be accessible in memory, and that a n–TOT means the item is probably inaccessible or not in memory store. I do not duplicate here what was reviewed earlier, but I briefly make the case for monitoring.

Many studies show that TOTs are accurate predictors of resolution. During a TOT a rememberer is more likely to retrieve target words than when not experiencing a TOT. Diary studies show extremely high resolution rates for naturally occurring TOTs (e.g., Burke et al., 1991; Heine et al., 1999). In laboratory studies, TOT target resolution has consistently been shown to be superior to resolution after n–TOTs (e.g., James & Burke, 2000; Schwartz, 1998; Smith, 1994). In Smith's study, 40% of all TOTs were successfully resolved, whereas only 11% of n–TOTs were resolved, supporting the contention that TOTs are good monitoring tools.

TOTs also are good predictors of whether the target will be recognized, again supporting the idea that TOTs are good monitors. Table 3.2 recaps 15 experiments, showing higher recognition for unrecalled items following TOTs than those following n–TOTs. In terms of computable gamma correlations, my research generally shows correlations of around .6 between TOTs and recognition (Schwartz, 2001; Schwartz et al.; 2000 Schwartz; 1998). Although the target word is not recallable at the time of the TOT experience, TOTs predict eventual successful resolution as well as later recognition.

It is also possible to adapt the metacognitive perspective to reinterpret the findings that partial information is more likely to be retrieved during a TOT. In particular, in chapter 4, the retrieval of partial phonological and partial syntactical information was discussed at length. From a metacognitive perspective, the TOT may serve the function of informing the rememberer when such partial information is accessible. Although the entire word may not be retrieved, partial information is often important in cueing retrieval. Experiencing a TOT may prompt the rememberer to look for partial information. Indeed, the studies discussed in chapter 4 showed that rememberers are far more likely to retrieve phonological (Brown & McNeill, 1966; Brown, 1991) and syntactical information (Miozzo & Caramazza, 1997; Vigliocco et al., 1999) when experiencing a TOT than when not.

MONITORING AND CONTROL THEORY AND INFERENTIAL MODELS OF TOT ETIOLOGY

The metacognitive view of monitoring and control and inferential theory concerning the etiology of TOTs are compatible views. In inferential theory, the rememberer uses a host of clues to determine future memorability. The metacognitive view supplies the importance of this function. The clues can serve to inform the rememberer whether a word will, in fact, be retrieved. Nonetheless, although monitoring has been shown to be generally accurate, it is not perfect. This, too, is consistent with inferential approaches, which postulate that the clues that people use to determine future memorability are heuristic in nature.

If monitoring and inferential theory are correct, there should be identifiable situations in which TOTs distort the metalevel model of the retrieval situation. In chapter 4, I discussed two studies in particular, in which metacognitive judgments mispredicted performance (Benjamin et al, 1998; Koriat, 1995). This misprediction was based on a misapplied heuristic. In the case of the Benjamin et al. (1998) study, participants based their JOLs on the ease in which they answered general-information questions. This did not prove to be an accurate heuristic for predicting free recall. Judgments were made on the basis of information that did not inform the experimental task. Thus, if TOTs are also based on inferential clues, which are systematically invalid, then the monitoring will be inaccurate, leading to TOTs that do not correctly predict future performance. Recent research of my own has attempted to identify situations in which TOTs do not signal accurate monitoring. Similar to the Koriat (1995) procedure, which used questions for which most participants made commission errors, I used nonanswerable general-information questions. These nonanswerable questions sometimes produce TOTs, which I call *illusory TOTs* (Schwartz, 1998; Schwartz et al., 2000). Illusory TOTs occur when the inferential clues mislead the participants into experiencing TOTs when they do not know the target answer. I describe these studies next.

From the perspective taken here, a TOT means the feeling that a particular word will be recalled. The word *feeling* refers to a subjective state of the individual and not "cold" judgments that they make based on logic and conscious inference. The feeling is produced by an unconscious inference based on clues of memorability because, in general, the inference is accurate and the TOT feeling serves as a good predictor of future recall. If we manipulate clues to cause the person to make a TOT inference when they do not have an item in memory store, illusory TOTs result. Therefore, illusory TOTs are phenomenological experiences in which the person feels that the target is recallable, but the target memory is either unavailable, forgotten, or indeed, was never acquired (Schwartz, 1998; Smith, 1994).

Illusory TOTs expand on the earlier concept of subjective TOTs (Burke et al., 1991; Jones & Langford, 1987; Perfect & Hanley, 1992). Subjective TOTs refer to TOTs reported by the participants, which are not followed by successful memory performance. The target is neither resolved nor recognized, nor is any partial information retrieved. In contrast, objective TOTs are those in which there is evidence of target knowledge. The distinction between subjective and illusory TOTs is a theoretical one. With a subjective TOT it is possible that, under the right retrieval conditions, rememberers may be able to evidence knowledge of the target. In an illusory TOT, no knowledge of the target is possible. Therefore, some subjective TOTs, but not all, may be illusory, but all illusory TOTs are subjective.

To illustrate this point, consider the following question: "What is the name of the capital city of Canada?" A person may experience a TOT for this name. An objective TOT is one in which the person retrieves the partial information that the first letter is "O" and that the city is located along the Ontario–Quebec border, or a TOT in which the person later recognizes "Ottawa" from a list of alternatives. A subjective TOT is one in which the person experiences the TOT but actually has no supporting objective knowledge and may later misidentify the capital, perhaps because the person thought the capital was Vancouver. In contrast, if the question is "What is the capital city of Bormea?" any TOT is necessarily subjective and necessarily illusory because no such country exists. In the lab, we can test illusory TOTs with fictional questions such as these.

I conducted two experiments designed to document the existence of illusory TOTs (Schwartz, 1998). In the first study, I used TOTimals as stimuli (see Smith, 1994; Smith et al., 1994; Smith, Brown, & Balfour, 1991). Rememberers were presented with a series of six pictures of fictional animals (drawn to resemble real animals), combined with some biographical information about the animals, such as diet, size, and habitat (see Fig. 3.3). Four animal pictures were paired with two-syllable fictional names (e.g., Yelkey, Rittle, etc.). Two of the animals were not paired with names. Later, the rememberers were presented with only the pictures and were asked to recall the animals' names. If they could not recall the names, they were asked whether they were experiencing TOTs. The critical question follows: Would rememberers experience TOTs for the names of the unnamed animals? The answer was yes—illusory TOTs occurred and at a rate almost comparable to TOTs for targets with names. Rememberers experienced more TOTs of the unrecalled, but named, animals (23%) than for the unnamed animals (16%). Thus, 16% of items for which no name had been provided induced a TOT for the name of the TOTimal.

In the second study, I used general-information questions to elicit illusory TOTs. Remembers gave answers to 100 general-information questions (Schwartz, 1998). Of these questions, 80 were adapted from Nelson and Narens' (1980) norms and had one-word answers. I added 20 questions to which there was no correct answer (unanswerable questions). Thus, rememberers could not possibly retrieve targets because there were no targets to retrieve. For example, one question was, "What is the name of the Canadian writer who wrote the novel *The Last Bucket*? The only correct answers are "nobody" or "no such novel." Participants read the questions, both answerable and unanswerable, and typed in their response on a computer keyboard. Any guess on the unanswerable questions were treated as errors of commission. Following errors of commission or of omission, participants made TOT judgments. For the unanswerable questions, any TOTs were considered illusory. Once again, findings show more TOTs for the answerable than for the unanswerable, but there were still a great many illusory

TOTs. Illusory TOTs occurred for 18% of the unanswerable questions, less than half than after answerable questions, but significantly above zero.

In a follow-up study, Schwartz et al. (2000) examined illusory TOTs for unanswerable general-information questions, using a paradigm nearly identical to the work just described. However, in this study, because we were interested in the phenomenological characteristics of TOTs, participants were asked to judge emotionality, strength, and imminence for their TOTs. Thus, the phenomenology of TOTs using both answerable and unanswerable general-information questions were compared on each of these phenomenological characteristics. Replicating Schwartz (1998), illusory TOTs were less common than TOTs following answerable questions. However, illusory TOTs did occur, and again at comparable rates.

There were differences in the experienced phenomenology of the TOTs of answerable and unanswerable items. Illusory TOTs were more likely to be judged less emotional, weaker, and less imminent than were the TOTs for answerable items. Nonetheless, some illusory TOTs were judged to be strong, emotional, or imminent. That strong and emotional experiences did occur for some illusory TOTs suggest that their phenomenology can be quite compelling. We were curious as to why, however, the illusory TOTs were less subjectively powerful in general. We suspected that the answerable questions led to more retrieval of partial and related information, thus providing more clues for the answerable questions than for the unanswerable questions.

It is possible to interpret illusory TOTs within a direct access or lexical access framework. Perhaps for each illusory TOT, the participant has an (incorrect) answer in mind that is not accessible. Thus, the participant may be experiencing a TOT for "loggerhead" for the turtle that lays its eggs underwater. Although the answer is wrong, the participant has a real target in mind. Thus, illusory TOTs are not inconsistent with most direct access models. However, even so, they do support a monitoring perspective on TOTs. Illusory TOTs do occur, so even if they are based on direct access to an incorrect answer, they do lead to errors both of prediction and of memory. Therefore, researchers interested in lexical retrieval must be careful that TOTs are "objective" ones. Illusory TOTs support a monitoring perspective because they indicate monitoring failures, regardless of whether one assumes an inferential or direct access basis for TOT etiology.

TOTs AS CONTROL MECHANISMS

Control refers to the decisions that are made based on monitoring cognitive processes. In the previous chapter, the relation among judgments such as FOKs, JOLs, and learning behaviors was discussed. Numerous studies have now shown that metacognitive judgments are closely correlated with various

learning and retrieval strategies (see Son and Metcalfe, 2000, for a recent review). In this section, I discuss some putative control functions for TOTs and
review the nascent research on TOTs and the control of retrieval.

My assumption is that a major function of TOTs is the control of the retrieval process. Because TOTs usually indicate successful monitoring recall
and recognition, it is now important to ask the question, How do TOTs control behavior? With regard to retrieval, the following questions may be addressed: How do TOTs direct or redirect the retrieval process for it to be
successful? Do TOTs cause us to search our memory for targets longer, or do
they drive us to ask friends or consult dictionaries and encyclopedias to
search for the missing target? Do they cause us to cue ourselves in various
ways to aid in effective retrieval? Most of these question remain unanswered
partially because the monitoring and control approach to TOTs is so new. In
this chapter, I propose a few preliminary answers to some of these questions.

TOTs and Retrieval Time

One possible metacognitive function of the TOT is to cause one to search
longer for an item that is currently inaccessible. To be more specific, the
TOT tells us that the unrecalled word is both in memory store and imminent, so we devote more time in our attempt to retrieve the item. Research
on feelings of knowing reviewed in the previous chapter found that feeling-of-knowing judgments are related to the amount of time people spend
attempting retrieval of the target (Barnes et al., 1999, Costermans et al.,
1992; Nelson et al., 1984). Items that are high in feeling of knowing will
elicit longer retrieval attempts because rememberers think they can retrieve the item if they keep trying. Similar logic can also be applied to TOTs
and retrieval time. TOTs might effect retrieval by causing people to direct
more search time to the TOT targets. Presumably, if TOTs indicate that the
item is stored in memory and could be located, a plausible strategy would be
to spend more time attempting retrieval of those items for which one is in a
TOT than for an item for which one is not in a TOT.

In a recent set of studies (Schwartz, 2001), I examined the relation of
TOTs to the time it took people to retrieve answers or decided that they
could not retrieve the answers. Thus, like the FOK studies, I explored the
relation between a metacognitive judgment (the TOT) and retrieval latency. These latencies were measured by computer, and they meant something slightly different depending on condition. For correct recall, retrieval
time refers to the amount of time needed to initiate the response on the
computer keyboard. For incorrect recall or errors of commission, retrieval
time was defined in the same way: time to initiate memory response. However, for errors of omission ("don't know" responses), retrieval time was the

amount of time necessary to initiate the "don't know" response (a question mark in the experiments) on the computer keyboard.

Once again, I used the standard Brown–McNeill (1966) paradigm, in which participants were asked general-information questions. Following omission and commission errors, the computer asked the participants whether they were experiencing a TOT. In the series of four experiments, two called for emotionality judgments along with the TOTs, whereas the other studies asked for dichotomous ("yes" or "no") TOT judgments. Finally, in all experiments, an eight-alternative forced-choice recognition test was presented. The critical variable was the amount of time participants spent attempting retrieval during TOTs and during n–TOTs.

All four studies showed a clear association between retrieval time and the likelihood of a TOT (see Table 6.1; Schwartz, 2001). TOTs were associated with longer retrieval times than were n–TOTs. Although this effect appeared to be moderated by other factors, which I discuss later, there was a positive correlation between the presence of a TOT and the amount of time spent attempting retrieval of unrecalled targets, particularly those that would become omission errors. There was a general trend in this direction for TOTs after commission errors as well. Although the data are only correlational, they clearly support the notion that one control function of TOTs is to direct the amount of time participants spend in retrieval search.

I also examined whether emotionality in TOTs would influence retrieval times (Schwartz, 2001). In one experiment (Exp. 1), participants were asked to rate their TOTs as either emotional or nonemotional. The initial hypothesis was that both emotional and nonemotional TOTs would be correlated with longer retrieval times, but that emotional TOTs might elicit even longer times than the nonemotional ones. The data supported this hypothesis. The emotional TOTs (13.3 sec) were the longest, followed by the nonemotional TOTs (8.1 sec), and n–TOTs (7.3 sec) were the shortest. This basic pattern was found to be statistically significant for both TOTs induced by general-information questions and those induced by word definitions.

When I submitted this article to *Memory & Cognition* for publication, I received an interesting set of reviews. The reviewers were generally positive about the study but had many questions about the methodology, in particular, that I collected TOTs following commission errors, a practice generally not used in TOT experiments. It led one reviewer (Alan Brown) to reflect on the common experience of brief TOTs that occur before we retrieve a word. Brown claimed that many TOTs go unmeasured because resolution occurs so quickly. Moreover, if my view of metacognitive control was correct, TOTs followed by rapid resolution should also show longer retrieval times than those successfully recalled without a TOT experience.

TABLE 6.1

Retrieval Times

	Correct	Emotional	Nonemotional	N–TOT
		Experiment 1		
omission		13.3 (1.07)	8.1 (.56)	7.3 (1.00)
commission		12.3 (1.17)	8.2 (.56)	8.8 (.33)
correct	7.7 (.28)			
		Experiment 2		
	Correct	TOT		N-TOT
omission		13.8 (1.13)		7.6 (.42)
commission		12.3 (.89)		11.0 (.72)
correct	8.9 (.48)			
		Experiment 3		
	Correct	Emotional	Nonemotional	N–TOT
omission		25.2 (2.60)	16.1 (1.77)	12.7 (1.11)
commission	16.9 (1.26)	15.0 (1.70)	17.3 (1.53)	
correct	12.6 (.87)			
		Experiment 4		
	Correct	TOT		N–TOT
omission		14.9 (.92)		7.7 (.34)
commission		16.3 (1.03)		11.3 (.53)
retrospective		16.0 (.84)		10.0 (.54)
correct	11.1 (.46)			

Note. Retrieval times in seconds (standard errors in parentheses) as a function of correct retrieval, TOT substate, and the type of error. From Schwartz (2001). TOT = Tip-of-the-tongue phenomenon.

Thus, at the suggestion of Brown, I conducted Experiment 4 (Schwartz, 2001), in which participants were asked to make retrospective TOT judgments after successful retrieval had occurred. In this study, if people correctly recalled the target, they were asked if they had temporarily experienced a TOT before they retrieved it. Thus, retrospective TOTs are those made following correct retrievals, in which people indicate that they experienced a quick TOT in advance of correct retrieval. Many people report that TOTs can be quite short-lived and quickly followed by resolution (e.g., Burke et al., 1991), but no lab study had examined retrospective TOTs. Experiment 4 showed that the presence of a TOT can be correlated with retrieval time of correct answers as well as with the unrecalled items.

As far as I know, this represented a unique contribution to the TOT literature. Although some questionnaire studies have been done retrospectively (Burke et al., 1991; Read & Bruce, 1982), this represented the first lab study to rely on participants' reports as to whether they had experienced a momentary TOT before they retrieved the correct answer. The results suggested that the methodology was tapping into something not all that different than the more typical TOTs after retrieval failure.

In the study, TOTs were experienced following 37% of failures to recall the answer, averaging across both omission and commission errors. However, for the retrospective TOTs, their rates were much lower. Participants rated 22% of their correct answers as having been preceded by momentary TOTs. Although significantly lower than the TOT rates for omissions and commissions, this represented a large enough TOT rate to compare retrieval latencies.

Retrieval latencies, measured in seconds, were longer for TOTs than n–TOTs for both omission and commission errors. Furthermore, retrospective TOTs also showed longer retrieval times for correct answers than did retrospective n–TOTs, which were also for correct answers (see Table 6.1). Thus, the retrospective TOTs indicated a relation between TOTs and retrieval latencies in a way that was similar to the more typical TOTs after retrieval failure. These data also support the theory that TOTs are involved with metacognitive control. Presumably, the temporary experience of the TOT directed the rememberer to continue searching for the missing target, rather than make a fast "don't know" response. The extra time led to a successful retrieval of the target. This is the essence of metacognitive control.

An important caveat to these findings must be acknowledged, and that is the experiments from my study (Schwartz, 2001) only demonstrate a correlation between retrieval times and the likelihood of TOTs. Causality cannot be inferred from the study. It is likely that being in a TOT causes the person to spend more time attempting retrieval, but other explanations are possible. For example, because TOT judgments were made after the retrieval attempt, it is conceivable that participants may have given TOT judgments to those items that took them a long time to decide that they did not know the answer. However, this reasoning begs the question; that is, what processes lead them to take longer to retrieve? It is, of course, also possible that a third unknown factor, such as familiarity, drives both the long retrieval latencies and the likelihood of a TOT (Metcalfe et al., 1993; Nelson et al., 1984). Nonetheless, I prefer the notion that the TOT drives the long retrieval latency, as this is most consistent with the monitoring and control framework.

To summarize, at this juncture we have some tentative evidence that TOTs direct retrieval. My data (Schwartz, 2001) showed a strong association between TOTs and retrieval times. Although other explanations are possible, it is most reasonable to interpret this within the metacognitive framework. However, it is likely that TOTs also serve other control functions. I discuss two lines of evidence that suggest this. One line comes from studies that were interested in other aspects of the TOT but can be reinterpreted in light of monitoring and control theory. The other line includes some specific experiments currently ongoing (at the time of writing), which directly test the idea that TOTs inform or control retrieval. I start first with the earlier studies.

TOTs AND OTHER CONTROL FEATURES

TOTs Ensure Greater Processing

A possible function of TOTs is that they may inform the rememberer that a particular item is prone to being forgotten. Thus, if it is inaccessible at one point in time, it may be inaccessible at another point in time. To counter the perceived tendency of a word to be forgotten, a TOT may be produced to make the word more distinctive. Once the item is made more distinctive, it may become more memorable and so more easily retrieved in the future, consistent with a great deal of research on memory and distinctiveness. In essence, the TOT is a self-fulfilling prophecy—by making a forgettable item distinctive, it enhances its future memorability.

Some evidence for this hypothesis comes from an interesting experiment conducted by Gardiner et al. (1973), also discussed earlier in this volume. Their original interest was in the relation of initial retrieval difficulty and subsequent recall (see Benjamin et al., 1998). Gardiner et al. asked participants to provide the target words for 50 dictionary definitions. If the participants did not know the target word, they were asked to judge whether they knew the item on a 4-point Likert-type scale. The highest two values on the scale were explicitly equated to TOT feelings. If the participant had not recalled the answer, it was then shown to them. After all 50 definitions had been tested, the participants were asked to recall, without cues, the 50 words that they just retrieved, had been in a TOT for, or had been shown.

There was no difference in final recall for words that had been retrieved by the participant versus those that had been supplied by the experimenters. However, surprisingly, TOT words, regardless of whether they had been resolved by the participant, were recalled at a higher rate than n–TOT words. The final recall was 59% for retrieved TOT words and 49% for unretrieved TOT words, whereas final recall was 27% and 36%, respectively, for n–TOT words. Note again that this is free recall, not cued recall, and therefore the final recall scores are a measure of episodic memory of test materials and not semantic memory of word knowledge. Episodic memory indicates the memory of the particular items shown at a particular time, whereas semantic memory indicates the person's general knowledge.

Thus, TOT words were rendered more memorable in this experiment, supporting the view that experiencing a TOT creates the kind of processing that leads to a more distinctive or elaborative encoding of the item, ensuring its future memorability. It is also possible that this effect is mediated by the retrieval time involved in TOTs. TOTs, in Gardiner et al. (1973), were associated with longer retrieval times. Thus, the TOTs could have been causing the participant to spend more time on those items, thereby providing the opportunity for increased processing. Gardiner et al. reported that the final recall advantage for items that took more time initially only occurred for TOT items. This suggests that it is the TOT that ensures greater processing and not simply the extra retrieval time. Other explanations are possible. Brown (1991) suspected that the Gardiner et al. effect might be because remember-ers pay more attention to their TOTs than to other items. This suggestion is intuitive, but still untested. Brown's view is also consistent with the metacognitive view, which hypothesizes that TOTs serve a control function to improve learning. If a TOT increases attention to those items, it also improves their memorability.

TOTs as Motivational States

Ryan et al. (1982) conducted an interesting study of TOTs that is often ignored by other researchers in the area, but is very relevant from the perspective of metacognition. Ryan et al. were interested in whether the TOT served a "motivational" function. What they meant by motivation is that the TOT alerts a person that an item is potentially accessible, and that the TOT drives the person to want to remember that item. This is certainly intuitive—resolving a TOT seems much more satisfactory when one does it by oneself than when someone else provides the target word. One nonobvious implication, however, is that TOTs may be distracting when one needs to concentrate on another task. If attention is diverted or motivation is elsewhere, the TOT may interfere with performance on nonretrieval tasks. Thus, they predicted that rememberers in TOTs will be distracted from other tasks because of a conscious or nonconscious drive to resolve the TOT.

They conducted a clever experiment to test this notion. In the experiment, the participants studied lists of paired associates, such as "trumpet–green." In an initial learning phase, the participants studied 52 word pairs for either 7, 5, or 3 sec each. Not surprisingly, it was difficult to learn the words in the set time, and overall recall was rather poor.

In the recall phase of the experiment, the participants were given the stimulus (or cue) word and asked to retrieve the target word. If they could not recall the target word, they were asked if they were experiencing a TOT. Then, for both TOTs and n–TOTs, the participants were given a number-probe task. A set of digits was presented on and then disappeared from a computer screen. The participant had to decide as quickly as possible whether the set that they had just seen was a member of six test sets now which had replaced it. They responded "yes" or "no" as quickly as possible. This test was repeated for 20 sec, and then the participants were given feedback as to their performance on the number-probe task. The number-probe task was repeated until each participant made eight correct decisions during three consecutive 20 sec intervals. When the participants passed the number-probe task, they were given the next stimulus term in the paired-associate task.

Now here is the interesting part. Ryan et al. (1982) hypothesized that if the TOT was motivating participants to continue searching, either consciously or nonconsciously for the unretrieved target, then more cognitive resources would be drawn away from the probe task following TOTs than following n–TOTs. If a participant experienced a TOT, then it would be more difficult to concentrate on the number-probe task than if the participant was not experiencing a TOT. Thus, Ryan et al. predicted that participants experiencing a TOT for the previous word would make more errors on the number-probe task during TOT trials than during n–TOT trials.

This is exactly what Ryan et al. found. The mean number correct following n–TOTs was 7.23 number-probes, significantly higher than the mean number correct following TOTs, which was 7.00 number-probes. Ryan et al. concluded that TOTs are "associated with changes in capacity-allocation" (p. 144). Because some cognitive capacity is focusing on the resolution of the TOT, there is less than full capacity left for the number-probe task. Thus, Ryan et al. concluded that TOTs "control memory processing" (p. 144).

I think Ryan et al. (1982) were ahead of their time. I suspect their research was neglected for several reasons. First, most studies use real-world materials like word definitions and general-information questions. They used word associates, and therefore, their data lack some of the ecological validity that other studies have. Second, at the time, most of the TOT research was directed at the retrieval process per se, or the kinds of information accessible during a TOT. Ryan et al. were already thinking about control processes. Ryan et al.'s work is an important and convincing study demonstrating one function of the TOT, providing the motivation to continue searching memory store.

Strategy Selection. The findings of Schwartz (2001), Gardiner et al. (1973), and Ryan et al. (1982) support the notion that TOTs act to control the retrieval process. TOTs cause us to search longer for an elusive target, they alert us to those items that we know but cannot recall, and they distract us from other tasks as we continue to ponder our fragmented memories. In the case described by Ryan et al., TOTs actually hinder us, by drawing attention away from the tasks at hand. Each of these studies hinted at a hypothesized control function of TOTs, not yet explored: the control of retrieval strategies. Brown (1991) also speculated that TOTs serve the function of directing our retrieval strategies, thereby helping us remember the inaccessible target.

For example, a person may just have experienced a TOT for a piece of information, say a trivia question asked during a time-out during sports coverage on TV (e.g., "Who was the only basketball player to average 50 points a game for a single season?"). The person is instantly seized with a TOT. The TOT alerts the person that this information is available, and starts that person thinking about how to render it accessible. He or she might then assess what kinds of partial information is accessible. The partial information may be visual, phonological, semantic, or some combination of these. For example, the person might wonder if he or she has a visual image of the person. Or perhaps she may be able to retrieve partial phonological information. If semantic blockers are occurring (e.g., Michael Jordan, Kareem Adul-Jabbar), he or she might wonder whether it is better to continue searching now, or return to it later, after thinking about something else. The occurrence and nature of the TOT would therefore drive the nature of the retrieval process. Hopefully, these retrieval processes will act fast enough that the person will remember "the late great Wilt Chamberlain" before the answer is given by the TV announcers. Thus, the question that can be asked is whether TOT experiences cause us to search our memories in different manners, or if they cause us to abandon memory search and to use different kinds of retrieval strategies altogether.

Diary studies find that TOTs are resolved in three main ways (e.g., Burke et al., 1991; Schwartz, 1999a). We usually resolve our TOTs by directed search, concentrating or cueing ourselves to remember the item. The second method is spontaneous resolution, that is, allowing ourselves to experience a "pop-up" at some later time. The final common method is to seek the information from a secondary source, whether another person, a dictionary, or some other source. One might ask why rememberers direct their search immediately for some TOTs, but for others try to forget it for the time being in the hope of a pop-up later, and finally, why for some TOTs, rememberers go right to their friends. Is there some element of the TOT itself that tells us which is the best method? And, do we allocate these strategies differently for TOTs than n–TOTs in the first place?

We have just begun to examine the issue of retrieval strategy in my laboratory. We wondered if participants experiencing TOTs and n–TOTs in the laboratory could choose the strategy that was most likely to generate a satisfactory resolution of the TOT. Would participants know when it was most adaptive to continue to search now despite the inaccessibility of the word, and would they know when to return to it later and rely on spontaneous recovery? Would a more sensible option be to ask someone else to tell them? Furthermore, would differences among the phenomenological aspects of the TOT direct this choice? Would imminent TOTs be followed by a decision to continue the search, and emotional TOTs by a decision to wait until later?

We do have some data suggesting that TOTs do influence retrieval strategy (Schwartz, 2000). The experiment follows a similar pattern of many other experiments on the TOT. First, the participants were given general-information questions. If the answer was known, the participants moved on to the next question. If the answer was not known, the participant was asked if they were experiencing a TOT. At this point, the new twist was introduced. The participants were given a choice: (a) they could elect to continue search on the item immediately (*search strategy*); (b) they could opt to return to the question later (*return strategy*), after all the other questions had been presented; or (c) they could choose to see the answer immediately (*see strategy*). The decision was completely left up to the participants. However, in an experimental control condition (not to be confused with metacognitive control), a group of individuals had no choice about which strategy to use. The decision to search now, return to the question later, or see the answer now was determined randomly by a computer. Thus, we were able to compare TOT resolution when participants had control over retrieval strategy to a condition in which participants did not have control over the retrieval strategy. If TOTs successfully direct us toward the right strategy, then more TOTs should be resolved when the participants have control over their own strategies.

The results of the first experiment were intriguing (Schwartz, 2000). The TOT rate was 27% of the initially unrecalled items, consistent with earlier data from my lab. When participants had control over their strategy choice, the most chosen strategy was a return strategy. Fifty-seven of the TOTs were followed by the return strategy, whereas only 21% of the TOTs were followed by the search strategy, leaving 22% in the see strategy category. In contrast, for n–TOTs, 57% of the time the participants chose the see strategy, 32% chose the return strategy, and 11% chose the search strategy. This supported the idea that TOTs serve as motivational states. The participants were far more likely to attempt to self-retrieve the answer than opt to have it provided for them when they were experiencing a TOT.

The most startling finding came when the comparison was made between resolution of TOTs for which the participants had control over strategy and those for which they did not. When the participants had control over their retrieval decisions they resolved 60% of the items for which they chose the return strategy, and they resolved 67% of the items for which they choose the search strategy. For the group for which strategies were randomly assigned, participants resolved only 42% of the items in the return strategy and only 44% of the items in the search strategy. The difference between the participant control and randomly assigned conditions was statistically significant. Thus, giving people control over the strategies that they use to resolve TOTs allows them to resolve those TOTs much better, in this study more than 20% better. However, for n–TOTs, exercising control over retrieval strategies did not help resolve more TOTs. In the participant-controlled condition, 20% of n–TOTs were resolved, whereas 16% of n–TOTs were resolved in the randomly assigned condition, a nonsignificant difference. Therefore, it is the TOT experience itself that appears to be directing rememberers toward the correct retrieval strategy.

An interesting aspect of the strategy selection data is that neither pop-up or search were better at driving resolution; they both did equally well. Nonetheless, exercising control over the strategy improved resolution. Thus, the advantage for the control condition must reflect that TOTs direct us toward different retrieval strategies for different items. Therefore, it is likely that differences in TOT phenomenology may cause us to choose different retrieval strategies. Currently, we are investigating what variables (discussed in chap. 2) are correlated with the decision to choose different retrieval strategies.

TOTs as Social Motivators

Another hypothesis concerning the control functions of TOTs is that TOTs may serve to facilitate certain social interactions. Indeed, TOTs may be the grease that smoothes the way for us to be friendly with people that we barely know. For example, a person whom you have met cannot remember your name. You remember his, but he cannot remember yours; not a good start to a positive interaction. At conferences, many feel snubbed when somebody does not remember their name, and often experience embarrassment when they cannot remember somebody else's name. Consider a second person who cannot remember your name but claims to be in a TOT for your name. If she acts convincingly as if your name is on the tip-of-her-tongue, you may be more likely to think positively of her than the person who did not experience a TOT and simply drew a blank when they greeted you. Thus, a genuine TOT may work to convince others that forgotten knowledge is present, even if it cannot be recalled right away. Unfortunately, there have been no studies on how people detect TOT experiences in others.

Pinker (1997) considered much of human behavior in light of evolutionary theory. He argued that in order for one human being, the person must be sincere. Pinker argued that humans are complex lie detectors, as this aids us in our evolutionary success. For example, most people can easily tell the difference between a real and a fake smile (see Pinker, 1997). The TOT fits nicely into this approach. If it is adaptive to convince others that we have knowledge although we cannot show it, then a genuinely felt TOT is just the thing for which we are looking. A TOT is a strong subjective state with noticeable behavioral consequences, including motoric ones (i.e., Beattie & Coughlan, 1999). Thus, we may be able to convince others that we know more than we do if we experience a TOT. Like a real smile, a TOT experience may convince people that the forgetful person really does have information about the forgotten target.

Consider the results of Widner et al (1996), first reviewed in chapter 2. Widner et al. found that demand characteristics affected TOT rates. Two groups of participants were given the same general-information questions. However, one group was told that the questions were normatively easy, whereas another group was told the questions were normatively difficult. More TOTs were reported in the normatively easy group, suggesting that social factors play a role in TOTs. Indeed, the participants in the normatively easy group may have been motivated to not appear less knowledgeable (or indeed, less intelligent) than the average student. One way to compensate for a lack of knowledge is to feel as if one is in a TOT for the knowledge one cannot recall. No such social pressure exists when one feels that one is doing average or better than average on the task, and thus there is greater social pressure for TOTs in the normatively easy group. Therefore, the Widner et al. (1996) data can support a view that another function of TOTs is the social communication that knowledge exists when that knowledge cannot be demonstrated.

Schacter (2000) offered a cautionary note concerning the interpretation of metacognitive control, particularly in light of its potential evolutionary adaptiveness. Schacter made the distinction between control functions, that is, design features of a system, which have a particular function for the individual and control consequences, which suggest that metacognitive control may be an incidental by-product of other adaptive processes. It is unclear, given the present state of research, how one would distinguish between metacognitive control that was a function of design features or a consequence of other adaptive systems, particularly given that most of the research is correlational. Nonetheless, the thought is provocative and worth addressing.

Overview of TOT Control Functions

In this chapter, I discussed the idea that TOTs are not just monitors of our memory failures. Rather, TOTs actively direct our retrieval processes in such a way as to resolve TOTs, maximize our recall performance, and perhaps even ease awkward social situations. The first function of TOTs that was discussed was that TOTs may cause us to spend more time trying to retrieve an unrecalled target (Schwartz, 2001). This was supported by longer retrieval attempts during TOTs than n–TOTs. The second function discussed was that TOTs may ensure greater processing of TOT targets, promoting better retrievability of those targets in the future (Gardiner et al., 1973). A third function is that TOTs may motivate us to work harder to retrieve those items (Ryan et al., 1982), and a fourth function may be that they help us direct retrieval strategies (Schwartz, 2000). Finally, they may also serve as social motivators.

Now, it may be possible to reinterpret each of the individual findings reviewed in this chapter. However, I think a convincing case has been made that TOTs do serve a control function for the rememberer. If this is so, it strongly supports the Nelson–Narens (1990) model, which claims that metacognition evolved so that effective monitoring could inform an effective control system to maximize performance of the rememberer.

SUMMARY

Overall, TOTs are remarkably accurate metacognitive monitors. Most studies showed that resolution and recognition rates are much higher for TOTs than for n–TOTs (see Brown, 1991; Schwartz, 1999b; Smith, 1994). Furthermore, recent research has also begun to show that this monitoring is not only accurate, but it leads to effective control of retrieval behavior. A variety of studies demonstrated that TOTs serve both to monitor and to control. Control functions include increasing motivation to remember (Ryan et al., 1982), allocating resources for attention to TOT items (Gardiner et al., 1973), and determining retrieval time (Schwartz, 2001). Moreover, Schwartz (2000) showed that TOTs influenced retrieval strategy. Thus, Nelson's model of metacognition is useful when discussing TOTs (Barnes et al., 1999; Nelson, 1996; Nelson & Narens, 1990, 1994). TOTs serve both a monitoring and control function, as predicted by the model.

7

TOTs, Development,
and Neuropsychological Issues

Throughout the first six chapters of this book, the discussion has mainly focused on TOTs in normal adults. Most of the data discussed so far has been drawn from younger adults, mostly students in introductory psychology courses. It is now time to consider developmental and neuropsychological perspectives on TOTs, concentrating on TOTs in "special" populations. TOTs among older adults, children, and neuropsychological patients are instructive for several reasons. Naturally, it is important to understand cognitive processes in each of these populations. It is also important to understand the development of TOT etiology and phenomenology. Beyond that, each group may offer insights into both the nature of lexical theory and the nature of monitoring and control processes. In this chapter, I first consider the literature on TOTs and aging, primarily because it is the most extensive and well-articulated. Following discussion of TOTs and aging, I discuss the limited research on TOTs in children and the limited literature on TOTs and neuropsychological patients.

We have seen throughout this volume the role that TOTs play in two bodies of thinking: theories of lexical retrieval and theories of metacognition. In theories of lexical retrieval, TOTs are seen as a "window" into the process of retrieval, an opportunity to study retrieval when the process is slowed or halted (e.g., A. S. Brown, 1991; Kohn et al., 1987). In contrast, in metacognitive theory, the TOT is an experiential feeling that allows rememberers to monitor and control their retrieval processes. Each of these perspectives has led to great many interesting facts, theories, and unexplored questions. Research on older adults, children, and neuropsychological patients may inform and refine each of these theoretical perspectives.

132

Unfortunately, the TOT has not been much of a focus in neuropsychological circles. There a few scattered articles looking at TOTs in clinical populations, and no published neuroimaging studies. Thus, given the paucity of studies and the paucity of replications, it is hard to conclude anything from the neuropsychological literature. However, TOTs and normal aging have been well studied with some oft-replicated findings. Thus, some firm conclusions can be drawn based on the aging data. Nonetheless, none of the existing studies on TOTs and aging have been conducted with metacognitive theory in mind. Thus, one of my goals in this chapter is to add a metacognitive spin to some of the research on TOTs and aging, suggesting how such research could be accounted for by a monitoring and control perspective. However, it should be kept in mind that all of the studies on TOTs and aging were originally designed to address issues of word memory or lexical retrieval theory.

TOTs AND AGING

In many informal discussions with regard to my research, I often hear some variant of a single basic complaint: "I experience many more TOTs now than I did when I was young." I have heard it from people in their 80s, from people in their 60s, and even from some people still in their 40s. I have heard it from people with advanced degrees, from waiters, and from cab drivers. It seems to be an experience imbedded in our folk psychology. And, for good reason. Research tells us that this bit of folklore is correct—older adults do experience more TOTs than younger adults. The reasons for this are elusive and controversial.

There are two major theories that have been introduced to explain age-related increases in TOT: the decrement model and the incremental knowledge model. The two theories highlight basic differences in the perception of old age. In the one view, aging is seen as a time of biological and mental decline, whereas the other view sees aging as the culmination of knowledge, wisdom, and experience. In the first view, there are those that argue TOTs are more common among older people because their memory networks are beginning to deteriorate, and TOTs reflect these weakened associations (e.g., Brown, 2000; Burke et al., 1991; Heine et al., 1999; Rastle & Burke, 1996). I will refer to this class of theories as the *decrement model*. On the other hand, others argue that TOTs reflect the increased knowledge base and vocabulary of older adults. Because they know more, they have more words for which they can experience a TOT (Dahlgren, 1998). I will call this class of theories the *incremental knowledge model*. This second intriguing view has only been advanced recently by Donna Dahlgren (Dahlgren, 1998), but there appears to be some data to support it, although many disagree (see Brown, 2000).

Before we get to the theory, it is important to review some of the basic data in the area. The first few studies on the phenomena were mostly designed to simply confirm the suspicion that TOTs are more common among older adults than younger adults. The TOT and aging literature has combined the use of laboratory investigation with a series of carefully conducted diaries studies (see chap. 2). The use of the two methodologies and the general consistency of findings from one lab to another has built a strong foundation of solid empirical evidence. Also, Brown (2000) recently reviewed the TOT and aging literature.

TOT Frequency

Do people experience more TOTs as they age? Most research suggests that TOTs increase with age from young adulthood to the oldest adults (see Table 7.1). Although there has not been a longitudinal study, of 11 cross-sectional studies that have been conducted, 10 show clear evidence of age-related increases in TOT frequency (see Brown, 2000). The exception (Maylor, 1990a) compared people in their 50s, 60s, and 70s. It is conceivable that the Maylor (1990a) study did not have sufficient age range to document age-related increases in TOTs. The bottom line, however, is that across all of these studies, it is apparent that TOT frequency increases as people age from young adulthood through middle age to older adults to oldest adults.

Despite the null results from Maylor (1990a), the trend appears to be a steady increase in TOTs over time. For example, Burke et al. (1991) found more TOTs in their middle-aged group (mean age = 38.7) than for the young adult group (mean age = 19.4). Heine et al. (1999) found more TOTs in their oldest adult group (range 80 to 92) than in the young–old group (60–74). Thus, increases in TOT rates occur with advancing age and well into late life.

TOT Resolution

Do older and younger adults differ in the rate at which they resolve TOTs? It is known that TOT rates increase with aging. However, the issue of whether TOT resolution differs with age does not naturally follow. From the decrement view, it might be expected that, given the general breakdown in associative networks, older adults would show a deficit in resolution. For example, if older participants are experiencing more TOTs because of breakdowns in phonological activation, as suggested by Burke et al. (1991), one might hypothesize that failure to activate sound representations would persist and TOT resolution would be low. Alternatively, from the incremental knowledge view, older adults may have more and better cueing strategies

TABLE 7.1

TOTs and Aging

Study	Method	Age Groups	TOT Differences
Cohen & Faulkner (1986)	diary	Young, middle-aged, old	Young = middle-aged < old
Finley & Sharp (1989)	experiment	Old	Not about developmental differences
Gollan & Silverberg (in press)	experiment	Old and young	Young < old
Maylor (1990a)	experiment	50s, 60s, 70s	No effect of age
Maylor (1990b)	experiment	50s, 60s, 70s	Unresolved TOTs increased with age
Burke et al. (1991)	diary	Young, middled-aged, old	Young < middle-aged < old
Burke et al. (1991)	experiment	Young and old	Young < old
Brown & Nix (1996)	experiment	Young and old	Young < old
Rastle & Burke (1996)	Experiment 1	Young and old	Young < old
Rastle & Burke (1996)	Experiment 2	Young and old	Young < old only for proper names
Dahlgren (1998)	experiment	Young, middle-aged, old	Young = middle-aged < old
Heine et al. (1999)	experiment	Young, young–old, oldest	Young <Young–old < oldest

Note.   Across 11 studies, 10 show higher TOT rates for older adults. TOT = Tip-of-the-tongue phenomena.

with which to resolve TOTs. Unfortunately, the data are ambiguous with respect to differences in TOT resolution and aging.

Three diary studies (Burke et al., 1991; Cohen & Faulkner, 1986, Heine et al., 1999) found increases in TOT resolution with aging, although in none of the studies was the difference found to be statistically significant. Cohen and Faulkner (1986) found an 81% resolution rate for young participants, a 66% resolution rate for middle-aged participants, and an 87% rate for older adults. Burke et al.'s (1991) rates for young, middle-aged and older participants were 92%, 95%, and 97%, respectively. Heine et al. (1999) found a 91% rate for younger adults, a 95% for young–old participants, and a 98% rate for the oldest adults. Thus, the diary findings show trends that older adults are actually better than younger adults at resolving TOTs. This is consistent with incremental knowledge views of TOTs and aging, which suggest that there are aspects of TOT performance in which older adults will do better than younger adults.

Alternately, the experimental studies suggest a different story. Burke et al. found that, in their laboratory experiment, when the participants had produced alternate responses (intrusions or blockers), the young participants resolved 15.9% of their TOTs, whereas the older participants resolved 5.3% of their TOTs. When TOTs without alternatives were considered, the younger participants resolved 53.6 of the TOTs, whereas the older participants resolved 37.6. Similarly, Heine et al. (1999), in their lab study, found that the oldest participants showed the lowest rate of resolution. When orthographic cues were provided, Heine et al. found that the young participants resolved 34% of their TOTs, the young–old 39% of their TOTs, but the old–old only 28% of their TOTs. However, both Maylor (1990b) and Brown and Nix (1996) found nonsignificant trends showing that older participants resolved more TOTs.

The reason why the diary studies and the laboratory studies contradict each other is not completely clear. One possible explanation is a speed-accuracy trade-off (Salthouse, 1993, 1996). In the lab, the retrieval must be made quickly, whereas at home, the rememberer can take his or her time.

Thus, it is likely that TOTs are resolved with differing time courses in the lab and at home. Studies of cognitive aging typically show age-related declines in cognitive speed (Salthouse, 1993; 1996). Thus, the low rate of resolution in the lab for older adults may only partially capture their actual ability to resolve TOTs given enough time.

Interestingly however, Burke et al. (1991) found that older adults are less likely to use search strategies than younger adults, and more likely to rely on spontaneous retrieval. The search strategy usage dropped 8% from the young to the old, whereas the spontaneous retrieval rate increased 15%. The hypothesis that older adults resolve more TOTs would have predicted that older adults would have used a search strategy more than the younger adults. Alternatively, older adults may just be more patient with their normal retrieval failures and await spontaneous retrieval.

A second explanation centers on the incremental knowledge model. If older adults have more in memory, any particular item may be in a lower state of accessibility than a given item might be for a younger adult (e.g., Bjork & Bjork, 1992). Hence, older adults will show greater fluctuations in the accessibility of words, and this fluctuation may elicit more TOTs. The greater fluctuation in accessibility can account for both the higher rate of TOTs and the increased reliance on spontaneous retrievals. Spontaneous retrievals will occur as the items fluctuate from low accessibility to high accessibility. TOTs may occur when accessibility temporarily fluctuates to a lower state. This explanation accounts for Burke et al.'s (1991) finding concerning the use of retrieval strategies, but is clearly speculative.

Further research must address the issue of TOT resolution as a function of age. In terms of application of this research, the issue of resolution is paramount because memory loss is an important issue to older adults. Thus, more studies need to be directed at the processes by which older and younger adults retrieve TOT words, as well as whether there are age-related differences in the control processes used to resolve TOTs.

Partial Information Retrieval.   The retrieval of partial information has played an important role in the development of theories concerning the etiology of TOTs. Lexical retrieval theory postulates that partial information represents the access to the lemma with only partial access or no access to the lexeme. Inferential theories postulate that TOTs are based on the amount of information that is retrieved. Similarly, theories of age differences in TOTs also hinge on access to partial information. According to the Burke et al. (1991) model, based on decrement theory, aging weakens connections between the semantic level and the phonological level. TOTs arise when semantic activation is not accompanied by phonological activation. Thus, according to the model, older participants should access less phonological information during a TOT, including fewer retrieved blockers that are phonologically related to the TOT. Incremental knowledge theory does not make predictions that are substantially different from the decrement theory here.

The data here strongly support the view that during a TOT less phonological information is accessible for older participants than younger participants (see Table 7.2a). Also, more persistent alternates or blockers are accessible for younger than for older participants. The one exception is the study by Brown and Nix (1996), who found the opposite pattern for alternates, with the older participants experiencing more blockers. They also

TABLE 7.2a

TOTs and Aging

Study	Method	Age Groups	Partial Information
Cohen & Faulkner (1986)	diary	Young, middle-aged, old	Young = middle-aged > old
Maylor (1990a)	experiment	50s, 60s, 70s	Negative correlation with age
Burke et al. (1991)	diary	Young, middled-aged, old	Young > middle-aged > old
Burke et al. (1991)	experiment	Young and old	No differences
Brown & Nix (1996)	experiment	Young and old	Young > old (amount, not accuracy)
Rastle & Burke (1996)	Experiment 1	Young and old	Young > old
Dahlgren (1998) (First letter)	experiment	Young, middle-aged, old	Young > middle-aged > old
Heine et al. (1999)	diary	Young, young–old, oldest	Young > young–old = oldest

Note. Evidence suggests that younger adults retrieve more partial information than older adults.

found that younger participants reported more first-letter information, but this information was not more accurate than that of the older participants.

Why does the Brown and Nix (1996) study find a different pattern than the other studies? There is no immediately obvious answer. However, there are several procedural differences that may point to why this pattern occurred. In particular, all of the older participants in the Brown and Nix study were alumni of Southern Methodist University (SMU), and therefore, they all had more years of education than the SMU students, whereas in the other studies addressing this question, the older participants were more widely selected. It is unclear exactly how this would change the rate of persistent alternates, but it seems to have done so. Second, the Brown and Nix procedure was, by and large, simpler for the participant. It is possible that the older participants could therefore devote more attention to the retrieval of each item. Finally, Cohen and Faulkner (1986), Burke et al. (1991), and Heine et al. (1999) had specific hypotheses that there would be fewer persistent alternates for the older participants. Brown and Nix's instructions were decidedly more neutral. Therefore, it is possible that participants may have been picking up on the experimenter's biases in the former studies.

DECREMENT THEORY VERSUS INCREMENTAL KNOWLEDGE THEORY

To review the theories from the beginning of the chapter, decrement theory postulates that age-related increases in TOTs are a function of normal biological decline that takes place in aging. For example, Burke et al.'s (1991) theory suggests that with aging, breakdowns occur in the associations between semantic representations and phonological representations, leading to increased TOTs. Incremental knowledge theory postulates that increases in TOTs with advancing age occur because older adults have more knowledge of words, and thus a greater set of materials for which to experience TOTs. Indeed, findings show that older adults have greater vocabulary and greater general world knowledge than do younger adults (Dahlgren, 1998; Maylor, 1994, Salthouse, 1991).

Incremental Knowledge Theory

I consider the evidence for the incremental knowledge theory first. The theory is newer, and there are less data that support it. The data we do have are convincing. However, the main empirical evidence comes from a study by Dahlgren (1998), which I review later. First, I share my experience in trying to induce TOTs in older adults, during an unsuccessful experiment, which now leads me to favor the incremental knowledge view.

The difference in knowledge base between older and younger adults was recently vividly demonstrated to me. In my work on illusory TOTs (see Schwartz, 1998; Schwartz et al., 2000) I developed a set of trick questions, for which there was no correct answer (e.g., "What is the name of Mercury's moon?"). These questions were carefully designed so that college students would not suspect the questions to be unanswerable, and they might be susceptible to illusory TOTs. In the four experiments reported in Schwartz (1998) and Schwartz et al. (2000), only one college student out of nearly 200 detected a discrepancy (the participant knew that Mercury had no moons). However, when I tried to conduct the study at a local senior citizen center, I was overwhelmed with the participants approaching me to tell me I had made a mistake on the question sheet. Others asked if they could answer "no possible answer." The study was a washout because virtually every older adult detected the falsity of the questions. Daunted by the task of having to reconstruct my illusory questions, I abandoned the project. The relevance here is that the older adults showed both a better vocabulary and greater knowledge, albeit of trivia, than did the younger college-age adults. Although the data from this experiment were long ago discarded, I suspect that both the correct recall rates and the TOT rates were higher for these older adults, probably in part because of their greater knowledge of the world. I did not analyze normative data on these older adults, so one cannot rule out cohort effects or differences in education or intelligence between the younger and older adults. Nonetheless, it does serve as an interesting anecdote on the knowledge level of older adults.

Unfortunately, Dahlgren's (1998) work has not received the attention it deserves. Nonetheless, her theory, the incremental knowledge theory, seems to be an excellent way of thinking about age-related increases in TOTs. She was interested in whether the higher TOT rates among older adults were related to their greater knowledge base compared to younger adults. In her sample, she matched old and young participants on education level. The older adults averaged 13.9 years of schooling, the middle-aged adults had 14.5 years, and the younger adults had 14.0 years of schooling. These differences were not statistically significant. However, on the Wechster Adult Intelligence Scale (WAIS–R) vocabulary score, the older adults (50.35) outperformed the younger adults (41.27) and the middle-aged adults (48.19). The WAIS–R served as the measure of knowledge of English vocabulary.

As in all of the other studies addressing TOTs and aging, Dahlgren (1998) found that older participants experienced more TOTs than did middle-aged and younger participants, thus replicating the central finding of this literature. However, when vocabulary score was entered as a covariate in an analysis of covariance, no differences in TOT rates were found among the age groups. Furthermore, when she used age as a covariate to detect TOT differences among people with high or low vocabulary, she found that high vocabulary participants experienced more TOTs than low vocabulary participants. Based on these data, Dahlgren (1998) argued that age alone is insufficient to account for differences in TOTs. Rather, age covaries with knowledge of the world, and those with more knowledge are more likely to experience TOTs, regardless of age.

However, one problem with Dahlgren's view is that other studies have not found the same relation between aging, knowledge and TOTs. In fact, Burke et al. (1991) found results that run contrary to it. Burke et al. found that older adults experienced more TOTs, as did Heine et al. (1999) in a similar study a few years later. However, in contrast to Dahlgren (1998), Burke et al. found that the age difference in TOTs was not related to greater education or higher vocabulary scores. Age was the only predictor of TOT frequency, casting doubt on the increment view. Brown (2000) conducted analyses across a number of TOT and aging studies. When he partialed out vocabulary size, there was still a correlation between TOTs and aging, but Brown did not report how many studies were used.

Interestingly, the differences between the two samples may be illuminating and may explain the discrepancy between the findings. The ages of the participants in the younger, middle-aged, and older adult groups were similar in both studies. However, Burke et al.'s (1991) participants had more education and higher WAIS–R vocabulary scores. Burke et al.'s older adults scored an average of 71 on the Wechster Adult Intelligence Scale (WAIS) and had 15.8 years of education. Dahlgren's older adults scored an average of 50 on the WAIS–R and had 13.9 years of education. Dahlgren's younger adults had equivalent education to Burke et al.'s younger adults (14.0 vs. 13.7). Therefore, the contradiction between their results may have been caused by differences in their samples. In the more knowledgeable group studied by Burke et al., age differences swamped knowledge differences. Indeed, given their participants' higher scores, ceiling effects may have ruled out the observation of knowledge differences. In the less knowledgeable group studied by Dahlgren (1998), knowledge differences were observable that overwhelmed the age differences. In particular, because only one study empirically supports the incremental knowledge hypothesis, further research is necessary to test and refine the theory.

Decrement Theory

Decrement theory states that TOTs increase with advancing age because of failures and breakdowns in the retrieval systems of older adults. Most of the data supporting this view come from studies that start from a lexical theory perspective, based on direct access models. In this section, I evaluate direct-access models in addition to decrement theory. Recall that direct-access theory postulates that the TOT is based on access to the unretrieved but present target word. Thus, TOTs are influenced by variables affecting retrieval. Direct-access views are divided into blocking, one-stage, and two-stage views. The one-stage models mirror the activation models and the two-stage models refer to variants of the transmission deficit theory (e.g., chap. 3).

With respect to aging, the dominant theory has been transmission deficit theory (Burke et al., 1991; Rastle & Burke, 1996), and all of the studies on TOTs and aging since 1991, except Dahlgren's (1998), have been linked to it. Therefore, the folowing section will be an evaluation of the transmission deficit model as the prototypical direct-access model.

Aging in the Transmission Deficit Model.   Recall that the transmission deficit model is considered a two-stage model because it postulates two distinct levels of representation, a semantic level and a phonological level (Harley & Bown, 1998). TOTs occur when semantic activation is insufficient to activate a phonological representation (Burke et al., 1991). MacKay and Burke (1990) argued that aging weakens the connections between nodes in the model, reducing the amount of priming that can spread from semantic to phonological levels. Because of this, older adults with weaker connections will experience more TOTs, consistent with the decrement model. Another prediction of the transmission deficit model, according to Burke et al. (1991), is that older adults will experience fewer persistent alternates (or blockers) during a TOT than will younger adults. This hypothesis is made because the deficit that causes TOTs may also "reduce bottom-up priming to the lexical nodes for alternates, making activation of an alternate less possible" (Burke et al., 1991, p. 549). As we have seen, this too, is supported by the empirical evidence. Four of five studies demonstrated significantly more persistent alternates for younger adults than for older adults. Similarly, older adults should retrieve less partial information than younger adults, according to the model. This is also supported by the data (see Table 7.2b). Burke et al.'s data are among the strongest that support the decrement model of TOTs in aging.

The strong association between age and decreased retrieval of partial information supports the transmission deficit models, and it also argues against the incremental knowledge view. If older adults experience more TOTs because they have a greater vocabulary, as incremental knowledge theory suggests, then it is likely that they will also experience more semantic blockers or partial semantic retrieval. Thus, it is likely that at least some of the increase in TOTs with age is a function of decrements in associative networks, as suggested by Burke et al. (1991).

TABLE 7.2b

TOTs and Aging

Study	Method	Age Groups	Alternates (Blockers)
Cohen & Faulkner (1986)	diary	Young, middle-aged, old	Young = middle-aged > old
Burke et al. (1991)	diary	Young, middled-aged, old	Young = middled-aged > old
Burke et al. (1991)	experiment	Young and old	Young > old
Brown & Nix (1996)	experiment	Young and old	Old > young
Heine et al. (1999)	diary	Young, young–old, oldest	Young = young–old > oldest

Note. Most studies suggest that older adults retrieve fewer blockers than do younger adults.

With respect to TOT resolution, Burke et al. (1991) claimed that the transmission deficit model did not make relevant predictions. However, if aging causes weakened connections between semantic and phonological representations, it is likely that older adults should resolve fewer TOTs than do younger adults. The data, however ambiguous, actually suggest the opposite—that older adults are better at resolving TOTs, or at the very least, TOT resolution is about the same in younger adults than it is in older adults. None of the studies found significant age advantages for TOT resolution, so this issue also requires future study. If these nonsignificant trends hold up under future testing, the better resolution of older adults would be damaging to decrement theory and would support incremental knowledge theory.

Inferential Models. Inferential models claim that TOTs are the result of unconscious inferences that a target is known, based on the recognition of cues or the retrieval of clues (e.g., Koriat, 1993; MacLin, 2000; Schwartz & Smith, 1997). Inferential theory is compatible with either decrement theory or incremental knowledge theory. If decrement theory is correct, older adults experience more TOTs because, despite the breakdown of connections, the clues that an item is in memory are still there. In inferential models, it is the clues, not the breakdown, that induces the TOTs. If the incremental knowledge theory is correct, the increase in knowledge that occurs with aging will be accompanied by an increase in the number of clues that people can use to infer TOTs. Or, simply put, more knowledge means more clues and more cue familiarity, which in turn means more TOTs.

To date, however, inferential theory has not been specifically tested in studies looking at age effects on TOTs. How well can inferential models explain the relation of aging to TOT effects? I generate a set of plausible hypotheses based on what we know about inferential models and cognitive aging. I then apply them to the known data on TOTs and aging.

Inferential models can handle the age differences in TOT frequency very easily. If the familiarity of the cue is a factor in producing a TOT, as suggested by the literature (Metcalfe et al., 1993; Schwartz & Smith, 1997), then TOTs should increase when cues (questions) are more familiar to the participants. In general, studies have shown that older adults are more knowledgeable and familiar with the stimulus materials usually used than are younger participants. The cue familiarity hypothesis (see chap. 3) predicts more TOTs with age. In fact, cue familiarity postulates that the more familiar the cue, the greater the likelihood of a TOT. It should be familiarity (or general knowledge) that correlates with TOTs, not simply age. This is exactly the pattern observed by Dahlgren (1998).

On the other hand, inferential theory also predicts that the amount of related information is correlated with the production of TOTs (Koriat, 1993;

Schwartz & Smith, 1997). More TOTs should occur when more partial or related information is retrieved. Inferential theory predicts that older adults experience more TOTs, and that these TOTs will be accompanied by increased partial and related information. However, the literature suggests that this is not the case. Older adults experience more TOTs but retrieve less related and partial information (in general; see Brown & Nix, 1996, for an exception). It is difficult for inferential theory to account for this.

Inferential theory also includes the idea that nonmnemonic variables, such as social motivation, play a role in producing TOTs. If older participants are motivated to appear as if they are not suffering from cognitive decline, they may reduce their threshold for reporting a TOT (Brown & Nix, 1996). Because they perceive self-declines in memory (see Sunderland, Watts, Baddeley, & Harris, 1986), they are motivated to report TOTs, thereby increasing the rate of reported TOTs for older adults relative to younger adults. Hopefully, future research will elucidate these issues.

Monitoring and Control of TOTs in Older Adults

Because the work on TOTs among aging adults has centered on the lexical retrieval issues, the role of monitoring and control functions of TOTs among older adults has not received any attention. It is possible to speculate how some of the literature can be parsimoniously explained by metacognitive models of monitoring and control.

Research in other metacognitive domains has shown that older adults monitor their memory at least as well as younger adults, particularly for JOLs (e.g., Connor, Dunlosky, & Hertzog, 1997; Dunlosky & Connor, 1997; Dunlosky & Hertzog, 1997). Similarly, in TOT studies, it is possible to argue that older adults show no deficit in monitoring. For example, in the diary studies, TOT resolution is generally higher, if not significantly higher, for older adults than it is for younger adults. Other studies have found similar trends in laboratory studies (e.g., Brown & Nix, 1996). Therefore, it is likely that TOTs serve to monitor accessibility in memory at least equally well for older adults as for younger adults.

With respect to control, research in other areas of metamemory often reveal age-related declines in the strategic control of memory as people age. For example, Dunlosky and Connor (1997) found that older adults showed equivalent monitoring skills on a JOL task as the younger adults, but did not use the JOLs as efficiently to control learning behavior, and thereby showed lower recall. Older adults may have an impairment in metacognitive control relative to younger adults. No research on TOTs is directly relevant here. However, the switch from directed search to a reliance on spontaneous retrieval in resolving TOTs as found in older adults may reflect age-related changes in the control processes used for TOTs. It is not clear whether the increased use of spontaneous-retrieval strategies represents good or poor control because it is not known what would happen if older adults were encouraged or forced to use direct search at the expense of spontaneous retrieval. This is another area of TOT research ripe for further investigation.

To summarize, the literature shows that older adults do experience more TOTs than younger adults, but resolve them at least equally well, despite having retrieved less partial information. There is some evidence to suggest that the increase in TOT frequency with age is due to a decline in the strength of associative networks, particularly the connection between semantic and phonological levels. In contrast, there is evidence to suggest that TOTs increase with age because older people simply know more. Little research on TOTs and aging has been conducted from a metacognitive perspective, but I believe this is a fruitful area of inquiry. We now turn our attention from older adults to children.

TOTs IN CHILDREN

When do children experience their first TOT? At what age, and why? Do children experience more TOTs because they have not strengthened the associations between semantic and phonological aspects of a word? Or do they experience fewer TOTs because their vocabularies are smaller? Are accuracy rates the same because TOTs are a function of direct-access to an unretrieved target, or are accuracy rates lower because children have not learned which clues to pay attention to? Again, when we talk about TOTs in children, we encounter yet another unexplored area in the TOT research. Although theoretically, the issue of TOTs in children is important for both metacognitive and psycholinguistic theory, there has been little attempt to address these issues in developmental studies. The issues of partial knowledge, access to knowledge, and awareness of that knowledge clearly have important educational implications. However, to my knowledge, only three studies of limited scope have asked if and how children experience TOTs (Elbers, 1985; Faust et al., 1997; Wellman, 1977). Two of those studies (Faust et al., 1997; Wellman, 1977) were conducted in an experimental fashion, but neither study specifically asked children to report on TOT states. I also discuss a fourth study, by Butterfield, Nelson, and Peck (1988), designed as a follow-up to the Wellman (1977) study, but which used FOKs.

Elbers (1985) recorded several conversations with her 2½-year-old son concerning a single difficult retrieval in their native language, Dutch. On the previous day, the child and his mother had visited the aquarium, where the child saw dolphins for the first time. The next day, when seemingly trying to retrieve the word for dolphins, the child could not. On several occasions, blocking words intruded ("soldier," which sounds similar to the word for "dolphin" in Dutch), but the child could not retrieve the word "dolphin" even though it was clear that he was talking about them. On the basis of this anecdote, Elbers concluded that TOTs occur in children younger than 3 years old.

In an experimental study, Wellman (1977) looked at the accuracy of FOKs in young children. In addition to collecting FOKs, Wellman also looked for evidence of actual TOT states by observing when the children experienced frustration because they could not recall the target word for which they were searching. Although explicit TOT judgments by the children were not included, Wellman clearly wished to address the issue of TOT phenomenology.

Wellman (1977) was one of the earliest researchers interested in metacognition, and his 1977 article was specifically designed to look at metacognition in young children. One of his concerns was the accuracy of the childrens' FOKs, which was to serve as a measure of the children's monitoring abilities. Wellman, like later metacognitive researchers, was interested in the nature of the judgments and how well they predicted performance. In his study, he asked kindergarten, first-, and third-grade children to name pictures taken from the Peabody picture vocabulary test. He prescreened the pictures into easy, medium, and difficult categories to see which would be more likely to elicit feelings of knowing when the name could not be recalled. If the children could not name the object, the experimenter asked them for a FOK by asking the following question: "What if I told you a lot of names, could you pick out the right name for the picture?" Most of the children understood this question and did not answer either all "yes" or all "no." In a final recognition test, the children were given the names and had to pick which of nine pictures was the correct one.

The children's FOKs predicted correct recognition at greater than chance levels. Furthermore, the third-graders were significantly more accurate than the kindergarten and first-grade children. The younger and older children showed equivalent recognition and familiarity, suggesting that the older children's increase in accuracy was due to better metacognitive monitoring. Wellman (1977) also looked at verbalizations, which included clear statements of metacognitive intent by the children. For example, some children, particularly the third-graders, said when indicating a feeling of knowing, "I know I know that," or "I know, I just can't remember." Wellman also reported that some of the third-graders "became agitated and frustrated with their inability to recall the name." (p. 20). Although, Wellman specifically looked at FOKs rather than TOTs, the anecdotal reports suggest that some of the children were experiencing TOTs.

In a study by Butterfield et al. (1988), that only partially replicated Wellman's (1977) findings, accuracy differences were not significantly different between older and younger children. The 6-year-olds showed equivalent accuracy to the 10-year-olds and to the 18-year-olds using gamma correlations. Butterfield et al., therefore, suggested that metacognitive accuracy was invariant across these developmental periods. Because of the failure to replicate from one study to the next, and because neither study really asked children to report what was on the "tip of the tongue," the nature of TOTs in tots remains a mystery.

Faust et al. (1997) were also interested in TOTs in young children. They examined TOT rates and TOT accuracy in normal and language-impaired children. They suspected that the language-impaired children might show more TOTs than did the normal children because word retrieval is often a problem for children with impairment.

Faust et al. (1997) looked at comparable samples of normal and impaired children who were either in the second or third grade (the children were all approximately 8 years old). Like Wellman (1977), they showed children pictures of objects or animals and asked them for the names of the items. If the children could not recall the name of the item, they were asked whether they knew the item and might be able to remember it later. If they said they could remember it later, they were asked to make a FOK (with instructions that were very close to those normally given for TOTs). The children were subsequently given a recognition test.

Both language-impaired and normal children quite frequently indicated that they knew an item that they could not recall right away. Indeed, the language-impaired children gave the TOT response on 30% of all the items, and the normal children indicated a TOT response 11% of the time, indicating that by 8 years of age, children are routinely experiencing TOTs.

Faust et al. (1997) examined the accuracy of TOT judgments in both the normal and the language-impaired children. There were some stunning differences between the two groups with respect to accuracy. The normal children resolved 36% of their TOTs, comparable to adults. However, the language-impaired children resolved only 18%. The recognition results were even more striking. Normal children correctly recognized 45% of their TOTs, and 0% of their n–TOTs, thus demonstrating good metacognitive accuracy. The language-impaired children actually recognized more n–TOTs (39%) than they did TOTs (27%), thereby demonstrating very poor, if any, monitoring capability. Also, the language-impaired children recalled more false phonological information than did the normal children.

This study demonstrates that children as young as 8 years old experience TOTs, and that these TOTs can predict both recall and recognition. The Faust et al. (1997) study also suggests that there is a relation between TOT accuracy and language impairment, although the nature of that relation is unclear. One important implication, discussed by Faust et al., is that clinicians may be able to overcome language impairment by teaching good metacognitive skills.

From any perspective, TOTs in children could be seen as an important line of research. Consider lexical retrieval theory. Research in children could demonstrate how connections between semantic nodes and phonological nodes form and develop. If TOTs arise from failures between semantic and phonological nodes, then as yet unformed connections in children may give rise to similar phenomena as with the very old. The pattern of TOTs in younger children may mirror that of older adults.

From the point of view of metacognition, TOTs in children are also of interest. If metacognition is a complex and late-developing skill, there should be little evidence of TOTs in young children. However, if TOTs are in place at quite a young age in fully-formed format, it may suggest an early development of metacognitive skills and perhaps emphasize the role of nonconscious processes in metacognition (e.g., Reder & Schunn, 1996). Furthermore, it would be important to determine if TOTs have the same etiology in children and adults or if childhood TOTs are qualitatively different from those of adults. Nonetheless, this research remains in the future.

With respect to TOT phenomenology, it is also interesting to know when children start using the expression "its on the tip-of-my-tongue," given that this expression exists in most languages (Schwartz, 1999b, chap. 2). Although it may have just not occurred to Wellman (1977) to quote any child as saying it, he does not report any anecdotes in which children used the expression "on the tongue." If TOTs really are universal, it would be expected that the phrase would be used by children. However, once again, I must say "alas" because the research is not done.

TOTs IN PATIENT POPULATIONS

Perhaps the most promising avenue of research on TOTs, the one with the least amount of research actually accomplished, is in the domain of Neuropsychology. Neuropsychology should give us some tremendous insight into the TOT, if we can bring its tools bear. First, patient studies need to address the nature of the TOT in both aphasic and amnesic patients. Second, neuroimaging studies would also enhance our understanding of TOTs considerably. Indeed, the prominent neuropsychologist, Schacter wrote that, "Although no neuroimaging studies of TOT states have yet been reported (and may be difficult to carry out because of the relative infrequency of the TOT phenomenon), such studies could provide novel insights into the neural correlates of retrieval blocking." (Schacter, 1999, p. 188). I could not agree more and would only add that novel insights would also occur concerning the nature of TOT etiology and phenomenology as well. D. L. Schacter assured me that such studies are on the agenda in his lab, but have not yet been completed at the time of this writing (personal communication, June 9, 2000).

A few studies have discussed the TOT in neuropsychological patients. Many of them, however, do not explicitly ask the patients to report if they are experiencing a TOT. Rather, the TOT is inferred from their behavior, as we saw with Vigliocco et al.'s (1997) study of syntactic access during Italian TOTs. I urge caution in interpreting these studies because what may seem like a TOT to an outside observer may not feel like one for the neuropsychological patient. I discuss these studies here, but remind the reader that the TOTs are third-person defined, and not first-person subjective TOTs.

Before reviewing the studies, let me strengthen the argument for their importance. Patient groups could allow for some careful testing of the different theories outlined in this volume. For example, consider the comparison between direct-access theory and inferential theory. Direct-access theory postulates that TOTs are a function of access to an unretrieved word, but with a failure to access its phonological component. Direct-access theory might predict that Broca's aphasics and anomic aphasics, therefore, should experience TOTs very frequently, as their chief problem is one of access to phonological form. Because of their intact semantic knowledge, their TOTs should show high accuracy when measured by recognition tests. Inferential theory suggests that TOTs are based on piecing together clues. Inferential theory, therefore, makes a different prediction, at least for the Broca's aphasics. Broca's aphasics do not retrieve much partial information because of the extreme deficit in their retrieval systems. According to inferential theory, two of the clues we use to infer a TOT are the amount and the intensity of retrieved partial and related information. Because Broca's aphasics do not retrieve much partial information, they may experience very few TOTs. In contrast, inferential theory might predict that patients with prefrontal damage may have a more difficult time with accurate TOT judgments. Prefrontal damage is often associated with monitoring difficulties (Schacter, Harbluk, & McLachlan, 1984), so it is likely that TOT accuracy will decline as well.

TOTs in Aphasia

Aphasia is a general term referring to acquired language deficits (Kolb & Whishaw, 1996). It is frequently divided into aphasia that affects language comprehension, referred to as Wernicke's aphasia, and aphasia that affects production, referred to as Broca's aphasia. Anomic aphasia refers to an acquired deficit in lexical retrieval, which is usually accompanied by fluent speech and good comprehension: just an endless inability to find the right word.

All of the studies, save one, on TOTs in aphasia inferred their presence from retrieval behavior. Funnell, Metcalfe, and Tsapkani (1996) relied on FOKs. Thus, the aphasic literature, unfortunately, does not address etiology or phenomenology of TOTs, although the studies are relevant from the perspective of lexical retrieval. The studies have addressed a range of aphasic conditions, including Wernicke's aphasia (Goodglass, Kaplan, Weintraub, & Ackerman, 1976), Broca's aphasia (Bruce & Howard, 1988; Goodglass et al., 1976), conduction aphasics (Goodglass et al., 1976), and anomic aphasia (Funnell et al., 1996; Goodglass et al., 1976; Vigliocco et al., 1999).

Goodglass et al. (1976) were interested in the nature of word retrieval in aphasia. Following an all too familiar pattern, they inferred TOTs based on retrieval behavior rather than explicitly asking the patients about their experiences. The criterion for inferring a TOT was that phonemic information was partially, but not completely recovered. In the study, the patients were presented with line drawings of relatively common objects. If the patients were not able to recall the target word, they were asked to identify the first letter, syllables, and the length of the word. They were also asked if they had an "idea of the correct word," a judgment perhaps halfway in between a TOT and a FOK. Goodglass et al. found that conduction aphasics indicated the greatest number of partial phonological information (TOTs), whereas anomic aphasics reported the fewest. Broca's and Wernicke's aphasics were intermediate. Conduction aphasics also showed the most accurate reporting of partial phonological information, even though all groups were roughly equivalent in their ability to correctly name the target word. Therefore, Goodglass et al. concluded that the conduction aphasics were best able to use TOT information to help obtain partial information for a target word.

It is difficult to know what to make of these data. It was a group study, so some patients may have been more severely aphasic than others within each group. The Wernicke's patients, presumably, were relatively mild aphasics, as one might wonder how patients with more severe Wernicke's aphasia would handle these tasks at all. Clearly the study does not address differences among theories of TOT etiology.

Bruce and Howard (1988) were interested in whether Broca's aphasics could improve their naming ability through the use of phonemic cueing. Therefore, they tested 20 Broca's aphasics in a naming task. If the patients could not recall the name of a line drawing of an object, they were either given a phonemic cue or not given a cue. Bruce and Howard found that the Broca's aphasics benefitted from the phonemic cues. Like Goodglass et al. (1976), Bruce and Howard primarily used the label TOT in terms of the accessibility of partial information combined with the inability to retrieve the full target word.

The two most illuminating studies concerning the nature of TOTs during aphasia are recent ones involving single-subject designs with individual anomic aphasics. The first, Funnell et al. (1996), examined the nature of FOKs in a strongly anomic patient. Funnell et al. were interested in linking the experimental work on FOKs with the word-retrieval difficulties in anomia. The second study, conducted by Vigliocco et al. (1999), examined the nature of syntactic information that can be retrieved by an anomic patient during word-finding difficulties.

Funnell et al. (1996) studied the patient HW, who is a highly intelligent man but became densely anomic after suffering a left-hemisphere stroke in 1989. A Harvard MBA graduate, HW's poststroke WAIS–R IQ was still measured at 121 when it was given to him untimed. However, he has a very limited production vocabulary, and his speech is characterized by endless word-retrieval failures. Funnell et al. conducted a FOK experiment, in which HW was asked general-information questions such as "When something is chronologically out of place, it is called an _____ " (anachronism). HW was almost completely unable to recall any of the words that fitted the sentence. He usually gave very high feeling-of-knowing judgments and declared that he knew the word absolutely, but he just could not say it. Indeed, his recognition performance was extremely good. Thus, it seemed highly likely that HW did indeed have an image of the word and perhaps related semantic information, but that his deficit was in activating the phonological form of the word. Funnell et al. argued that their data supported Burke et al.'s (1991) position on TOT etiology, that is, that TOTs occur when there is semantic activation without phonological activation—this seemed to be the pattern in HW. However, Funnell et al. used FOKs, not TOTs, to assess metacognitive ability.

In a second single-subject study of TOTs and anomia, Vigliocco et al. (1999) was interested in whether anomics would access syntactic information for words that they could not recall. They studied the patient MS, a 31-year-old man rendered anomic after a bout with herpes encephalitis. MS is of normal intelligence aside from his verbal deficit. In Vigliocco et al.'s paradigm, MS was presented with pictures of items representing fruits and vegetables, or buildings and furniture. Half of the presented items were mass nouns ("asparagus"), whereas half of the presented items were count nouns ("artichokes"). Mass nouns refer to items that are not grammatically pluralized when speaking of many of the items, whereas count nouns are. If MS could not retrieve the name of the object, he provided whatever phonological information he could, guessed at the number of syllables, and indicated whether the unretrieved word was a mass or count noun.

Vigliocco et al. (1999) defined a TOT as occurring when the patient could not retrieve the target name but did retrieve partial information about the target. MS was not asked whether he thought that he was experiencing a TOT. Positive TOTs occurred when MS later recognized the correct word, whereas negative TOTs were those items for which recognition was incorrect. Vigliocco et al. found that MS was able to correctly identify whether a word was mass or count even when he could not actually retrieve the word. Because of the limited size of the item pool, Vigliocco et al. were not able to compare correct response rates for positive TOTs, negative TOTs, and n–TOTs. Nonetheless, the study does show that syntactical information is accessible to anomic patients. Given the general similarity between deficits in word retrieval in anomics and TOTs in normal people, Vigliocco et al. inferred that this study supports a model that includes syntactical information as important in the production and resolution of TOTs.

Both studies on anomic aphasia were directed at testing word-access theories. In both studies, the predominant problem of the patient was accessing the phonological form of target words. Both patients retained access to semantics, and Vigliocco et al. (1999) showed that the anomic had access to syntactical information as well. Therefore, both studies support the general notion that a complete lemma is accessed before the phonological representation, or lexeme, is retrieved. It is not clear what each study tells us about the TOT, as the first study substituted FOKs, and the second study did not measure subjective TOTs.

I suspect it is highly likely that anomic patients will experience TOTs quite frequently. This is a straightforward prediction from direct access theory, but also a prediction of inferential theory. According to inferential theory, TOTs are based on the number and intensity of clues that are retrieved by the rememberer. Anomic aphasics have no shortage of retrieved clues, although they are usually semantic, not phonological in nature. Therefore, both models predict high frequency of TOTs, and good predictive accuracy when recognition is used as the criterion measure. On the other hand, it is possible that direct and inferential theory will make different predictions for other population groups, particularly different aphasic groups. I find it very unfortunate that no labs are currently addressing these issues.

We now turn our attention to two studies that have been conducted on patients with neurological diseases. Parkinson's is a disease that attacks the substantia nigra of the basal ganglia, causing problems with the control of voluntary movement. Because the basal ganglia are connected to the prefrontal cortex, some Parkinson's patients also show dementia. Alzheimer's is a degenerative and eventually fatal neurological disorder, which first affects memory, but then degrades all cognitive functions.

TOTs in Parkinson's Disease

Matison, Mayeux, Rosen, and Fahn (1982) postulated that TOTs might be more common in Parkinson's disease, given that Parkinson's patients often have difficulties in articulating words. However, Parkinson's deficits are generally considered to be dysarthric deficits, that is, difficulties in motor control, and not aphasic deficits. Matison et al. tested 22 medically stable Parkinson's patients with standard neuropsychological testing, including the Boston naming test. They found that, like aphasics, the Parkinson's patients benefitted from phonological cueing of unrecalled words. Therefore, Matison et al. interpreted Parkinson's deficits in articulation as being similar to the problems of speech production in aphasia and in normal individual with TOT states. Matison et al. did not explicitly ask their patients to provide subjective TOT judgments. Because of possible frontal cortex damage in Parkinson's patients, one might suspect that the TOTs would show lower correlations to resolution and recognition, but this aspect was not tested by Matison et al.

TOTs in Alzheimer's Disease

Astell and Harley (1996) looked at explicit TOT judgments in patients suffering from Alzheimer's disease (AD). Astell and Harley gave simple word definitions to AD patients and asked them to supply the word. For example, one item used was "timepiece that is worn on the wrist" (watch). If the patients could not retrieve the target word, they were asked to provide any semantically or phonologically similar words. TOT states were only recorded if "they indicated that they knew the word and were unable to retrieve it, and if they carried out an active search in an attempt to locate the target word. These were often marked by phrases such as 'it's on my tongue' and 'I can't get my tongue around it.'" (p. 200). The patients were then given the target word and asked if that matched the word that they had in mind.

Compared to the age-matched controls, the AD patients experienced more TOTs (both resolved and unresolved). This result is partially because the control patients retrieved more words correctly, leaving a smaller pool available for TOT states. The AD patients retrieved few phonological blockers relative to the controls, although they were roughly equivalent for semantic blockers. Thus, like the other patient groups, the AD patients seemed to be revealing a phonological deficit while they were experiencing TOTs. Astell and Harley (1996) interpreted these results as consistent with a two-stage account of retrieval with an initial semantic phase followed by a subsequent phonological phase. Like Burke et al. (1991), Astell and Harley think of TOTs occurring when that phonological stage is impaired.

Unfortunately, Astell and Harley (1996) did not measure the accuracy of the TOTs. Although the low phonological retrieval in the AD patients supports the lexical access model, it does not address inferential model. Assuming that AD patients have frontal damage relatively early in the course of AD, we would then expect to see accuracy deficits in the TOT judgments, according to inferential theory. Astell and Harley did not consider this because their goal was to test the two-stage model of lexical retrieval in a patient group.

Ideas for the Future

What are we to make of these neuropsychological studies? From a lexical access perspective, the studies support a two-stage model of lexical retrieval, in which semantic and syntactical information is compiled before the rememberer retrieves the phonological information. However, from the standpoint of their nature, the studies tell us little about TOT etiology and phenomenology.

I next consider a few hypotheses about TOTs that can be tested in the neuropsychological domain. If TOTs evolved from a metacognitive mechanism for monitoring and controlling word retrieval, one may make several innovative hypotheses not addressed in the existing literature. With no current patient data to support them, I simply put forth the hypotheses and why they make sense here and leave it to future research to illuminate them. The focus is on relating TOT accuracy and frequency to functions of the prefrontal cortex.

The frontal lobes, prefrontal cortex in particular, have been implicated in some metacognitive functions. Janowksy, Shimamura, and Squire (1989) found that frontal lobe patients showed deficits in feeling-of-knowing accuracy whereas amnesic patients showed essentially normal accuracy. Shimamura and Squire (1986) found even greater deficits in accuracy of feeling-of-knowing judgments for Korsakoff patients, for whom frontal damage is not uncommon. However, amnesic patients with temporal lobe dysfunction do not show impairment in feeling of knowing accuracy. Thus, Shimamura and Squire suggested that metacognition may be a frontal phenomena not linked directly to the hippocampus and surrounding temporal lobe structures. More recently, Souchay, Isingrini, and Espagnet (2000) examined FOKs in young and older adults. They found that feeling-of-knowing accuracy correlated with assessments of frontal functioning.

A close relation between TOTs and feelings of knowing would indicate that TOTs perhaps originate in the prefrontal cortex. If so, frontally damaged patients should experience fewer TOTs and with less accurate prediction of resolution or recognition (i.e., more likely to be negative TOTs) than comparison groups with damage elsewhere. Frontal patients may also be less likely to connect TOTs with retrieved partial information. Unlike Broca's aphasia patients, frontal patients will not show impairments in the retrieval of phonological information during TOTs. However, retrieval of phonological information will not differ from TOTs to n–TOTs because the frontal patients can no longer distinguish between the two states.

Temporal-lobe amnesics, on the other hand, show no deficits in metacognitive monitoring (Shimamura & Squire, 1986). Therefore, their production of TOTs should be unimpaired. Given their memory deficits, it is likely that amnesics will generate more TOTs than comparison groups, and that the TOTs will predict recognition performance equally well (although given their general recall deficits, not resolution). Certainly, the amnesic group should show better TOT accuracy than the frontal-lobe patients. Although amnesics may also show deficits in the retrieval of related phonological and semantic information, it should be no worse for TOTs than for n–TOTs.

Relevant to these hypotheses is a recent study by Widner, Otani, and Falconier (1999). They classified normal participantsts as high frontal or low frontal as a function of their performance on the Wisconsin Card Sort. Participants then retrieved word definitions, and gave both FOKs and TOTs. Participants who scored low on the frontal tasks showed lowered FOK accuracy relative to those with better accuracy, consistent with the hypotheses of frontal lobe's role in metacognition. However, there were no differences in either TOT rates or TOT accuracy. Thus, their data did not support a role of frontal lobes in TOT judgments. On the other hand, Widner et al. (1999) tested only unimpaired people who all scored higher than neuropsychological patients with frontal damage. They did, however, find that FOKs correlated with frontal functioning, similar to the findings of Souchay et al. (2000). Thus, it is possible that there simply was not enough variance in the participants to reveal deficits in TOT accuracy. This hypothesis needs to be tested with patients whose frontal lobes are truly damaged, not simply inefficient.

Another manner in which to test these views would be to conduct neuroimaging studies of normal adults. As the quote by Schacter (1999) at the start of this section indicated, there have been no published studies looking at TOT formation with neuroimaging equipment, although such studies would be terribly interesting. It is likely that neuroimaging data would be extremely important in elucidating issues in TOT etiology and lexical retrieval. Given that the left prefrontal cortex appears to be implicated in retrieval from semantic memory, one hypothesis is that TOTs will selectively activate this area relative to n–TOTs (see Nyberg, Cabeza, & Tulving, 1996). Such a finding would also support the role of frontal lobes in metacognitive monitoring. If the deficit causing a TOT is the lack of retrieval of phonological information given the retrieval of semantic information, one might expect TOTs to activate areas posterior in the frontal lobe, perhaps Broca's area. Broca's area activation during TOTs would support direct-access models of TOTs. However, all such notions remain speculation.

Some very preliminary data from D. L. Schacter's (personal communication, June 9, 2000) lab points to a role for the anterior cingulate gyrus of the frontal lobe as being involved in TOT and "don't know" judgments. Although preliminary, this data is highly intriguing. The anterior cingulate is involved in both emotional processing, supervisory attention, and the detection of errors (Dehaene, Posner, & Tucker, 1994). These are three functions quite compatible with a metacognitive view of the TOT because TOTs allow us to detect errors of retrieval, monitor and control retrieval, and frequently involve emotional experiences. I find this line of research highly interesting.

SUMMARY

In this chapter, issues related to TOTs and aging, children's TOTs, and TOTs in neuropsychological patients have been addressed. I contrasted the decrement theory of TOTs and aging with the incremental knowledge theory of TOTs and aging, and discussed the support for each in the literature. I then discussed how both direct-access and inferential models of TOT etiology account for the aging literature. The literature on TOTs in childhood and neuropsychological patients, unfortunately, is still in its infancy, but some interesting avenues of research in those domains were suggested.

8

Conclusions and Directions for the Future

In the first seven chapters, I present a synopsis of what is known about TOTs and also illustrated how much is not known. I suspect that my readers were frequently disappointed that issues could not be resolved and that so many interesting questions remain unsolved. Despite the gaps, loose ends, and open holes in our knowledge about TOTs, there are solid data pointing to the importance of the phenomena for a range of psychological issues. More to the point, relative to many other subjective phenomena of human psychology, there has been a lot of research conducted on TOTs, which may serve as a model for other phenomenology-based investigations. In this closing chapter, I present some general thoughts, link TOTs to other phenomenological experiences, and offer a summary on TOTs.

I reiterate some of the important themes in the volume: On one hand, TOTs can be viewed as instances in which known words are not retrieved. In this view, TOTs serve as "windows" onto word retrieval (Kohn et al., 1987) and inform us about retrieval processes. On the other hand, TOTs can be thought of as phenomenological experiences, in which one has a feeling about the likelihood of retrieval. In this view, it may be better to categorize TOTs as experiences that provide a "lens" onto human phenomenology (Schwartz, 1999b). That is, because the phenomenology is so salient and occurs so often, the TOT can serve as a case study in the investigation of human phenomenology. In this volume, I do not argue against the former view, but argue strongly for the second view. Thus, to the extent that some researchers have exclusively endorsed the "window" view, my arguments have been critical of this singular approach.

Partially as a function of the two different views, different mechanistic explanations have been advanced to explain TOTs. On the one hand, direct-access models theorize that TOTs are based on access to the unrecalled target, usually semantic aspects of it. On the other hand, inferential models theorize that TOTs are based on clues and cues that a target might be in memory store. Psycholinguists who argued for a "window on retrieval" view, usually endorse the direct-access models, whereas metacognition researchers, such as myself, have stressed the inferential model. I think the jury is far from reaching its verdict on which, if either, theory should prevail, but all of us benefit from greater discussion. Regardless of the eventual explanation, future research must take into account TOT phenomenology.

In chapter 1, Tulving's doctrine of concordance was described. Tulving (1989) described how most researchers in cognition assumed a basic equivalence of cognitive processes and conscious experience. This means that if an experiment uncovers the cognitive mechanism, the nature of the phenomenology is understood.

I added TOTs to that list of phenomena for which the doctrine cannot hold. The TOT is too complex and multidimensional to be explained as simply a stage of lexical retrieval. Dimensions other than an unretrieved target play a role in determining TOTs, such as partially retrieved information, cue familiarity, social motivation characteristics, and a person's knowledge base. Moreover, TOTs play a role in the control of retrieval behavior, from motivating rememberers to work harder, to lengthening search times, to influencing strategy decisions. Throughout the last several chapters, I built a case to demonstrate that the doctrine of concordance does not hold true with respect to TOTs, and like Tulving (1989), we must search for models that account for both cognitive processes and phenomenology as potentially dissociable, if usually correlated, entities.

I view the TOT as a marker, superimposed by metacognitive processes onto the lexical retrieval process. The lexical retrieval process attempts to retrieve a word and comes up with semantic information, but less than complete phonological information. In response, the metacognitive process produces a TOT, which informs the rememberer that the word may be available in memory and may eventually become accessible. The metacognitive process can then suggest new ways in which to run the basic lexical retrieval process, which then initiates another search for the word. The evidence reviewed in this volume supports the idea that the "markers," or metacognitive processes, are accurate—they usually denote those items that are retrievable and memorable. Illusory TOTs are examples of when this processes is in error—when the markers say a word is in memory store when it is not.

At a neuropsychological level, the TOT remains a mystery. Nobody has any firm handle on what, if any, area of the brain is responsible for inducing TOTs. Based on the studies we do have, the TOT seems to persist in patients with various forms of aphasia, as well as in Parkinson's disease and AD. There is also some limited evidence that TOTs are present in patients with temporal-lobe amnesia and patients with frontal deficits (e.g., Widner et al., 1999). However, these studies have been weakened by methodological difficulties, most prominent among which is the failure to collect firsthand subjective TOT data. This precludes analysis of either TOT frequency or TOT accuracy in these patient groups.

It is possible that various patient groups may show differing selective deficits in TOT frequency and TOT accuracy. A brain region responsible for inducing the subjective experience of the TOT could become damaged, causing failure to experience the TOT, even when unrecalled words are potentially retrievable. Another brain region, responsible for linking those subjective experiences to the word retrieval process, could become damaged, causing indiscriminate TOTs without any link to successful resolution. In chapter 7, I argued that it is possible that damage to the prefrontal cortex may create difficulties in appropriately producing TOTs or linking TOTs to retrieval. Finally, TOT production, combined with a deficit in word retrieval, may result in patients who constantly experience TOTs for known words, but can only recognize but not recall those TOT targets. This scenario is probably the case in anomic aphasic patients. Future neuropsychological studies should be geared in this direction.

A WORD ON CONSCIOUSNESS

Tulving (1994) accused metacognition researchers of being cowards for not using the "big bad C word," that is, *consciousness*. He argued that metacognition is about conscious monitoring and conscious control, and he said that researchers hide behind jargon that is behaviorally and cognitively acceptable to avoid discussing the term consciousness. In Tulving's view, I have been a coward here because I find the term consciousness an overused and fuzzy term. I prefer the term *phenomenology*, which refers to the person's subjective experience. I have suggested throughout the volume that the TOT is a conscious phenomenological experience, but its production, either by direct or inferential means, is mostly likely hidden from consciousness. The experience of TOT may be conscious, even if it controls retrieval at a nonconscious level. Thus, I have avoided the term consciousness throughout the volume, and have discussed issues of phenomenology instead.

RELATED PHENOMENA

TOTs are advanced as a case study in phenomenology because the TOT research can serve as a model for thinking about a number of different psychological phenomena, such as déjà vû, the tip-of-the-nose, absent-mindedness, and perhaps, the remembering of dreams. These phenomena, not well studied or well understand, mirror the TOT in a number of important ways.

Like the TOT, déjà vû is characterized by a strong phenomenological experience. We sense that we have previously experienced something, although knowing objectively that it is not possible. Like the TOT, the important aspects of the déjà vû experience are twofold. On the one hand, it is important to determine what kinds of memory processes are activated during déjà vû experiences. On the other hand, déjà vû is essentially a phenomenological experience, which tells us we may know something but not how we know it. It is monitoring certain processes, which we cannot monitor consciously, and like the TOT, it serves a control function: It tells us we may have knowledge that is not currently accessible. It urges us to search memory store to bring the information into conscious accessibility.

Unlike TOTs, I suspect a diary study would reveal that déjà vû experiences are very rare, and probably not possible to induce in the lab. Thus, déjà vû experiences are more difficult to study than TOTs. Nonetheless, I think they probably shares basic features with the TOT in its phenomenological salience and in its probable function.

Engen and colleagues (Engen, 1987; Lawless & Engen, 1977; see Brown, 1991) described what they called the "tip-of-the-nose" phenomenon. This refers to a common experience in which one smells an odor that is very familiar, but cannot name the odor. Engen claimed that people have almost no lexical or phonological information for the odor, but are overwhelmed by its familiarity. In their studies, Engen and his colleagues showed that participants have knowledge about the odor, as they could identify objects associated with it. In the terms I have advanced, this is another example in which a strong phenomenological experience gives rise to an inference that one may have knowledge that is not currently accessible. In a functional sense, then, the "tip-of-the-nose" phenomenon can direct search and knowledge acquisition strategies.

"I don't know his name, but his face sure rings a bell" is the punch line to a children's joke about a paraplegic bell-ringer in the cathedral of Notre Dame. It also rings true as another phenomenon that may share features with the TOT. As discussed earlier, people generally have good memories for faces, but poor memories for names. Thus, we are often confronted with situations in which recall of a name is impossible, although the face is recognized. Indeed, Brennan et al. (1990) showed that presenting faces does not resolve TOTs for names. Nonetheless, a familiar face may inform us that we know something about the person and perhaps should mentally search for that information.

Earlier, the Chinese language phenomenon called the "tip-of-the-pen" phenomenon (TOP) was discussed (see Brown, 1991, for a discussion of slips of the pen). In the TOP, a person knows the phonological form of the word, that is, he or she can say it, but the written character is not accessible. Thus, the TOP informs the person to direct a mental search for the missing orthographic entry.

There is also the common feeling on awakening of having just had a dream, which slips away as your mind begins to change from its relaxed dream state to the awareness that you are already late for work. There is often a feeling that the whole dream is right on the tip of one's tongue. We usually feel that we can or should be able to remember the dream, but are seldom able to do so.

I argue that the TOT can serve as a model for these other phenomenological experiences. Unlike these other experiences, the TOT is quite common in everyday life and is easily amenable to laboratory methodology for study. It has been relatively well studied over the past 35 years since Brown and McNeill (1966) first asked a group of Harvard students to let them know if they were experiencing TOTs in response to obscure word definitions. I suspect that much of what we know about the TOT is generalizable, and at least in principle, to many other human phenomenological experiences.

A FINAL WORD ON TOTs

Over the last 10 years, my colleagues, students, and I have been on a quest to understand an odd but interesting aspect of cognition, the tip-of-the-tongue phenomenon. To understand just one small aspect of human cognition, it was necessary to synthesize theories in four domains: psycholinguistics, memory theory, cognitive aging, and metacognition. Unfortunately, a fifth domain, neuropsychology, has yet to contribute much. The research has carried me from interviewing Amharic-speaking cab drivers, to e-mailing Native American Web sites, to asking students to carry around diaries, to the more traditional work of running experiments in the lab.

If I can draw any one conclusion about TOTs, it is their strong subjective presence when we experience them. They can be frustrating, or exciting, or not at all emotional, but they cause us to rack our minds for unremembered words and names. And it is this strong subjective experience that deserves our attention as scientists. Thus, regardless of their etiology, and regardless of their role in word retrieval, monitoring, and control, more study is needed to understand why TOTs feel the way they do.

It is traditional to end a volume such as this with a quote from a famous person, perhaps a famous playwright or novelist, who may have casually made reference to the phenomena under discussion, or failing that, a quote from an old master such as William James, or failing that, at least a quote from a respected colleague. Instead, I end with a quote from the aphasic patient HW (Funnell et al., 1996), a man caught in a perpetual TOT state, always trying to remember words that he knows but whose retreival prove elusive. When asked to retrieve the furry animal that attacks snakes (mongoose), HW said: "The problem is I can't remember in my own head. It's not that I can't say it. I know what it is and I can't know how to say the name. I don't know what the name is of what they are" (Funnell et al., 1996, p. 190). And that, perhaps, is what TOTs feel like to us all: the wave of a magician's wand—now we know it, and now we don't.

References

Altarriba, J. (1992). The representation of translation equivalents in bilingual memory. In R. J. Harris (Ed.), *Cognitive processing in bilinguals* (pp. 157–174). New York: Elsevier.

Arbuckle, T. Y., & Cuddy, L. L. (1969). Discrimination of item strength at time of presentation. *Journal of Experimental Psychology, 81,* 126–131.

Askari, N. (1999). Priming effects on tip-of-the-tongue states in Farsi-English bilinguals. *Journal of Psycholinguistic Research, 28,* 197–212.

Astell, A. J., & Harley, T. A. (1996). Tip-of-the-tongue states and lexical access in dementia. *Brain and Language, 54,* 196–215.

Atkinson, R. C., & Shiffrin, R. M. (1968). Human memory: A proposed system and its control processes. In K. W. Spence & J. T. Spence (Eds.), *The psychology of learning and motivation* (Vol. 2; pp. 89–105). New York: Academic.

Bak, B. (1987). The tip-of-the-tongue phenomenon: A Polish view. *Polish Psychological Bulletin, 18,* 21–27.

Banaji, M. R., & Crowder, R. G. (1991). The bankruptcy of everyday memory. *American Psychologist, 44,* 1185–1193.

Barnes, A. E., Nelson, T. O., Dunlosky, J., Mazzoni, G., & Narens, L. (1999). An integrative system of metamemory components involved in retrieval. In D. Gopher & A. Koriat (Eds.), *Attention and performance XVII: Cognitive regulation of performance: Interaction of theory and application* (pp. 287–314). Cambridge, MA: MIT Press.

Beattie, G., & Coughlan, J. (1999). An experimental investigation of the role of iconic gestures in lexical access using the tip-of-the-tongue phenomenon. *British Journal of Psychology, 90,* 35–56.

Begg, I., Duft, S., Lalonde, P., Melnick, R., & Sanvito, J. (1989). Memory predictions are based on ease of processing. *Journal of Memory and Language, 28,* 610–632.

Benjamin, A. S., Bjork, R. A., & Schwartz, B. L. (1998). The mismeasure of memory: When retrieval fluency is misleading as a metamnemonic index. *Journal of Experimental Psychology: General, 127,* 55–68.

Berg, R. A. (2000). *Effect of delay of first interview and repetition of interview on accuracy and confidence of recall of a flashbulb-type memory.* Unpublished doctoral dissertation, Florida International University, Miami, FL.

Bjork, R. A. (1994). Memory and metamemory considerations in the training of human beings. In J. Metcalfe & A. P. Shimamura (Eds.), *Metacognition: Knowing about knowing* (pp. 185–205). Cambridge, MA: MIT Press.

Bjork, R. A. (1999). Assessing our own competence: Heuristics and illusions. In D. Gopher & A. Koriat (Eds.), *Attention and performance XVII. Cognitive regulation of performance: Interaction of theory and application* (pp. 435–459). Cambridge, MA: MIT Press.

Bjork, R. A., & Bjork, E. L. (1992). A new theory of disuse and an old theory of stimulation fluctuation. In A. F. Healy, S. M. Kosslyn, & R. M. Shiffrin (Eds.), *From learning processes to cognitive processes: Essays in honor of William K. Estes, Vol. 2* (pp. 35–67). Hillsdale, NJ: Lawrence Erlbaum Associates.

Brennan, T., Baguley, T., Bright, J., & Bruce, V. (1990). Resolving semantically-induced tip-of-the-tongue states for proper nouns. *Memory & Cognition, 18,* 339–347.

Brown, A. S. (1991). A review of the tip-of-the-tongue experience. *Psychological Bulletin, 109,* 204–223.

Brown, A. S. (2000, June). Aging and the tip-of-the-tongue experience. Paper presented at the meeting of the American Psychological Society Convention, Miami Beach, FL.

Brown, A. S., & Nix, L. A. (1996). Age-related changes in the tip-of-the-tongue experience. *American Journal of Psychology, 109,* 79–91.

Brown, R., & McNeill, D. (1966). The "tip of the tongue" phenomenon. *Journal of Verbal Learning and Behavior, 5,* 325–337.

Bruce, C., & Howard, D. (1988). Why don't Broca's aphasics cue themselves? An investigation of phonemic cueing and tip of the tongue information. *Neuropsychologia, 26,* 253–264.

Burke, D. M., MacKay, D. G., Worthley, J. S., & Wade, E. (1991). On the tip of the tongue: What causes word finding failures in young and older adults? *Journal of Memory and Language, 30,* 542–579.

Busey, T. A., Tunnicliff, J., Loftus, G. R., & Loftus, E. F. (2000). Accounts of the confidence-accuracy relation in recognition memory. *Psychonomic Bulletin & Review, 7,* 26–48.

Butterfield, E. C., Nelson, T. O., & Peck, V. (1988). Developmental aspects of the feeling of knowing. *Developmental Psychology, 24,* 654–663.

Butterworth, B. (1989). Lexical access in speech production. In W. Marslen-Wilson (Ed.), *Lexical representation and process* (pp. 108–135). Cambridge, MA: MIT Press.

Butterworth, B. (1992). Disorders in phonological encoding. *Cognition, 42,* 261–286.

Caramazza, A., & Miozzo, M. (1997). The relation between syntactic and phonological knowledge in lexical access: Evidence from the 'tip-of-the-tongue' phenomenon. *Cognition, 64,* 309–343.

Chen, H. C., & Ng, M. L. (1989). Semantic facilitation and translation priming effects in Chinese–English bilinguals. *Memory & Cognition, 17,* 454–462.

Cohen, G., & Faulkner, D. (1986). Memory for proper names: Age differences in retrieval. *British Journal of Developmental Psychology, 4,* 187–197.

Connor, L. T., Dunlosky, J., & Hertzog, C. (1997). Age-related differences in absolute but not relative metamemory accuracy. *Psychology & Aging, 5,* 291–303.

Conway, M. A. (1995). *Flashbulb memories.* Hillsdale, NJ: Lawrence Erlbaum Associates.

Costermans, J., Lories, G., & Ansay, C. (1992). Confidence level and the feeling of knowing in question answering: The weight of inferential processes. *Journal of Experimental Psychology: Learning, Memory, and Cognition, 18,* 142–150.

Dahlgren, D. J. (1998). Impact of knowledge and age on tip-of-the-tongue rates. *Experimental Aging Research, 24,* 139–153.

Dehaene, S., Posner, M. I., & Tucker, D. M. (1994). Localization of a neural system for error detection and compensation. *Psychological Science, 5,* 303–305.

Dunlosky, J., & Connor, L. T. (1997). Age differences in the allocation of study time account for age differences in memory performance. *Memory & Cognition, 25,* 691–700.

Dunlosky, J., & Hertzog, C. (1997). Older and younger adults use a functionally identical algorithm to select items for restudy during multi-trial learning. *Journal of Gerontology: Psychological Sciences, 52B,* 178–186.

Dunlosky, J., & Nelson, T. O. (1994). Does the sensitivity of judgments of learning (JOLs) to the effects of various study activities depend on when JOLs occur? *Journal of Memory and Language, 33,* 545–565.

Dunlosky, J., & Nelson, T. O. (1997). Similarity between cue for judgments of learning (JOLs) and the cue for test is not the primary determinant of JOL accuracy. *Journal of Memory and Language, 36,* 34–49.

Ecke, P. (1997). *Tip of the tongue states in first and foreign languages: Similarities and differences of lexical retrieval failures.* Proceedings of the EUROSLA 7 Conference (pp. 505–514). Barcelona, Spain.

Ecke, P., & Garrett, M. F. (1998). Lexical retrieval stages of momentarily inaccessible foreign language words. *Ilha do Desterro: Special issue on the cognitive aspects of foreign/second language acquisition/learning, 35,* 157–183.

Elbers, L. (1985). A tip-of-the-tongue experience at age two? *Journal of Child Language, 12,* 353–365.

Engen, T. (1987). Remembering odors and their names. *American Scientist, 75,* 497–503.

Faust, M., Dimitrovsky, L., & Davidi, S. (1997). Naming difficulties in language-disabled children: Preliminary findings with application of the tip-of-the-tongue paradigm. *Journal of Speech, Language, and Hearing Research, 40,* 1026–1036.

Finley, G. E., & Sharp, T. (1989). Name retrieval by the elderly in the tip-of-the-tongue paradigm: Demonstrable success in overcoming initial failure. *Educational Gerontology, 15,* 259–265.

Freedman, J. L., & Landauer, T. K. (1966). Retrieval of long-term memory: "Tip-of-the-tongue" phenomenon. *Psychonomic Science, 4,* 309–310.

Frick-Horbury, D., & Guttentag, R. E. (1998). The effects of restricting hand gesture production on lexical retrieval and free recall. *American Journal of Psychology, 111,* 43–62.

Funnell, M., Metcalfe, J., & Tsapkani, K. (1996). In the mind but not on the tongue: Feeling of knowing in an anomic patient. In L. M. Reder (Ed.), *Implicit memory and metacognition* (pp. 171–194). Mahwah, NJ: Lawrence Erlbaum Associates.

Gardiner, J. M. (1988). Functional aspects of the recollective experience. *Memory & Cognition, 16,* 303-313.

Gardiner, J. M., Craik, F. I. M., & Bleasdale, F. A. (1973). Retrieval difficulty and subsequent recall. *Memory & Cognition, 1,* 213–216.

Gardiner, J. M., & Java, R. I. (1993). Recognizing and Remembering. In A. F. Collins, S. E. Gathercole, M. A., Conway, & P. E. Morris (Eds.), *Theories of memory* (pp. 163–188). Hillsdale, NJ: Lawrence Erlbaum Associates.

Garrett, M. (1975). The analysis of sentence production. In G. H. Bower (Ed.), *The psychology of learning and motivation* (pp. 133–177). New York: Academic.

Garrett, M. (1992). Disorders of lexical selection. *Cognition, 42,* 143–180.

Glucksberg, S., & McCloskey, M. (1981). Decisions about ignorance: Knowing that you don't know. *Journal of Experimental Psychology: Human Learning and Memory, 7,* 311–325.

Gollan, T., & Silverberg, N. (in press). Tip-of-the-tongue states in Hebrew–English bilinguals. *Bilingualism: Language and Cognition.*

Goodglass, H., Kaplan, E., Weintraub, S., & Ackerman, N. (1976). The "tip-of-the-tongue" phenomenon in aphasia. *Cortex, 12,* 145–153.

Guralnik, D. B. (1984). *Webster's new world dictionary* (2nd College Ed). New York: Simon and Schuster.

Harley, T. A., & Bown, H. E. (1998). What causes a tip-of-the-tongue state? Evidence for lexical neighbourhood effects in speech production. *British Journal of Psychology, 89,* 151–174.

Hart, J. T. (1965). Memory and the feeling-of-knowing experience. *Journal of Educational Psychology, 56,* 208–216.

Hart, J. T. (1967). Memory and the memory-monitoring process. *Journal of Verbal Learning and Verbal Behavior, 6,* 685–691.

Heine, M. K., Ober, B. A., & Shenaut, G. K. (1999). Naturally occurring and experimentally induced tip-of-the-tongue experiences in three adult age groups. *Psychology and Aging, 14,* 445–457.

Hulms, K. (1983). *The bone people.* New York: Penguin.

Iwasaki, N., Vigliocco, G., & Garrett, M. F. (1998). Adjectives and adjectival nouns in Japanese: Psychological processes in sentence production (pp. 555–568). *Japanese/Korean Linguistics.* Stanford, CA: CSLI.

Jacoby, L. L. (1991). A process dissociation framework: Separating automatic from intentional uses of memory. *Journal of Memory and Language, 30,* 513–541.

Jacoby, L. L., & Dallas, M. (1981). On the relationship between autobiographical memory and perceptual learning. *Journal of Experimental Psychology: General, 110,* 306–340.

James, L. E., & Burke, D. M. (2000). Phonological priming effects on word retrieval and tip-of-tongue experiences. *Journal of Experimental Psychology, LMC, 26,* 1378–1391.

James, W. (1890). *The principles of psychology: Vol. 1.* New York: Holt.

Janowsky, J. S., Shimamura, A. P., & Squire, L. R. (1989). Memory and metamemory: Comparisons between frontal lobe patients and amnesic patients. *Psychobiology, 17,* 3–11.

Jones, G. V. (1988). Analyzing memory blocks. In M. M. Gruneberg, P. E. Morris, & R. N. Sykes (Eds.), *Practical aspects of memory: Current research and issues* (Vol. 1; pp. 215–220). New York: Wiley.

Jones, G. V. (1989). Back to Woodworth: Role of interlopers in the tip-of-the-tongue phenomenon. *Memory & Cognition, 17,* 69–76.

Jones, G. V., & Langford, S. (1987). Phonological blocking in the tip of the tongue state. *Cognition, 26,* 115–122.

Kahneman, D., & Tversky, A. (1973). On the psychology of prediction. *Psychological Review, 80,* 237–251.

Kahneman, D., & Tversky, A. (1984). Choices, values, and frames. *American Psychologist, 39,* 341–350.

Klin, C. M., Guzman, A. E., & Levine, W. H. (1997). Knowing that you don't know: Metamemory and discourse processing. *Journal of Experimental Psychology: Learning, Memory, & Cognition, 23,* 1378–1393.

Kohn, S. E., Wingfield, A., Menn, L., Goodglass, H., Berko Gleason, J., & Hyde, M. (1987). Lexical retrieval: The tip-of-the-tongue phenomenon. *Applied Psycholinguistics, 8,* 245–266.

Kolb, B., & Whishaw, I. Q. (1996). *Fundamentals of human neuropsychology, 4th edition.* New York: Freeman.

Kolers, P. A., & Palef, S. R. (1976). Knowing not. *Memory & Cognition, 4,* 553–558.

Koriat, A. (1993). How do we know that we know? The accessibility account of the feeling of knowing. *Psychological Review, 100,* 609–639.

Koriat, A. (1995). Dissociating knowing and the feeling of knowing: Further evidence for the accessibility model. *Journal of Experimental Psychology: General, 124,* 311–333.

Koriat, A. (1997). Monitoring one's own knowledge during study: A cue-utilization approach to judgments of learning. *Journal of Experimental Psychology: General, 126*, 349–370.

Koriat, A., & Goldsmith, M. (1996). Monitoring and control processes in the strategic regulation of memory accuracy. *Psychological Review, 103*, 490–517.

Koriat, A., & Lieblich, I. (1974). What does a person in a "TOT" state know that a person in a "don't know" state doesn't know. *Memory & Cognition, 2*, 647–655.

Koriat, A., & Lieblich, I. (1977). A study of memory pointers. *Acta Psychologica, 41*, 151–164.

Kozlowski, L. (1977). Effects of distorted auditory and of rhyming cues on retrieval of tip-of-the-tongue words by poets and nonpoets. *Memory & Cognition, 5*, 477–481.

Krauss, R. M., Dushay, R. A., Chen, Y., & Rauscher, F. (1995). The communicative value of conversational hand gestures. *Journal of Experimental Social Psychology, 31*, 533–552.

Larsen, S. F. (1998). What is it like to remember? On phenoemal qualities of memory. In C. P. Thompson, D. J. Hermann, D. Bruce, J. D. Read, D. G. Payne, & M. P. Toglia (Eds.), *Autobiographical memory: Theoretical and applied perspectives* (pp. 163–190). Mahwah, NJ: Lawrence Erlbaum Associates.

Lawless, H., & Engen, T. (1977). Associations to odors: Interference, mnemonics, and verbal labeling. *Journal of Experimental Psychology: Human Learning and Memory, 3*, 52–59.

Leonesio, R. J., & Nelson, T. O. (1990). Do different metamemory judgements tap the same underlying aspects of memory. *Journal of Experimental Psychology, LMC, 16*, 464–470.

Levelt, W. J. M. (1989). *Speaking: From intention to articulation.* Cambridge, MA: MIT Press.

Loftus, E. F., Donders, K., Hoffman, H. G., & Schooler, J. W. (1989). Creating new memories that are quickly accessed and confidently held. *Memory & Cognition, 17*, 606–616.

MacKay, D. G., & Burke, D. M. (1990). Cognition and aging: A theory of new learning and the use of old connections. In T. Hess (Ed.), *Aging and cognition: Knowledge, organization, and utilization* (pp. 213–263). Amsterdam: North-Holland.

MacLin, O. H. (2000). *The relationship between feeling of knowing and tip of the tongue: Effects of perceived difficulty, cue familiarity, and partial information.* Manuscript submitted for publication.

Maki, R. H. (1998). Test predictions over text material. In D. J. Hacker, J. Dunlosky, & A.C. Graesser (Eds.), *Metacognition in educational theory and practice* (pp. 117–144). Mahwah, NJ: Lawrence Erlbaum Associates.

Marsh, S., & Emmorey, K. (2000, July). *Tip-of-the-finger experiences in deaf signers.* Paper presented at the Theoretical Issues in Sign Language Research Conference, Amsterdam, the Netherlands.

Martin, N., Dell, G. S., Saffran, E. M., & Schwartz, M. F. (1994). Origins of paraphasias in deep dysphasia: Testing the consequences of a decay impairment to an interactive spreading activation model of lexical retrieval. *Brain and Language, 47*, 609–660.

Matison, R., Mayeux, R., Rosen, J., & Fahn, S. (1982). "Tip-of-the-tongue" phenomenon in Parkinson disease. *Neurology, 32*, 567–570.

Matlin, M. W. (1998). *Cognition* (4th ed.). Orlando, FL: Harcourt Brace.

Maylor, E. A. (1990a). Recognizing and naming faces: Aging, memory retrieval, and the tip of the tongue state. *Journal of Gerontology, 45*, 215–226.

Maylor, E. A. (1990b). Age, blocking and the tip of the tongue state. *British Journal of Psychology, 81*, 123–134.

Maylor, E. A. (1994). Ageing and the retrieval of specialized and general knowledge: Performance of master minds. *British Journal of Psychology, 85*, 105–114.

Mazzoni, G., & Cornoldi, C. (1993). Strategies in study time allocation: Why is study time sometimes not effective? *Journal of Experimental Psychology: General, 122,* 47–60.

Mazzoni, G., Cornoldi, C., & Marchetilli, G. (1990). Do memorability ratings affect study-time allocation? *Memory & Cognition, 18,* 196–204.

Mazzoni, G., & Nelson, T. O. (1995). Judgments of learning are affected by the kind of encoding in ways that cannot be attributed to the level of recall. *Journal of Experimental Psychology: Learning, Memory, & Cognition, 21,* 1263–1274.

Metcalfe, J. (1993). Novelty monitoring, metacognition, and control in a composite holographic associative recall model: Interpretations for Korsakoff amnesia. *Psychological Review, 100,* 3–22.

Metcalfe, J. (1996). Metacognitive processes. In E. L. Bjork & R. A. Bjork (Eds.), *Memory* (pp. 383–411). San Diego, CA: Academic.

Metcalfe, J. (2000). Metamemory: Theory and data. In E. Tulving & F. I. M. Craik (Eds.), *The Oxford handbook of memory* (pp. 197–214). New York: Oxford University Press.

Metcalfe, J., Schwartz, B. L., & Joaquim, S. G. (1993). The cue familiarity heuristic in metacognition. *Journal of Experimental Psychology: Learning, Memory, and Cognition, 19,* 851–861.

Metcalfe, J., & Wiebe, D. (1987). Intuition in insight and noninsight problem solving. *Memory & Cognition, 15,* 238–246.

Miozzo, M., & Caramazza, A. (1997). Retrieval of lexical-syntactic features in tip-of-the-tongue states. *Journal of Experimental Psychology: Learning, Memory, and Cognition, 23,* 1410–1423.

Meyer, A. S., & Bock, K. (1992). The tip-of-the-tongue phenomenon: Blocking or partial activation? *Memory & Cognition, 20,* 715–726.

Mulligan, N. W., & Hirshman, E. (1997). Measuring the bases of recognition memory: An investigation of the process-dissociation framework. *Journal of Experimental Psychology: Learning, Memory, and Cognition, 23,* 280–304.

Murakami, Y. (1980). On the memory unit within kana-letter and kanji-letter words in the tip of the tongue phenomenon. *Japanese Journal of Psychology, 51,* 41–44.

Neisser, U. (1978). What are the important questions? In M. M. Gruneberg, P. E. Morris, & R. N. Sykes (Eds.), *Practical aspects of memory: Current research and issues* (Vol. 1; pp. 3–24). New York: Wiley.

Nelson, T. O. (1984). A comparison of current measures of the accuracy of feeling-of-knowing predictions. *Psychological Bulletin, 95,* 109–133.

Nelson, T. O. (1988). Predictive accuracy of feeling of knowing across different criterion tasks and across different subject populations and individuals. In M. Gruneberg, P. Morris, & R. Sykes (Eds.), *Practical aspects of memory: Current research and issues* (Vol. 1; pp. 190–196). New York: Wiley.

Nelson, T. O. (1993). Judgments of learning and the allocation of study time. *Journal of Experimental Psychology: General, 122,* 269–273.

Nelson, T. O. (1996). Consciousness and metacognition. *American Psychologist, 51,* 102–116.

Nelson, T. O., & Dunlosky, J. (1991). The delayed-JOL effect: When delaying your judgments of learning can improve the accuracy of your metacognitive monitoring. *Psychological Science, 2,* 267–270.

Nelson, T. O., Dunlosky, J., Graf, A., & Narens, L. (1994). Utilization of metacognitive judgments in the allocation of study during multitrial learning. *Psychological Science, 5,* 207–213.

Nelson, T. O., Gerler, D., & Narens, L. (1984). Accuracy of feeling of knowing judgments for predicting perceptual identification and relearning. *Journal of Experimental Psychology: General, 113,* 282–300.

Nelson, T. O., Graf, A., Dunlosky, J., Marlatt, A., Walker, D., & Luce, K. (1998). Effect of acute alcohol intoxication on recall and on judgments of learning during the acquisition of new information. In G. Mazzoni & T. O. Nelson (Eds.), *Metacognition and cognitive neuropsychology: Monitoring and control processes* (pp. 161–180). Mahwah, NJ: Lawrence Erlbaum Associates.

Nelson, T. O., & Leonesio, R. J. (1988). Allocation of self-paced study time and the "labor-in-vain" effect. *Journal of Experimental Psychology: Learning, Memory, & Cognition, 14,* 676–686.

Nelson, T. O., & Narens, L. (1980). Norms of 300 general-information questions: Accuracy of recall, latency of recall, and feeling-of-knowing ratings. *Journal of Verbal Learning & Verbal Behavior, 19,* 338–368.

Nelson, T. O., & Narens, L. (1990). Metamemory: A theoretical framework and new findings. In G. Bower (Ed.), *The psychology of learning and motivation* (Vol. 26; pp. 125–141). San Diego, CA: Academic.

Nelson, T. O., & Narens, L. (1994). Why investigate metacognition? In J. Metcalf & A. Shimamura (Eds.), *Metacognition: Knowing about knowing* (pp. 1–26). Cambridge, MA: MIT Press.

Nisbett, R. E., & Wilson, T. D. (1977). Telling more than we can know: Verbal reports on mental processes. *Psychological Review, 84,* 231–259.

Nyberg, L., Cabeza, R., & Tulving, E. (1996). PET studies of encoding and retrieval: The HERA model. *Psychonomic Bulletin & Review, 3,* 135–148.

Perfect, T. J., & Hanley, J. R. (1992). The tip-of-the-tongue phenomenon: Do experimenter-presented interlopers have any effect? *Cognition, 45,* 55–75.

Piattelli-Palmarini, M. (1994). *Inevitable illusions: How the mistakes of reason rule our minds.* New York: Wiley.

Pinker, S. (1997). *How the mind works.* New York: Norton.

Pinker, S. (1999). *Words and rules: The ingredients of language.* New York: Basic.

Pitcher, H. (1999). *Chekhov: The comic stories.* Chicago: Ivan Dee.

Priller, J., & Mittenecker, F. (1988). Experimente zum Unterrschied von "Wort auf der Zunge" und "Gefuhl des Wissens." *Zeitshrift fur Experimentelle und Angewandte Psychologie, 35,* 129–146.

Rastle, K. G., & Burke, D. M. (1996). Priming the tip of the tongue: Effects of prior processing on word retrieval in young and older adults. *Journal of Memory and Language, 35,* 586–605.

Read, J. D., & Bruce, D. (1982). Longitudinal tracking of difficult memory retrievals. *Cognitive Psychology, 14,* 280–300.

Reason, J. T., & Lucas, D. (1984). Using cognitive diaries to investigate naturally occurring memory blocks. In J. Harris & P. E. Morris (Eds.), *Everyday memory, actions, and absent mindedness* (pp. 53–70). London: Academic.

Reder, L. M. (1987). Selection strategies in question answering. *Cognitive Psychology, 19,* 90–138.

Reder, L. M. (1988). Strategic control of retrieval strategies. In G. Bower (Ed.), *The psychology of learning and motivation* (Vol. 22). San Diego, CA: Academic.

Reder, L. M., & Ritter, F. E. (1992). What determines initial feeling of knowing? Familiarity with question terms, not with the answer. *Journal of Experimental Psychology: Learning, Memory, and Cognition, 18,* 435–451.

Reder, L. M., & Schunn, C. D. (1996). Metacognition does not imply awareness: Strategy choice is governed by implicit learning and memory. In L. M. Reder (Ed.), *Implicit memory and metacognition* (pp. 45–78). Mahwah, NJ: Lawrence Erlbaum Associates.

Riefer, D. M., Kevari, M. K., & Kramer, D. L. (1995). Name that tune: Eliciting tip-of-the-tongue experience using auditory stimuli. *Psychological Reports, 77*, 1379–1390.

Roediger, H. L. (1996). Memory illusions. *Journal of Memory and Language, 35*, 76–100.

Rubin, D. C. (1975). Within word structure in the tip-of-the-tongue phenomenon. *Journal of Verbal Learning and Verbal Behavior, 14*, 392–397.

Rubin, D. C. (1998). Beginnings of a theory of autobiographical remembering. In C. P. Thompson, D. J. Hermann, D. Bruce, J. D. Read, D. G. Payne, & M. P. Toglia (Eds.), *Autobiographical memory: Theoretical and applied perspectives* (pp. 47–68). Mahwah, NJ: Lawrence Erlbaum Associates.

Ryan, M. P., Petty, C. R., & Wenzlaff, R. M. (1982). Motivated remembering efforts during tip-of-the-tongue states. *Acta Psychologica, 51*, 137–147.

Salthouse, T. A. (1991). *Theoretical perspectives on cognitive aging.* Hillsdale, NJ: Lawrence Erlbaum Associates.

Salthouse, T. A. (1993). Speed mediation of adult age differences in cognition. *Developmental Psychology, 29*, 722–738.

Salthouse, T. A. (1996). The processing-speed theory of adult age differences in cognition. *Psychological Review, 103*, 403–428.

Schachter, P. (1990). What's in a name? Inferences from tip-of-the-tongue phenomena. In L. M. Hyman & C. Li (Eds.), *Language, speech, and mind: Studies in honour of Victoria A. Fromkin* (pp. 295–321). New York: Routledge & Kegan Paul.

Schacter, D. L. (1996). *Searching for memory: The brain, the mind, and the past.* New York: Basic.

Schacter, D. L. (1999). The seven sins of memory: Insights from psychology and cognitive neuroscience. *American Psychologist, 54*, 182–203.

Schacter, D. L. (2000). Commentary on perspectives on the tip-of-the-tongue phenomenon. Paper presented at the American Psychological Society Convention, Miami Beach, FL.

Schacter, D. L., Harbluk, J . L., & McLachlan, D. R. (1984). Retrieval without recollection: An experimental analysis of source amnesia. *Journal of Verbal Learning and Verbal Behavior, 23*, 593–611.

Schwartz, B. L. (1994). Sources of information in metamemory: Judgments of learning and feelings of knowing. *Psychonomic Bulletin & Review, 1*, 357–375.

Schwartz, B. L. (1998). Illusory tip-of-the-tongue states. *Memory, 6*, 623–642.

Schwartz, B. L. (1999a). The phenomenology of naturally-occurring tip-of-the-tongue states: A diary study. *Abstracts of the Psychonomic Society, 4*, 24.

Schwartz, B. L. (1999b). Sparkling at the end of the tongue: The etiology of tip-of-the-tongue phenomenology. *Psychonomic Bulletin & Review, 6*, 379–393.

Schwartz, B. L. (2001). The relation of tip-of-the-tongue states and retrieval time. *Memory & Cognition, 29*, 117–126.

Schwartz, B. L. (2000). The strategic selection of retrieval strategies during tip-of-the-tongue states. Unpublished data.

Schwartz, B. L., & Castillo-Andrade, Y. (1999). Access to plural forms in subjectively-defined tip-of-the-tongue states. Unpublished data.

Schwartz, B. L., Castillo-Andrade, Y., & Gonzalez, J. (1998). Access to grammatical gender in Spanish tip-of-the-tongue states. Unpublished data.

Schwartz, B. L., & Metcalfe, J. (1992). Cue familiarity but not target retrievability enhances feeling-of-knowing judgments. *Journal of Experimental Psychology: Learning, Memory, and Cognition, 18*, 1074–1083.

Schwartz, B. L., & Metcalfe, J. (1994). Methodological problems and pitfalls in the study of human metacognition. In J. Metcalfe & A. Shimamura (Eds.), *Metacognition: Knowing about knowing* (pp. 93–114). Cambridge, MA: MIT Press.

Schwartz, B. L., & Smith, S. M. (1997). The retrieval of related information influences tip-of-the-tongue states. *Journal of Memory and Language, 36,* 68–86.

Schwartz, B. L., & Smith, S. M. (1998). Fluctuation and stability in tip-of-the-tongue states. Unpublished manuscript.

Schwartz, B. L., Travis, D. M., Castro, A. M., & Smith, S. M. (2000). The phenomenology of real and illusory tip-of-the-tongue states. *Memory & Cognition, 28,* 18–27.

Shimamura, A. P., & Squire, L. R. (1986). Memory and metamemory: A study of the feeling-of-knowing phenomenon in amnesic patients. *Journal of Experimental Psychology: Learning, Memory, and Cognition, 12,* 452–460.

Silverberg, N., Gollan, T., & Garrett, M. F. (1999). What you can get from a TOT and what NOT. *Abstracts of the Psychonomic Society, 4,* 11.

Smith, S. M. (1994). Frustrated feelings of imminent recall: On the tip-of-the tongue. In J. Metcalfe & A. P. Shimamura (Eds.), *Metacognition: Knowing about knowing* (pp. 27–46). Cambridge, MA: MIT Press.

Smith, S. M. (2000, June). Blocking, tip-of-the-tongue states, and incubation in word retrieval. Paper presented at American Psychological Society Convention, Miami Beach, FL.

Smith, S. M., Balfour, S. P., & Brown, J. M. (1994). Effects of practice on tip-of-the-tongue states. *Memory, 2,* 31–49.

Smith, S. M., Brown, J. M., & Balfour, S. P. (1991). TOTimals: A controlled experimental method for studying tip-of-the-tongue states. *Bulletin of the Psychonomic Society, 29,* 445–447.

Smith, S. M., Ward, T. B., & Finke, R. A. (1995). *The creative cognition approach.* Cambridge, MA: MIT Press.

Spellman, B. A., & Bjork, R. A. (1992). People's judgments of learning are extremely accurate at predicting subsequent recall when retrieval practice mediates both tasks. *Psychological Sciences, 3,* 315–316.

Son, L. K., & Metcalfe, J. (2000). Metacognitive and control strategies in study-time allocation. *Journal of Experimental Psychology: Learning, Memory, & Cognition, 26,* 204–221.

Souchay, C., Isingi, M., & Espagnet, L. (2000). Aging, episodic memory feeling-of-knowing, and frontal functioning. *Neuropsychology, 14,* 299–309.

Sun, Y., Vinson, D. P., & Vigliocco, G. (1998). Tip-of-the-tongue and tip-of-the-pen in Chinese. *Abstracts of the Psychonomic Society, 3,* 32.

Sunderland, A., Watts, K., Baddeley, A. D., & Harris, J. E. (1986). Subjective memory assessment and test performance in elderly adults. *Journal of Gerontology, 31,* 376–384.

Thiede, K. W., & Dunlosky, J. (1999). Toward a general model of self-regulated study: An analysis of selection of items for study and self-paced study time. *Journal of Experimental Psychology: Learning, Memory, & Cognition, 25,* 1024–1037.

Tooby, J., & Cosmides, L. (1995). Mapping the evolved functional organization of mind and brain. In M. S. Gazzaniga (Ed.), *The cognitive neurosciences* (pp. 1185–1197). Cambridge, MA: MIT Press.

Tulving, E. (1983). Elements of episodic memory. New York: Oxford University Press.

Tulving, E. (1985). Memory and consciousness. *Canadian Psychologist, 26,* 1–12.

Tulving, E. (1989). Memory: Performance, knowledge, and experience. *European Journal of Cognitive Psychology, 1,* 3–26.

Tulving, E. (1994). Foreword. In J. Metcalfe & A. Shimamura (Eds.), *Metacognition: Knowing about knowing* (pp. vii–x).

Tulving, E., & Colotla, V. A. (1970). Free recall of trilingual lists. *Cognitive Psychology, 1*, 86–98.

Tulving, E., & Pearlstone, Z. (1966). Availability versus accessibility of information in memory for words. *Journal of Verbal Learning and Verbal Behavior, 5*, 381–391.

Tversky, B. (1981). Distortions in memory for maps. *Cognitive Psychology, 13*, 407–433.

Tversky, B. (1991). Spatial mental models. *The Psychology of Learning and Motivation, 27*, 109–145.

Tweney, R. D., Tracz, S., & Zaruba, S. (1975). Slips of the tongue and lexical storage. *Language and Speech, 18*, 388–396.

Underwood, B. J. (1966). Individual and group predictions of item difficulty for free learning. *Journal of Experimental Psychology, 71*, 673–679.

Vigliocco, G., Antonini, T., & Garrett, M. F. (1997). Grammatical gender is on the tip of Italian tongues. *Psychological Science, 8*, 314–317.

Vigliocco, G., Vinson, D. P., Martin, R. C., & Garrett, M. F. (1999). Is "count" and "mass" information available when the noun is not? An investigation of tip of the tongue states and anomia. *Journal of Memory and Language, 40*, 534–558.

Vinson, D. P., & Vigliocco, G. (1999). Can independence be observed in a dependent system? The case of tip-of-the-tongue states. *Brain and Language, 68*, 118–126.

Wellman, H. M. (1977). Tip of the tongue and feeling of knowing experiences: A developmental study of memory monitoring. *Child Development, 48*, 13–21.

White, K. K., & Abrams, L. (1999). The role of syllable phonology and aging in priming tip-of-the-tongue resolution. *Abstracts of the Psychonomic Society, 4*, 68.

Widner, R. L., Otani, H., & Falconier, C. (1999). The contribution of the prefrontal cortex to feeling-of-knowing and tip-of-the-tongue reports. *Abstracts of the Psychonomic Society, 4*, 13.

Widner, R. L., Smith, S. M., & Graziano, W. G. (1996). The effects of demand characteristics on the reporting of tip-of-the-tongue states and feeling-of-knowing states. *American Journal of Psychology, 109*, 525–538.

Xu, Y., Pollatsek, A., & Potter, M. C. (1999). The activation of phonology during silent Chinese word reading. *Journal of Experimental Psychology: Learning, Memory, and Cognition, 25*, 838–857.

Yaniv, I., & Meyer, D. E. (1987). Activation and metacognition of inaccessible stored information: Potential bases for incubation effects in problem-solving. *Journal of Experimental Psychology: Learning, Memory, and Cognition, 13*, 187–205.

Yarmey, A. D. (1973). I recognize your face, but I can't remember your name: Further evidence on the tip-of-the-tongue phenomenon. *Memory & Cognition, 1*, 287–290.

Zhang, S., Perfetti, C. A., & Yang, H. (1999). Whole word, frequency-general phonology in semantic processing of Chinese characters. *Journal of Experimental Psychology: Learning, Memory, and Cognition, 25*, 858–876.

Author Index

Subject Index